To Diane,
Friend for decades.
[My] Haircutter Extra-
ordinaire for decades
Kindred Spirit from
The 60s — Adventures.

A Little Help

ESSAYS AND STORIES

Travelor, Explorer of

Denis Clifford

Outside and Inner
Worlds and a Great
Soul.

Love,

Denis

$15.95

Front Cover: The Sponson, Old Forge. Oil on canvas, Denis Clifford
Back Cover: Self-Portrait in Red. Oil on canvas

ISBN: 0692255184
ISBN 13: 9780692255186
Library of Congress Control Number: 2014920886
The Boathouse Press, Albany, CA

Dedication: TO NAOMI, ONCE AGAIN

PREFACE

This is a collection of some of my writings over roughly a twenty-five year span. A few were published by little literary magazines. Most received only rejection slips, sometimes with encouraging notes, from other literary magazines, Happily, various friends who read one or more pieces often expressed approval. As part of celebrating seventy-five years of living, I decided I wanted these writings to become a book.

The title, *A Little Help*, comes from a phrase used on street-basketball courts, where I played for decades. When a ball rolled off-court, we'd call out, "A Little Help..." to players on other courts, spectators, bystanders, or anyone near the ball, and the ball would be quickly returned to us. The title reflects a major aspect of most of the book's essays and stories: Someone is getting or giving help, or both. Which brings up The Beatles' *A Little Help from my Friends,* a delightful song, though not the inspiration for the title—in street ball, *A Little Help* can come from anyone, not only friends.

Most of these writings, however, are about myself and friends and family. Somewhere, Thoreau wrote that he wouldn't write so much about himself if he knew much about anyone else. Me too. Many of these writings contain elements of autobiography, and there is sometimes overlap between different pieces. I like to think that any overlap includes a new perspective, or at least a new context.

Reading is and has been one of the greatest and deepest pleasures of my life. I hope reading *A Little Help* brings some pleasure to you.

THANK YOU to the many family and friends who have helped me with my writings in many ways, from editing to inspiration, over many years—indeed decades: Naomi Puro, Catherine Clifford, Steve Clifford, Phil Spitzer (superb literary agent and my best basket-ball-playing partner ever), Belinda Breyer, Jack Bursk, Roger Sale (my best English teacher at Amherst College, and later friend for thirty years and counting), Paul Samberg, Kit Duane, Dan Klein, Dick Duane, Laura King, Carol Kizziah, Betsy Simmons Hannibal, Ellen Hawkes, Missy Cusick, Mark Greenside, Dave Hamilton, Karin Jannson, Mark Peery, Steve Ronfeldt, Howard Schecter, Steve Antler, Carla Jupiter, Mary Spitzer, Jan Beyea, Merv Cherrin, Daniele Spellman, Mollie Katzen, Stephanie Clifford, Suzy Ronfeldt, Simone Knowlton, Tina Smelser, Ken Fischer, Priscilla Grant, Pat Ramsey, Patsy Vigderman, Kris Hafner, Annette Walt, Toby Furash, Toni Ihara, Bob Spilka, Richard Nagler, Gene Seltzer, Preston Maring, Rick Millikan, Nona Refi and Bay Area Models for the Arts, Amy Pine, Bob Campbell, Chris Peterson, Stan Jacobsen, Alan Greenbaum, Ben Pomeranz, Lewis Leader.

Merci Mille Fois

TABLE OF CONTENTS

Preface   v

ESSAYS
AN IRISH-AMERICAN FROM THE SUBURBS   1
MOM   13
ALMOST A HIPPIE   26
BERKELEY IN 2000   39
LESSONS IN LOVE   53
DRAGGED TO PARIS   66
SIXTEEN THINGS I LOVE ABOUT THE FRENCH
(AND A FEW I DON'T)   75
FOREVER WILD   84
CLIFFORD'S MAXIMS   92
A MORE MODEST PROPOSAL
(UPDATING JONATHAN SWIFT)   95
SHORT STORIES
THE PARKING LOT   101
THE RIGHT THING   113
A SENSE OF ACCOMPLISHMENT   127
THE BIG GUY   139
MACHO   151
ESSAYS
THIRTEEN TRUE TALES OF THE SAN FRANCISCO
BAY AREA   163
SEVEN TRUE TALES OF MANHATTAN   171

HAYDEN CURRY. IN MEMORIAL	174
REREADING LUCKY JIM	178
FOR MY AMHERST 50TH REUNION (2011)	188
ON TIPPING	192
THE FAN WHO LEFT	199
ROCK AND ROLL	201

AN IRISH-AMERICAN FROM THE SUBURBS

I'm 100% Irish-American. Which means what? Almost nothing for me while growing up in a prosperous, mostly Protestant New Jersey suburb in the 1950's. As a kid, I knew my mother's parents and my father's grandparents "came over on the boat" from Ireland. So? All my buddies' ancestors came from somewhere, and it didn't matter where. I never felt I came from the wrong side of the tracks, and indeed I didn't. If there were any old-line WASPs in town who scorned "Micks," I never heard that insult.

During college I pondered whether my childhood fit under the label "alienation." Paul Goodman's *Growing Up Absurd* described a core of my experience. But simultaneously, I first discovered romantic pride in being Irish. Feeling an instinctive loathing for the Anglo-Protestant codes Amherst was trying to coerce onto me (in my junior year I was suspended for two weeks for "excess chapel cuts") I was drawn to Irish rebellion. From an early age, I'd contested public grade school teachers, Cub Scout masters, Little League coaches, even Sunday School nuns (but not priests), usually slyly, occasionally overtly. During seventh grade I came home and proudly announced that our homeroom teacher had angrily put it to a class vote: either I and Timmy went, or he did. Of course, the class voted that he did. Mom, more pleased at my defiance than bothered by my naiveté in believing I'd prevailed, shook her head, saying that now she'd have to call the Principal and help straighten things out. Smiling, she reaffirmed the message: Stand up to them, Rebel.

The message was never stated explicitly. Only later on did I understand that Mom grew up in a family mistrustful of authority, particularly British authority. An old picture of Mom as a child with her brothers in a donkey cart, taken at some Democratic Party rally in the Bronx, included a large Sinn Fein sign Grandpa had taped on the cart. An uncle of Grandpa's had been executed by the British in the 1880s. Grandpa himself, I learned only after he died, would never allow an Englishman inside his home.

My continuing rebellions at Amherst were not received approvingly at home. My parents had deep faith in prestigious colleges. We weren't supposed to merely rebel, but to succeed as well. Thumb our noses at the British lords, but be dukes ourselves. When I was officially branded an "underachiever" by Amherst, and continued my unrepentant grumbling about how stuffy the place was, I seemed in danger of blowing the duke bit.

Mom and Dad needn't have worried. I too believed I had to graduate with honors from Amherst. Then I'd land a good job (doing what?) and shield myself from a tragedy like Uncle Martin's, who never went to college. Mom told us many tales of Martin, her younger brother. Charming and creative, a gifted writer, he produced his own plays for neighbors when he was a teenager. He married a beauty. People cleared the floor when they danced. The Duke of Windsor once told them, "You are poetry in motion." By his late forties, he was unemployed, drinking, and separated—of course divorce was impossible. The summer I turned twenty, while my parents worked and traveled in Peru with their youngest kids, Martin stayed with the rest of us in our summer home. I discovered pitchers of straight vodka in the icebox. Martin sat mute on the porch swing much of the day. Once an empty gin bottle rolled across the sloping porch floor. As one of my brothers put it after Martin died, he was the Irish nightmare, the man you didn't want to become.

Most of the Irishness of my childhood wasn't nearly as mythic, just everyday. Of course, we were a big family. I'm the oldest of seven. In many small ways, my parents encouraged us to be dismissive of dominant

WASP codes. Table manners: not only did we never learn "proper" manners, but somehow, without ever directly stating it, Mom and Dad conveyed that all those proprieties were silly. Who cared where Emily Post or the Queen of England proclaimed the knife and fork went? You grabbed them and ate.

Meticulous house cleaning was another denigrated WASP obsession. Mom, physically active and busy with local politics and magazine writing, as well as the kids, didn't think much of women devoted to a ceaseless war against dust. Days before her marriage, her mother had told her, "Remember Dear, you never saw a statue of a great housekeeper." Far more disapproved of were parents who forbid children to play in living rooms, so that the rooms stayed immaculate. That violated the cardinal rule of hospitality.

In my freshman college year, I invited a roommate to our family's Thanksgiving dinner. Bright and driven, he'd grown up in a family of rigid controls He had to give his father a detailed accounting of his monthly college expenses. We arrived at my home, and I announced that he'd be having dinner with us. Aghast, he asked, "You didn't tell them before?" Cavalierly, I answered no, reassuring him that I knew it was okay. Within a few years, I'd concluded that the moral of that story was how self-absorbed I was in college. Though true, the real moral now seems that my parents were profoundly hospitable and my behavior had indeed been okay.

The center of our family culture was talk, stories, and laughter. My mother's first words on my birth were "I hope he has a sense of humor." She loved to tell tales of my father's prickly wit. At a tedious dinner party, he drank several cups of coffee; a man asked if that didn't keep him awake. "It helps," my father replied. My parents seemed to regard dullness as the worst of sins. They'd come back from a dinner party and moan, "Oh, are they boring!" and I knew I must <u>never</u> become that.

Talk was performance. Unconsciously, you learned to use your body, hands, face, as well as your voice and mind, to hold attention. When you performed, you did not make eye contact, or reveal emotions. Nothing personal. Mom had grown up in the Irish political-civil-servant culture of New York City, so the major subject of our talk, aside from personal trivia like school events or golf scores, was U.S. politics. Irish politics, present or past, wasn't mentioned. Nor did we talk about Irish history or traditions. I never heard of dreams of "visiting the auld sod."

Though my family's processes may have been drenched in Irishness, the content wasn't. The arts my parents valued were an American-European mix, with little drawn from Ireland. Music was Mozart or operas on Saturday radio, pop songs or Gilbert and Sullivan. The one John McCormack record we had was never played. The only singing we did was Christmas carols, not "Galway Bay" or "A Nation Once Again." Our bookshelves held an eclectic mix, from mountain climbing sagas to tough-guy mysteries to Jane Austen, but no Irish works I recall, except a stray *As I Was Going Down Sackville Street*.

We didn't participate in any "Irish community"—no Irish-American parades, clubs, newspapers, or celebrations. Indeed, though the number of Irish-Americans in our town steadily increased, there didn't seem to be any Irish community, aside from attendance at Sunday mass. Which, I later concluded, was the point: Irish-Americans wanted to leave their historical baggage behind. Dad left his hometown of Bismark, North Dakota when he was eighteen. He returned once, for his mother's funeral.

Mom's parents, raised in Manhattan's Hell's Kitchen, now lived in a respectable New York suburb. Every Christmas day we crossed the Hudson to visit Grandma's and Grandpa's for a family gathering. Mom worshipped Grandpa. Each year, she spent considerable energy and thought trying to find him a present he'd love. Whatever she gave him, he'd open it, at best barely nod, then ignore it, saying nothing. One Christmas Mom believed she'd finally done it. Grandpa had retired from his job in the New York City Dock Department, and suffered from serious arthritis. He'd transferred much of his intensity to bird watching. Mom researched and searched until she found the perfect birdhouse, just right for the birds flying near his house, for the weather, and for attaching it to his back window.

Grandpa unwrapped the birdhouse and held it out, eyeing it skeptically as his lip curled. "That's silly," he snapped. "What would I want that for?" and dropped it down. Mom erupted in tears, sobbing that he'd never loved her. Dad, standing beside me, shook his head pensively and said quietly, "I don't understand how two people who love each other so much can hurt each other so much." Adults quickly bustled us kids upstairs. When we were called back down, the grownups presented themselves cheerfully, and it was Christmas again.

When my grandfather died, every present my mother had ever given him was found hidden away in his attic. Each present was carefully preserved, and dated with the year he'd received it.

I absorbed a diluted version of Grandpa's code, accepting without reflection that I'd never reveal anything really intimate (including to myself). I knew my parents loved each other, but rarely saw them hug. Strong people, they rarely displayed troubled feelings, or negative emotions, except temper. Mom sporadically erupted in anger, like a tea-kettle boiling over. Dad was darker, prone to rage at us kids, though never at Mom, as far as I saw. But with either, angers passed like sudden storms, and then it was back to normal: strength. You didn't ask for anything, because you never needed anything. If sickness wasn't exactly a disgrace, it certainly was not a cause for attention. Like a wounded animal, you healed best when left alone. The family doctor was not to be bothered unless you were alarmingly ill. On one level, my parents subscribed to American cheerfulness; things will work out. But at their core they were more Celtic stoics than optimists. When Dad's back went out, he carried on until unbearable pain forced him to him a chiropractor, who snapped his back into place and he returned promptly to work. All her life, when she went to a dentist my mother refused Novocaine, or any painkiller.

My parents drew strength from their Catholicism. Dad, a man sometimes plagued by his inner demons, once told me that praying in church helped him feel peaceful. Their Catholicism wasn't a matter of obeying rules. They read Monsignor Knox and Cardinal Newman. Subscribers to the liberal Catholic magazine Commonweal, they spoke of its editor, a friend, as a successful man, though his success clearly wasn't financial. A friend of mine once asked Mom if she'd had so many children because she was a Catholic. She replied no, that she'd wanted to have many children since she was eight years old and had visited a big family. She added, "I'm the kind of Catholic who would have had one child if that's what I wanted."

I acquired none of their faith. To me, religion was pointless rituals: church, confession, Sunday school. We attended mass at St. Cassians (whoever he was). Inside the attractive wood building, stained glass windows shed beautifully colored light, while a priest conducted service in mysterious Latin. On Fridays, you could "confess your sins." I'd kneel in the small, enclosed confessional, the priest would slide a wood panel open and I'd speak through a mesh screen. "Bless me Father for I have sinned..." After hearing my transgressions, the kindly, elderly parish priest would give his standard penance: "Ten Our Fathers, Ten Hail Marys. Now make a good Act of Contrition."

In puberty, I had to reveal that, "I had impure thoughts and deeds." We now had a second priest, young and earnest, who responded to my code phrase with "Alone or with others?" How I longed to answer, "With others. Several others. At the same time!" But no, I had to respond with the humiliating "Alone." The young priest spoke to me at length about how I could resist my urges, how deeply sins of the flesh hurt God. And I'd get a stiff penance. After several sessions with him, I decided I'd never go back. I'd go to the old priest or, increasingly, not bother.

From age six, I went to Sunday school classes run by nuns, where we studied the Baltimore Catechism. I puzzled over that "Baltimore;" it seemed an odd city for God to fix on. But it was never explained. Indeed, nothing was explained. "Study" meant we were supposed to memorize rules about God and man. I remember two: "Who made you? God made you. Why did God make you? To know, love, and serve Him in this world and be happy with Him ever after in Heaven." Catechism held hundreds more rules: the difference between a mortal sin and a venial sin, the difference between actual grace and sanctifying grace, the seven attributes of something or other. The worst sins—surprise!—had something to do with sex. Not that sex was mentioned, but we all knew that when a nun warned vehemently against "near occasions of sin," the sin sure wasn't gluttony.

By the time I was nine, I sat in the back pews at Sunday school and goofed with some buddies. The nuns usually ignored us. When I became an adolescent, Catholicism had dwindled to a gathering of teenagers outside church during Sunday mass. Then, when I was fourteen, Dad got a consulting job in Europe and we spent a year living in Paris. I saw people kissing in the streets and ads for the Folies-Bergére. Dad laughed that French priests seemed unconcerned with "sins of the flesh." What? Sexual morality was relative? My first clue that the Catholicism I'd grown with was distinctly Irish, and not, as it proclaimed, "universal."

A friend once spoke with me about the Jewish history he'd learned growing up. "Well, you learned yours too, in church," he sensibly added. Not a word of it, I replied. Nor did I learn any Irish history in the public schools I attended, nothing about the English conquest and enslavement of Ireland, or Cromwell's devastation (I was told he was a good guy). No troubling questions about why millions starved to death during the potato famine while Ireland exported immense amounts of food to England.

During my twenties, I grew interested in understanding what, if anything, it meant that I was an Irish-American. I began to read Irish literature, and also learned a few nuggets of family history. Some relative had traced Dad's Clifford family back to a legend that an Episcopalian Priest from England ran off with his Irish housemaid. Dad's grandfather was a lad of sixteen when he set out from near Cork for Boston. Somehow, when he got off the boat he was in New Orleans. No one knew anymore how he made it to North Dakota.

Mom's family were Corbetts and McDonalds, from western Ireland. Grandpa's Dad was known as the best jig dancer in county Tyrone. A gamekeeper (and, some said, a poacher) in Ireland, in the U.S. he got a civil service job as keeper of the buffalo herd in Van Cortland Park in the Bronx. Mom grew up in an extended Irish family of parents, brothers, aunts, uncles, grandparents, cousins, a world that vanished in one generation. Well, I had forebears, but, beyond a few good stories, so what?

In 1973, I and my love Linda left California to live in Ireland for several reasons, including curiosity. Why not explore the country of my ancestors?

After dreary days apartment hunting, we found a flat in Monkstown, Dublin, with only a park occupied by a Tinker's wagon separating us from the Irish Sea. Joyce's tower was a couple miles south.

Ireland was poor. The ten-gallon bathtub we had was a luxury, not found in working class homes. Electricity was costly. Our landlord told us that by government decree the heat was on only from twelve at night to eight in the morning.

An aspiring writer, I'd lugged my typewriter from the U.S., planning to buy a transformer to adapt Irish electrical current to my machine. Trudging around Dublin searching for a transformer, I met several shop owners who charmingly assured me they used to have transformers, surely they'd have them tomorrow... but right now, no ... but ... just go up the road, make a left and I'm sure... Finally, I arrived at a major electrical supply store and located the manager, who greeted me cheerily. I told him what I wanted. He was baffled. Several minutes of my fumbling explanations didn't help, but he retained his good spirits as I plugged on. Finally, he brightened.

"Ah, it's a transformer you're wanting."

I allowed that it was.

"Ah yes, well for that, you have to talk to Michael."

"Fine. Can you tell me where he is?"

"To tell you the truth," the man laughed, "I'm looking for him meeself."

Yes, they had a different attitude toward work here than in the U.S. I asked the owner of a hardware store if it was open on Saturdays. "Sometimes," he answered. So perhaps I could ascribe my aversion to the puritan work ethic to my heritage. Maybe it was even in my genes?

Love of talk and language was clearly Irish. People's voices had a lilt. They could speak with the brevity of poetry. When I asked the teenage daughter of a bed and breakfast proprietor why there weren't any Irish history books in their library, she replied, "Ah, it's all written in our hearts." Often, talk had a bite. In a restaurant, I overheard a woman say to her teary daughter, "Ah, love is blind, but marriage is an eye-opener."

The land was beautiful, often wild and harsh. Walking in the fierce winds and lonely hills of Donegal I thought: a man could get strong here—indeed he'd have to be to survive—but he'd never flower. I began to see Mom and Dad as only two generations from a vital, harsh, repressed country. Much about them was understandable as their U.S evolution from Irishness.

We drove back from Donegal through Northern Ireland. Machine-gun toting, full-battle-dressed British troops, mostly teenagers, halted us as we entered the border town of Strabane. The last remaining hotel in the central square had been blown up by the IRA Provos two nights before. Near the ruins, we picked up a hitchhiker, a handsome man who worked for a Dublin ad agency and regularly hitched home on weekends to see his pals and his ma. Driving out of Strabane, we were stopped by more troops. The road was littered with spent rubber bullets. Nearby walls were pockmarked from real bullets and covered with scrawled IRA slogans.

Stunned, I exclaimed my shock. "We're having a wee bit of a social problem," our passenger drawled. I laughed and looked at him, declaring that I was surprised he could joke about it. Smiling, he replied, "Ah, if you didn't laugh at it, you'd go mad."

There was much in Ireland I wasn't finding it easy to laugh at. Birth control and divorce were banned. Books and movies were censored. Beneath their charm, the Irish were essentially impenetrable to this outsider. The few glimpses beneath the surface I got weren't encouraging. In a pub, a guy who worked for an Irish bank said he was envious of me; he'd love to drop out for a while, but he never could. If he did, he'd never be hired again by an Irish bank. At a party, I met a stylishly dressed woman from fashionable Ballsbridge who worked for Irish TV. I asked her if she went to Sunday mass. She nodded yes. I asked why; we both knew she wasn't a believer. "Ah, if you didn't, people would talk."

My only real connection to Dublin life was my one Irish friend from California. Drinking heavily, he'd returned to living with his parents in the Coombe. Watching him tell stories in a pub, performing the same performance I'd seen many times, I felt weariness and yearned for intimacy.

Bitter rain fell on an October day. Sheets of icy water and knife-wind battered me as I ran to a little Monkstown food store. As I shook water from my rain jacket and shivered, the counter-woman said, without apparent irony, "Ah, 't'll be getting cold soon."

SOON! Hey, I'm a Californian. Within days, I was on a plane home. In New York, at JFK, I entered a cacophony of noise, colors, clothes, smells, an immense swirling whirl of peoples: Latinos, Whites, Blacks, Asians, Arabs. Languages and accents seemed innumerable. I recognized Spanish, Italian, Southern U.S., Bronx, French. I felt radiated with human energy, vitality. After I had passed through Customs, I overheard four black workers arguing about basketball, their voices rising above the bedlam of the crowd. "Reed? He'll never come back!" "Oh yeah, and The Celtics gonna stop Frazier with Jo-Jo?" Joyously, I felt, "I'm home!"

I returned to Ireland for a month's visit twenty years later. Much had changed. Urban crime had arrived; some Dublin streets were dangerous even during the day. Most changes, happily, seemed positive. Ireland, a member of the European Community, was actually becoming prosperous. Young men and women seemed freer, less fearful of the church. There was talk that divorce would be legalized. I stayed in several Irish homes, meeting people much more candid than those I'd encountered two decades before. And electricity wasn't controlled by the government. Indeed, I was assured that it never had been.

Much hadn't changed. The people remained witty, hospitable and wonderful talkers. The land, especially in the West, remained fierce. The scale of the country, of course, couldn't change. Ireland would always be small, without the space I loved in the U.S. west. Most of all, I remained clear that being Irish, or Irish-American, simply wasn't my core identity. Much of Irish culture, from its Gaelic sports to the intertwining of church and state, remained foreign to me. I returned to the U.S. with a renewed fondness for Ireland, but reinforced that I was an American.

Yeah, I'm happy to know I'm assimilated. In *Harp*, John Gregory Dunne asserts that the final stage of assimilation is "deracination," being fully uprooted. I suggest the final stage is the reverse, being fully re-rooted, at home (if not at ease) with U.S. oxygen. The immigrant's sense of being an outsider, or living in dual worlds, has vanished. "This land is my land, from California to the New York Island," from jazz and rock and roll to ghettos and gun nuts.

But for all its complexities, U.S. culture can be thin soil. Didn't I lose much of value because my sense of being "Irish" is so attenuated? Wouldn't I have grown up with a deeper sense of myself, less alienated, if my Irish heritage had been passed on to me?

I doubt it. Perhaps I would have had a more solid sense of identity if Grandma and Grandpa had told me stories of their lives, revealing their immigrant experiences. But they had walls against revealing. They brought those walls from Ireland. As Mary Gordon observed, until recently, the Irish inhibition against revealing resulted in curious dearth of writing about the Irish-American assimilation experiences—James T. Farrell, Edwin O'Connor, not many more.

Certainly my parents weren't concerned with passing on "Irishness," with the exception of Catholicism. They didn't want to be hyphenated Americans, they wanted to be Americans, plain and pure.

Beyond this, what heritage am I talking about? Since I was never told any, I can create my fantasy, a melange of history (tragic or heroic), family sagas and love of Irish writers. Hey, throw in Irish music and dance too. And make sure it's all transmitted by genuine enthusiasm. Nothing compulsory, or I'll hate it.

How romantic, a "heritage" with all pains, vindictiveness and oppressions removed from Irish life and character. If the truth could really be told, how dark was my heritage? And how varied? Does it make sense to lump my ancestors into a single "heritage?" All questions I'll never be able to answer. I suspect there was much darkness in my ancestors' Irish life, darkness still sometimes manifest in the U.S., as with the banning homosexuals from New York's St. Patrick's day parade.

Not that being an Irish-American feels meaningless. I enjoy using my ethnicity as one prism for viewing life, especially with Irish-American friends. A little deeper, I enjoy rummaging around in traditions of what's Irish, extracting what seems to fit: yeah, I've got the gift of gab, I'm a dreamer, a rebel. When I was younger, I'd offer being Irish as a convenient explanation, if not justification, for drinking too much. Deepest, I try to live those of my parents' Irish-American values that I value, from hospitality to love of reading to demand for freedom. On the other hand are Irish traits like melancholy or fear of intimacy that I'd like to move as far away from as I can. And how about the demons that can torment me? Are they inherited from my father? From Ireland?

Whatever those demons are, I don't—can't—define myself as "Irish." I do read Irish writers, and follow the country's politics with more interest than most Americans, but Ireland's not a country I feel a profound attachment to. I'm not a member of any Irish-American social group. My romantic dreams haven't included marrying an Irish-American woman to keep the genetic strain (whatever that is) pure. And I've surely never returned to the church.

I suspect mine is a typical evolution, and that ethnic origins, though interesting, will dwindle in significance as descendants of immigrants from any nation become fully Americanized. After years in Manhattan, whose residents are surely conscious of ethnicity, my brother Steve moved to Seattle. A Seattlite mentioned someone who had, to Steve, an ethnically puzzling name. He asked, "What kind of name is that?" The Seattlite looked puzzled. "It's an American name," he answered.

This is not to argue against diversity. How can you knock someone for feeling connected to an ethnic tradition? My friends who find richness in Berkeley's alternate Jewish community are fortunate. Sure, preserve all the "old ways," from rituals, custom, and ceremonies to music, dance, and art, that people care to. But all the while, the dominant U.S. culture will continue to absorb and alter values brought from other lands. Seen from the reverse perspective, formerly distinctive ethnic values evolve, blend and enrich the larger, amorphous U.S. culture. This process is far more liberating than sad, let alone tragic. As the artist Robert Henri wrote "The greatest American ... will be heir to the world instead of part of it, and will go to every place where he feels he may find something of the information he desires, whether it be in one province or another."

[1993]

MOM

Mom loved telling stories. Born to immigrant parents in 1912, she grew up in Manhattan's Irish-American culture and raised her seven children in the suburb of Upper Montclair, New Jersey. She had her last children, Justin and Catherine, when she was forty and forty-two, so in her late fifties she had two teenagers caught up in the tumult of "The Sixties."

Mom, myself, and my three-years-younger brother Steve were on the house porch of our funky, loved summer home in Old Forge in New York's Adirondacks. Mom, now in her seventies, remained as active as ever—rowing her aluminum rowboat three miles every evening, swimming regularly, riding her bike around town. I asked her what it had been like having two high schoolers in the 60s.

She laughed. "I was upstairs, changing Justin's sheets. His desk was open and I saw a plastic bag—two bags—with green leaves inside them. I knew it must be marijuana. I thought—how dare he bring that home! So I took them to the bathroom and flushed all the leaves down the toilet. That will teach him a lesson, I thought."

"That evening, Justin ran into the kitchen, hysterically asking if I had … if I had seen … any plastic bags on his desk. I told him that I found the marijuana while cleaning his room and flushed it down the toiled."

"'Mom,' he wailed. 'I haven't paid for that... I ....' He was shaking. "Now I haven't got it.'"

"'What?' I demanded."

"'I got it from two guys in Newark. If I don't pay them, they'll break my legs. Or kill me.'"

"Of course he didn't have any money. So I wound up paying $150 for it. Some lesson," she laughed.

Mom had been frugal since she was a young girl, long before being imprinted by the Depression. Family members had told her, "You're just like your Aunt Hattie," a well-known penny-pincher. Her father, a civil servant in the New York Dock Department, had uncharacteristically speculated on Florida produce in the late 20s, and lost. Without warning, one Sunday he put up a "For Sale" sign in front of their house, and Mom lost the only home she ever loved as a child.

Dad was a modestly-paid math professor at Montclair State, supporting a growing family. We surely weren't affluent. We only had the summer house in Old Forge because Grandpa bought it in 1947 for $4500. Yet somehow Mom and Dad managed to have a mortgage on their Montclair home for only three years. Mom economized on little things too. She regularly mixed powdered milk with fresh milk to cut down on our milk costs. In her old age, I learned that she had account books listing every single expenditure she'd made since being married in 1936. I laughed, "Ah, your skills were wasted. You should have been fiscal officer at the Pentagon."

Steve, a graduate of Harvard Business School, became a Special Deputy Controller of the City of New York during its fiscal crisis of 1975. That July, several of us kids gathered in Old Forge. (Mom later told us that she'd had mixed feelings about that: "A number of adults who used to be my children are coming to live in my house.") At a dinner, Mom served us dessert of ample raspberries and said: "This morning I was thinking about getting raspberries for dessert and wondering if I should buy one box or two. They're expensive. Then I was walking through the living room and I heard Steve talking on the phone, saying, 'No, not that $400 million. It's the other $700 million,' and I decided—if my son can talk about hundreds of millions of dollars, I'm going to buy TWO boxes of raspberries."

Our family culture valued humor, wit, and good conversation, especially about politics, and above all, telling good stories. Perhaps I was ten when Mom and Dad returned from a dinner out and sighed, "Oh, are they DULL." I wasn't sure what dull was, but I knew it was something I must never be.

As a teenager, I was occasionally supposed to assist Mom with household chores. I rapidly learned that what she truly wanted was an audience, not help. I'd lounge as she worked and told her stories: How she and her neighbor Parnell learned to read at age five and were rewarded by being advanced two grades, from first to third, when they started school. Or how the nuns at the high school and then the college of Mt. Saint Vincent had mercilessly picked on her because she was a scholarship student, not from a wealthy Catholic family as most of the girls were. (Both Imelda Marcos and the Cory Aquino went there).

Whatever the miseries of her adolescence, Mom had astonishing energy as an adult. A small woman, five feet, two inches, she had a pretty Irish face, brown hair and eyes, and a lithe figure. Intensely athletic, she loved to hike and rode her bicycle through the tree-lined streets of Montclair. I recall being horribly embarrassed, hanging out with some high school buddies, as she whizzed by on her bike. Why didn't she drive around in a car, as other moms did?

Active in local Democratic Party politics, Mom once told me that she was twelve before she understood that it wasn't a mortal sin to vote Republican. She was also active in the League of Women Voters. And a successful writer, publishing a column in the weekly Montclair Times and numerous articles in Parents' Magazine, including one article not only reprinted in the Reader's Digest, but featured on the Digest's front cover, along with two other authors—Truman Capote and Jean Stafford. Mom's article, published at the height of the '50 hysteria that "violent" comic books were warping young children, argued that what mattered was that kids learned to love reading. Comic books were not a threat— If kids started with them, they'd soon move on to the Hardy Boys and Nancy Drew, then further on to better books.

Our friends were always welcome at our house. Mom was not concerned with meticulous housecleaning nor interested in women who waged a ceaseless war against dust. On her wedding day, in 1936, her mother had told her, "Remember, Dear, you never saw a statue of a great housekeeper."

Mom didn't preach self-reliance and was sympathetic when I told her of childhood miseries like not being chosen for a baseball team, but we were not coddled. My favorite among Mom's many sayings was the words she'd often utter when one of her young children came sobbing to her after suffering a minor fall or slight bruise to the ego. "There, there," she'd say soothingly, while giving the child a soft hug, "Nothing trivial, I hope." While in high school, it was important to me that my chinos and shirts be freshly ironed. Which meant I learned to be a good ironer. Mom had made it clear she had no time for that.

When we were sick, we were generally left alone to heal, like a wounded animal. Being sick wasn't exactly a disgrace, but it surely didn't warrant coddling. The doctor was a very busy man, and not to be called unless we were seriously ill. Mom herself must have gotten sick sometimes, but I can't remember one occasion. She was, quietly, very tough. She always refused to use Novocaine at the dentist's. Why I never knew. Dad was equally stoic. Occasionally his back would "go out"—which was all he said about it. He'd go to his chiropractor who, I gathered, somehow snapped his back "back in" and Dad promptly returned to normal.

To say that Mom didn't believe in being overprotective only hints at the freedom she allowed her young children. Steve was allowed to roam freely when quite young, at age five, six, or seven. Sometimes he'd walk several blocks to the closest shopping street. At times, a policeman would stop and question him there, and he'd respond, "I'm allowed to be here." On rare occasions, a policeman would insist on taking him home, where my mother would tell the officer, "He's allowed to be there."

During our high school and college summers, I, my two-years-younger sister Joanne and Steve all worked at the Enchanted Forest, a woodsy amusement park on thirty-five acres in Old Forge. At various times during my summers there, Mom would drop off young Catherine, ages four to seven, at the Forest. Often dressed in a little princess costume, beautiful Catherine ranged freely through the Forest for hours. The employees knew her and loved her and, as far as I know, she had nothing but fun.

Sometimes, Mom's nurturing was inspired. Believing that much could be accomplished by a good letter, she wrote one to each of the three New York major league baseball teams, requesting that Steve and I be permitted to meet some players. Amazingly, the Brooklyn Dodgers responded, saying they would be pleased to allow Steve and I to visit the dugout before the game. We did, met some players—Jackie Robinson! And Gil Hodges, Peewee Reese, Preacher Roe— and we each got an autographed baseball (I've long since lost mine), and memories that have lasted a lifetime.

Though Mom was, in her own fashion, a devout Catholic, her deepest religion, as I understood when older, was that her children go to Ivy League colleges. We were to become members of the elite. In high school, I understood, without ever being told, that whatever else I could do wrong, I could not get bad grades. I got one C in one marking period in 11th grade math. Neither Mom nor Dad castigated me, but their disappointment was so deep and genuine that I vowed I would never get another high school grade below B. I didn't.

The first six of Mom's children all went to Ivy League colleges. Only Catherine, achievement-indifferent in the rebellious '60s, went to a less prestigious college—where she got as good an education as any of the rest of us, in her opinion and mine.

Once Justin and Catherine were in junior high, Mom decided to get a job, wanting to be more engaged in the world and to earn her own money, although our family was no longer financially pressed. Dad, one of the pioneers of Quality Control (the application of statistics to testing assembly-line products) had become a highly successful consultant, though he always retained his teaching job—and took the summers off. Mom got a masters degree in library science, then a job as the librarian in a ghetto junior high school in Newark. She loved reading, loved teaching kids reading, and loved young children. Soon the library had six copies of a kids' biography of Muhammad Ali and comic books about Malcolm X and Harriet Tubman. Mom happily reported that kids were starting to like coming to the library. A couple of years later she said that some teachers threatened unruly students that they would not be allowed to go to the library if they continued to make trouble.

In the late '70s, the entire family, all nine of us together, by then a rare event, were at a pre-Christmas dinner. Conversation was flowing when one of us kids blurted out, "Oh shit." Dad, looking stern, exclaimed, "Please—your mother is present." Mom glanced wryly at him and said, "If you knew how often I hear the word 'motherfucker.'"

During her first years in Montclair, Mom told me, she'd been so shy that she'd walked across the street to avoid saying hello to a woman she'd met. But she developed her social skills and facade, pursued her own societal ambitions, and eventually rose to top of the still-dominantly-WASP Montclair women's social ladder, becoming a member of the Art Museum Board—which provided her with new stories. At a Board meeting, an old-line dowager was deriding the Italians, who lived in the poorer Fourth Ward. "They breed like rabbits. That woman has eight children." Then, realizing that my mother was at the meeting, she said, "I mean seven is fine, but eight?"

As she aged, Mom became more relaxed and spoke more freely. She was interested in and followed the Women's Movement. She became overtly dubious of the Catholic (male-celibate) hierarchy. She once said about Pope John-Paul II, "Who does he think is listening to him?" In my forties, she and Dad joined a few friends in my Berkeley apartment for my birthday celebration. Near the end of dinner, my friend Hayden, who was gay, learned over to her and asked, "Did you have seven children because your are a Catholic?" Mom answered, "No, I'm the kind of Catholic who would have had one child if that's what I wanted." Hayden followed with, "What is it like to have seven children?' Mom smiled at him and said, "What is it like to be gay?" Hayden replied, "Do you want to talk?" Mom nodded yes. The two adjourned to the living room and talked with engaged intensity for over twenty minutes.

Mom also became more adventurous. With money from her librarian's job, she, stunningly, purchased a new car—a white Ford Galaxy 500 convertible, with red leather upholstery. Other adventures were more active, including mountain climbing, which she'd loved reading about for decades. Hillary and Tenzing, the first conquerors of Mt. Everest, were among her heroes. In her seventies, she attended a daylong mountain-climbing class on one of the high peaks of the Adirondacks. She returned thrilled—she'd actually climbed—though once seemed to satisfy her.

Mom did not discourage her kids' rebel streaks. During seventh grade I came home and proudly announced that our homeroom teacher had angrily put it to a class vote: either I and my buddy Timmy went, or the teacher did. Of course, the class voted that he went. Mom, more pleased at my defiance than bothered by my innocence in believing I'd prevailed, shook her head, saying that now she'd have to call the Principal and help straighten things out. Smiling, she reaffirmed the message: Stand up to them, rebel.

But her message of "rebel" was complicated. We were not only to rebel, but to succeed. Become an aristocrat, but not a WASP. Steve, who chose a straighter path than me, graduated from Harvard Business School. [Joanne had graduated from Harvard Law School, where she'd been the first woman Notes Editor of the Harvard Law Review.] Steve eventually became CEO of a major TV/radio/communications corporation. He enjoyed dressing the part and wore Saville Row suits elegantly. "You should have seen how proud Mom was when she saw me in one of those suits," he told me. "Finally, her son was a Duke. We'd bested the English at last."

Mom's message to rebel was never stated explicitly. Only as an adult did I comprehend that Mom grew up in a family mistrustful of authority, particularly British authority. An old picture of Mom as a child with her brothers in a donkey cart, taken at some Democratic Party rally in the Bronx, included a large Sinn Fein sign that Grandpa had taped on the cart. An uncle of Grandpa's had been executed by the British in the 1880s. Grandpa himself, I learned only after he died, would never allow an Englishman inside his home.

Mom professed to worship Grandpa. He was a strong, dominant man—a great athlete, champion rower, and swimmer—and (according to Mom) well-respected for his integrity as a high-level civil servant in the New York City Dock Department; during his tenure there, integrity was far from what the Department was commonly known for. As one encouragement to developing Mom's swimming prowess, Grandpa once had her swim across the Hudson River, with a canoe tied to her waist.

Grandpa and Grandma, raised in Manhattan's Irish-Immigrant Hell's Kitchen, now lived in respectable Riverdale. Every Christmas day we crossed the Hudson to visit them for a family gathering. Each year, Mom spent considerable energy and thought trying to find Grandpa a present he'd love. Whatever she gave him, he'd open it, at best barely nod, then ignore it, saying nothing. One Christmas when I was in my teens Mom believed she'd finally done it. Grandpa, now retired and suffering from serious arthritis, had transferred much of his intensity to bird watching. Mom researched and searched until she found the perfect birdhouse— just right for the birds that flew by his house, for the weather, and for attaching it to his back window.

Grandpa unwrapped the birdhouse and held it out, eyeing it skeptically as his lip curled. "That's silly," he snapped. "What would I want that for?" and dropped it down. Mom erupted in tears, sobbing that he'd never loved her. Dad, standing beside me, said quietly, "I don't understand how two people who love each other so much can hurt each other so much." Adults quickly bustled us kids upstairs. When we were called back down, the grownups presented themselves cheerfully, and it was Christmas again.

When my grandfather died, every present my mother had ever given him was found hidden away in his attic. Each present was carefully preserved and dated with the year he'd received it.

Though I'm fifteen years older than my sister Catherine, we became very close over three decades ago. Through Catherine, I learned much about Mom I wouldn't otherwise have known. Mom had been molested as a child, by an older male cousin. (God knows what that did to her.) She told Catherine and Joanne that if any boy or man ever touched her or bothered her she'd done absolutely nothing wrong, but be sure and tell Mom immediately. (I didn't press Catherine for details, but I understood that Mom had been sufficiently explicit so that Catherine knew what she was talking about.)

Catherine also reported that Mom had told her, early during Catherine's puberty, that sex was wonderful—but of course you waited until you were married.

Mom, Catherine told me, was sympathetic to the Women's Movement, although she disliked Betty Freidan, because of her dismissive view of housewives. Mom identified as a housewife, which included leading an active, involved life, as she and most all of her housewife friends did. Subservience, in Mom's view, was not part of being a housewife, although simultaneously she made it clear to Catherine that part of a woman's job was to support men's "fragile egos." Mom also didn't like that Freidan was homely. Mom much preferred the glamorous Gloria Steinem. Catherine observed that much as Mom agreed with the essence of the Women's movement, and loved earning her own money as a school librarian, she retained her rootedness in the value of being popular, which included being pretty.

Another Catherine story: She and Mom were discussing therapy, which Catherine had resumed in her late twenties. Mom said, "I know many of my children have been in therapy, and it seems to help, but I never saw any reason for therapy ... Well, there were those two years I was depressed all the time, but I knew I was happy, and ... besides, they'd just say something like I hated your grandfather, Ha Ha Ha."

When Catherine was fifteen, she went to Mom and told her that she was going to ask her something, "I know it will upset you, but I want you to think it over and let me know." Mom said, "Oh Catherine, I'm sure whatever it is will be fine." Catherine replied, "I'm going to get birth control, and I'd like your help and take me to Dr. N. (our family doctor)." Mom was distressed and shocked to her Irish-Catholic core. Catherine calmly responded, "Mom, I am going to get birth control. If you can, I'd like you to help. If you can't, I'll understand and I will go elsewhere." Three days later, Mom told Catherine that she would take her to Dr. N.

I could benefit from Catherine's family courage. Throughout my twenties, when I returned home, I went to Mass on Sunday, or at least pretended to, sometimes instead driving to a nearby diner during Mass time. Then, a couple of days before I was to go to another Sunday Mass, Mom announced that I didn't have to go. Stunned, I asked why. She said, "Catherine told me that she no longer believes in Catholicism, and she does not want to go to a church she doesn't believe in. So she isn't. And

I know that none of you (her older six children) have believed in it for years."

I also learned from Catherine that Mom come to understand the depth of Dad's ambition. By the start of World War II, Dad had become frustrated at the limits of his teaching job at Montclair State. Bright-side Mom reassured him that they were happy together, had two healthy children, a nice home and enough money, which was enough for her. Dad replied, "Well, It's not enough for me."

Mom and Dad were generally happy together. Many Sunday afternoons while I was growing up, they'd go for as long walk together. They'd return talking animatedly, alive with energy. Mom admired Dad's keen mind, and she loved to tell stories of his irreverent side. At a boring Montclair dinner Dad drank two full cups of coffee, and the man next to him asked, "Paul, doesn't that keep you awake?" "Well," Dad replied, "it helps."

They'd met at a Catholic Newman Club dance in the early 30s. Both were studying at Columbia—Dad working on his Ph.D. in math, and Mom getting a Master's Degree in Economics. They went out for three years, until as Mom told it, her parents were going on a long trip and her father told Dad that he couldn't come to her house while her parents were gone—unless the two were engaged. So engaged they became.

Late in her life, while Mom and I were waiting in a hospital for Dad to be brought out of surgery, she talked of the initial years of their marriage. She had often been tearful, even hysterical, fearing that the marriage was doomed, that something was dreadfully wrong. Dad, she said, had been a rock, always patient and loving, always assuring her that she was fine and they would be fine. And he remained patient, loving and positive during those first three years when she'd been unable to get pregnant, while she was bring treated by a fertility specialist in Manhattan, Dr. Berry.

Several times while I was growing up, I accompanied Mom to Dr. Berry's office. I don't recall Mom ever telling me what Dr. Berry did or why we were visiting him, but I definitely recall entering his waiting room, with a few to several women sitting there with tension so powerful even I could sense it. Then Dr. Berry would emerge and exclaim, "Ah,

Mrs. Clifford, my most successful patient!" I can't recall if I sensed tension dissipating then or if I simply much later understood that Mom and Dr. Berry were participating in a ritual of gratitude and hope.

Dad was often annoyed with his kids, though invariably compassionate if any were in serious trouble. Mom was generally cheerful, with occasional explosions; she'd become furious that her kids did little or nothing to help around the house. "There's going to be a New Regime around here!" Mom's New Regime phase usually lasted no more than a day or two. During that phase Dad made sure that no kid risked further offending Mom and that we volunteered to help with chores.

Mom was a myth-maker, and Dad was an important subject for her myths. During the rise of the Women's Movement, she told me, "Your father was always ahead of his time. Remember that article I wrote called 'Mom's Weekend Off' when you three oldest kids were little, and he took over." Actually, he took over for a weekend once. Though, to give him credit, he regularly washed the dinner dishes and cooked Sunday breakfast.

Mom could also be clear-eyed about Dad. In our summer home, he loved being in his workshop, making repairs and using tools (never power tools). He once told Mom, "You know, what I'd really like to do is run a junk shop." "For about two years," she replied.

Mom seemed to accept their differences without complaint. Dad was a heavy smoker, three packs a day from the time he was sixteen. Mom never smoked a single cigarette. I once asked her why, "It always seemed stupid," she replied. In her seventies, Mom said lightly to me, "Of course, your father is an unreconstructed chauvinist, but it's too late to change him."

As I grew older, I began to realize that Mom was more complex than I'd understood when younger. I'd moved to California in 1967, working as a lawyer for the poor in Oakland. During a return to Old Forge in the mid-70s I spoke enthusiastically with Mom about my Bay Area culture, especially my learning that I could be honest and intimate with truly close friends. Mom, looking at me as if I were distressingly naïve, pronounced, "Denis, everyone's always wearing a mask."

Her myth-making was more extensive and mysterious than I'd realized. I doubted that the Upper Montclair she spoke of—a sort of suburban Bloomsbury, full of brilliant, fascinating and yet untroubled adults—really existed. Deeper, several years after my divorce, Dad revealed that Mom was maintaining secret communications with my ex-wife. Mom, unhappy that there'd been a divorce in our family, hoped to restore it (ie, me) to her myth of what a Catholic family should be.

Late in Mom's life, I learned from Catherine that while at Columbia, Mom was one of the few female graduate students and had been a belle-of-the-ball, for the first time in her life. She was in no rush to become engaged, but Dad had insisted on it. I never learned why Mom chose to create the myth that it was Dad who'd been trapped—well at least pressured—into getting married.

As I grew my forties and beyond, I'd sometimes feel sad that Mom didn't like me to touch her. Even after she'd relaxed in many other ways, when I'd give her even a gentle shoulder hug she'd freeze, her body tense. Finally, I stopped trying.

Over many years, I slowly realized that Mom told many different stories that all had the same core: "They thought I was nobody, but found out I was somebody." One form of this was the Frank Lautenberg story. From Lautenberg's initial entry to elective politics as a New Jersey candidate for the Senate, Mom had been one of his first Democratic Party backers. Elected, he went on to serve as the long-time U. S. Senator. He retained a fondness for Mom. At various major Democratic Party functions over many years, Mom reported that she was generally being ignored, until Lautenberg came to her, hugged her and exclaimed, "Kay Clifford! I'm one of your biggest fans." And all around her were impressed—she was Somebody.

As she retold me that story once again, I felt almost embarrassed for her. Why her need to repeat, "They thought I was nobody, but found out I was somebody"? Then, in an atypical flash of intuition, I knew that need was from her childhood, and asked, "Mom, what was it like when you and Parnell skipped two grades?" She explained that Parnell's mother had taught him and her how to read before they started school, so, when Mom was just not quite seven, they were shot from first grade to third grade (back then, considered an honor). Third-grade math had been difficult for her. Making no school friends, beyond Parnell, had been much worse. "I was always the littlest and the smallest, always left out, never got chosen." I saw how wounded she'd been, and that part of her soul remained traumatized and continued to hunger for acceptance by the In-Group. I said, "That sounds horrible." She said it definitely had been, then became quiet. So I asked what Parnell had been like and she beamed, and began to tell me Parnell stories.

[2013]

ALMOST A HIPPIE

Hippies were cool—rebels, free. I'd first learned that in the mid-1960s, while living in Manhattan and finishing up a clerkship after law school. Reading Tom's Wolfe's *The Electric Cool-Aid Acid Test*, his tale of those archetypal hippies, Ken Kesey and the Merry Pranksters, stimulated my dreams of escaping stifling East Coast culture.

I arrived in San Francisco at the end of "The Summer of Love"— Labor Day weekend, 1967. But I was no hippie drop out. I was excited about my new job, working for Legal Services in an Oakland ghetto. Joining in the struggle for social justice was to live in the heart of my times.

My wife Ronnie had an old friend who knew a guy from the San Francisco Art Institute who played drums and had joined a band with some kids who lived near him. That first weekend, we set off to hear them play.

The band turned out to be Big Brother and the Holding Company, the singer Janis Joplin. The opening bands were the Jefferson Airplane and the Grateful Dead. A wild crowd jammed the Fillmore, dancing, leaping, laughing, hugging, kissing. Men wore Mexican shirts or loin clothes and bangles or billowing pantaloons or were bare-chested or wearing god knows what. In my Manhattan circles, men still wore ties to dinner parties. Luscious women writhed in see-through blouses or swirled in frayed gossamer gowns, or tie-died skirts, or gypsy garb or very little, with shiny silver things on their foreheads or tiaras or flowers in their flowing hair.

I smelled, then saw, marijuana everywhere. Strangers handed me joints. (Well, at least I wasn't a novice there; Ronnie, a bohemian Californian, had introduced me to dope a few years before.) After the first two bands finished, the crowd seemed exhausted; people sprawled on the floor or slumped against walls. Big Brother came on, Janis belted out the start of "Combination of the Two," and the instantly-frenzied crowd leapt in near unison to their feet, ecstatic. I felt excited, confused, and, deepest, unnerved. To paraphrase the prophet Bob Dylan, Something Was Happening Here and I Didn't Know What It Was, Did I, Mr. C?

For years, I'd managed to convince myself that I was cool; now I suddenly felt shaken. Real hippies were uninhibited, sexual, and at the glowing center—where I never managed to be. Worse, I sensed something ominous about their wildness, or perhaps wildness in me. But I was a twenty-seven year old Irish-American from a New Jersey suburb, reared to deny disturbing emotions. I told Ronnie I'd loved it all.

Within a few months, I had the hippie style down. My hair was growing towards shoulder length, I'd loved rock and roll since first hearing Elvis and Chuck Berry as a teenager, and I surely didn't have to fake the attitude that the grown-up world was a drag. I'd known since high school that joining what I was now sneering at as the "straight world" would break me. I'd read enough about alienation in college, lived it enough working two years for Manhattan publishers before going to law school. There must be some way I could live authentically, from my core.

Ronnie and I, drawn to hippie virtues of spontaneity and exploration, smoked more dope and roamed through San Francisco, meandering around Haight-Ashbury, the original hippie center, or hanging out in bohemian coffee houses in North Beach, or marveling at gorgeous stained glass windows in Victorian houses. With new friends, fellow seekers, including kindred spirits at Legal Services, we speculated on our futures, agreeing that Hippie could be more than escape, and deeper than sex-drugs-and-rock-and-roll. We were going to create a new, better world. I had little vision what that would be, beyond the elimination of corporate hierarchies and neckties.

Ah well, vision wasn't my job. Passionately working for legal changes benefiting poor people, I focused on Governor Reagan's "welfare reform laws" which were often illegal under controlling federal law, and sometimes unconstitutional as well. Within a year, I felt hopeful. We'd won some major cases. A federal judge had prohibited enforcement of the Reagan-rule allowing a welfare department to deny money for two months to an otherwise eligible family because the department previously had mistakenly "overpayed" them. Under the rule, it was immaterial that the parent—almost always, a single mother—had no idea she'd been overpaid, and had no other resources to support and feed her family.

I became head of a nine-attorney, twenty-employee neighborhood law office in East Oakland. Thirty, thirty-five, sometimes forty clients a day flooded into our office with their miseries. Aside from individual service work and law reform—law revolution was more my dream—we'd begun to work with some community groups, from the East Oakland Black Panthers to nascent welfare rights organizations.

As if I didn't see enough injustice at work to enrage me, the Vietnam War continued to poison my life, as well as the country. I screamed anger during protest marches, rallies, Stop the Draft Week, and admired both those committed to non-violent civil disobedience and the angrier radicals who called for moving "from protest to resistance."

In contrast to that fury, my hippie dream grew more alluring. Theodore Rozak's writings spoke of the new "Counterculture" hippies were creating. Charles Reich's *The Greening of America* described our new consciousness, free of materialistic values. The core would be community. "Men are free when they belong to a living, organic, believing community, active in fulfilling some unfilled, perhaps unrealized purpose," D. H. Lawrence had proclaimed. The essence of our new community would be cooperation, perhaps even love, not the destructive American competition I'd first experienced in Cub Scout baseball, when angry, uptight men (not my Dad) dominated our games and inflicted their "must-win" tensions on us kids.

As 1969 passed, I realized that I wasn't willing (yet?) to experiment with radical new forms of community. I didn't want to live in a commune, or become a member of a work collective or move "back to the land." (I joked that it was only three generations since my Irish forebears had wisely fled the land.) Happily, the hippie spirit, seething with change, also encouraged less radical experiments.

With Adrian, a friend from work, fellow book lover and East Coast escapee, as well as a dashing adventurer—he owned a motorcycle— I organized a weekly dinner meeting of several office colleagues and mates. Perhaps we'd evolve into a commune. Also, I signed up for a class in making stained glass windows, a craft just being liberated from church-guild secretiveness. Since I'd first seen stained glass windows in my hometown Catholic Church, they'd thrilled me. But—me, try to make some art? Fortunately, the liberating hippie *ethos* urged everyone to be creative. Why not try?

"Break on through to the other side," the Doors urged. I hadn't broken through yet, but perhaps soon … Curious about LSD, I held back. Smoking dope had occasionally released feelings of "paranoia." I'd instinctively smothered fears I'd felt at a rock show in 1968 with Ronnie and another couple. Stoned, anxiety throbbed inside me, screeching that I knew nothing of the core of any of them. Nor did I mention to Ronnie, who'd become increasingly remote since quitting her art history Ph.D. and becoming an aspiring actress, my experience at a workshop of Anna Halprin, dance experimenter. She'd directed our group to roll over onto each other. I'd rolled onto a woman's body, feeling illicit thrills as she'd writhed sensually, then languidly rolled on top of me. And I surely wouldn't divulge my attraction to beautiful Cathy, who I'd met at a meeting of a foundation-funded group trying to reform Oakland schools.

The War dragged on; Nixon was apparently impervious to dissent. The U.S. cultural war grew nastier. One night, walking in San Francisco's North Beach, I passed a crew cut, stocky, middle aged man who sneered "Hippie" at me. I turned toward him. "My kind hates your kind," he snarled. Asshole, I glared silently back, I'm not a kind—but I'm on the right side. Your world is dying.

Mine definitely had better music. Joan Baez sang at non-violent civil disobedience actions. The Grateful Dead played for hours at a benefit for radical lawyers. Protesting the War with tens of thousands at Golden Gate Park, I roared exuberantly with Country Joe and the Fish, "And it's one, two three, what are we fighting for? Don't ask me I don't give a Damn, next stop is Vietnam."

By 1971, my passion for Legal Services work was dwindling. The ocean of clients wore at me. What we really needed, our increasingly morbid office humor had concluded, was a drawer of money, so we could hand some to each client. Worse, practicing law, from handling an individual's case to law reform, was a cumbersome and rarely effective way to help our clients. Our welfare victories were usually negated by some new maneuver of Reagan's minions. The Reagan welfare overpayment rule, returning from the dead, was now a "presumption" that a recipient who'd received too much money knew that. The fight began again.

Major social/economic change was needed, which required a mass political movement. Which wasn't happening, "Counterculture" or not, aside from the still-surging force of the anti-war Movement. Beyond all that, I just wasn't enjoying lawyering. Legal struggles felt artificial and draining. Fighting the Man was frustratingly distant from evolving a saner, authentic life. So what to do?

Enjoy what I do have, I thought. At work, I'd made several good friends, including Al, the first close black friend I ever had. And I received a salary, so I could postpone figuring out what I'd do for a career.

I was well aware that I was riding two horses, as I had for years— the "real" (now the hippie) me and the conventional me who could maneuver in society. If I cut my hair, my resumé remained dressed-for-success: Cum laude at Amherst, Columbia Law Review, federal court clerkship. Perhaps I could become a law professor? At least I'd get summers off. Ah, I didn't want to teach law. Maybe, I groped, becoming a revolutionary was the answer. How about exploring Cuba, a revolutionary society?

A severe white woman and a stoic Asian man interviewed me for admission to the next Venceremous Brigade, radical gringos who went to Cuba to cut sugarcane. They asked me if I agreed that, "Black people were the vanguard of the revolutionary struggle in the U.S." I replied that I didn't, adding that, "Most of the welfare mothers I've worked with dream their children will to go to college." They scornfully dismissed me; yet once again, I'd flunked an attitude test.

Then—Boom! Ronnie announced she no longer loved me and was moving out. She stayed mostly gone, but returned occasionally for a cold, non-communicative night. For weeks, I catapulted between agony and lethargic despair. An excellent judge bawled me out for sloppy work I'd submitted in a test case. Knowing the judge was right, I was stunned at my indifference. I don't care, my soul's misery wanted to scream.

Struggling to understand Yeats' "the foul rag and bone shop of the heart," I sought comfort and insights from friends. After some time, their aid, plus introspection, and, eventually, glimmers of boredom with self-absorbed wretchedness, had revived my spirit so I could act. Weeks after I'd first tried to pick up the phone to call Cathy, I finally grasped the courage to make the call. Astonishingly, she said she'd love to go out. More astonishingly, on our date in San Francisco, we laughed heartily and talked merrily—not that I revealed my torments to her. Most astonishingly, soon we were lovers, making love with a passion I'd never felt before. Amazing—the "sexual revolution" was not mostly media hype as I'd thought, but real, and I was included.

Months after she'd first left, Ronnie returned one evening and announced that I was invited to join her at a party of her theater crowd. As we left on a warm spring afternoon, she produced some LSD. Afraid as I was of it, I impulsively decided to take some. What the hell—how much worse could I feel? Was I an explorer or not?

Standing near a tree, I felt extreme weirdness, as a sort of metallic energy coursed through my body. My knees trembled, as if I'd descended thousands of feet on a steep trail. My entire body vibrated. The party crowd swirled like a movie out of focus. Images, thoughts, feelings flashed though me at light speed. I sank down and gripped the ground, as frightened as a baby on a roller coaster.

Time crumbled. Unable to stand, I was engulfed in shuddering hysteria. Randomly, words emerged from the whirl: "fool," "real," "fear." Then the swirl roared on ominously. My face trembled; I was starting to whimper. I pressed my hands into my thighs, craving that the fact that I existed would halt this madness. It didn't. Some wall had crumbled in my soul, letting out hundreds of accusers. "You knew we were here all along," they cried in vicious triumph. "You fool!" "Look at Ronnie!" a voice howled, "Who is she?" When I looked, the stranger I saw chatting merrily with others terrified me.

Cowering under the tree, shaking, I snorted air through my nostrils. "What is it?" a stern voice demanded. "Love?" "You can't name it," a shrill voice mocked. "It doesn't have a cause. It is the cause." Images from my past—lies, public disgraces, cowardices, evasions, failures, most long forgotten—flashed in my mind. "And you think of yourself as a rebel," a voice sneered. "Fool. You've always taken the safe road."

Suddenly aware of my breathing, I poked my stomach—spongy, blubbery. Jabbing my shoulders, and my chest, I felt no strength there, no muscles. "And you pretend to be an athlete?" a voice sank beneath scorn to revulsion. "You've always been skinny, and now you're fat too."

I sat under the tree for hours, as waves of fear and self-loathing slowly receded, the babble of voices slowly subsided. But I knew they'd spoken the truth: I hated Ronnie, my body, and myself. I was alone and afraid—that was all I really knew.

A bad trip? Sure. But deeper, my profound introduction to LSD as the poor man's psychiatrist. With the mess that I'd discovered I was, I was going to change the world? Time to start trying to save myself. Some changes merely required discipline, like beginning regular workouts. But how to access my "feelings?" I was an emotional teen-ager. Could I love, or learn to love? Romantic love seemed to require such unfamiliar virtues as trust, candor, and openness.

What a joke the "cool" I'd hungered for turned out to be. There was no glowing center; cool was merely the pretense of emotionally invulnerability.

While I struggled to free myself from spiritual quicksand and leave Ronnie, Cathy and I remained lovers. She loved that I was a seeker, adding that the conversations of my dinner group were the most stimulating talks she'd ever been involved in. Even after I broke with Ronnie, and knowing Cathy wanted commitment—though she didn't ask for it—I floated, drawn to sexual adventuring. Then I met Liz, a sensual, insightful Cal English major. Our souls meshed in mutual love of books, as mine and Cathy's never had. And perhaps because I was starting fresh, I fully revealed myself to Liz. Still, for a few weeks I waffled between the two women, until the evening Liz and I walked from our apartments to meet each other. A half a block apart, a romantic-magnetic field enveloped us, drawing us together with energy that stunned us both. Within hours, I knew my decision had been made—I'd be with Liz. A decision based on instinct, and I had no trust in my romantic instincts. But trust or not, the decision was made.

After over three years running my Legal Services office, I demoted myself back to staff attorney and created a 2/3^{rds} work program: 8 months on, 4 months off, 2/3^{rds} pay. Freedom proved even more fun than I'd anticipated. Purchasing good equipment—pattern scissors, tapers, pliers, and beautiful hand-blown glass, I set up a mini-stained-glass studio in my and Liz's flat. Struggling to master the basic craft, I wrestled through pulling slivers of glass from my fingers or shattering a beautiful piece of glass or creating a lousy design. After a few months, I created my first windows, from designs based on things I loved—butterflies, human figures, rock singers, swirls of pure color. My favorites were hung in the front windows of our ground floor Berkeley apartment.

So much to do! Make love with Liz, or go for a ride on my new motorcycle, or go backpacking with Adrian, who'd introduced me to it. Talk, read, explore, connect, live to the fullest. "Be Here Now!" Ram Dass urged. Right on, I agreed, not that I was drawn to meditation.

So much to try! I dug and planted a vegetable garden—starting organic, getting overwhelmed by pests, ending up declaring "It's me and Dow Chemical against the invaders." OK, some experiments taught what I was not meant to do. In contrast, playing street basketball, a passion of my youth, revealed a new dream, "to be the world's oldest basketball player." And I risked LSD again. Experiencing ecstatic voyages into what Adrian call "the old cosmic perspective" unleashed many dreams, from spending time in Paris to becoming a writer.

Sadly, the evolving hippie world wasn't faring as well as my personal experiments. The Haight was degenerating into a district of lost souls and violence. Many of my almost-hippie friends were going through what we called "heavy stuff"—divorce, disorientation, identity crisis. Hippie life was splintering, fragmenting. People left—to travel to Guatemala or Morocco or to be with a guru or to move to the country, or, strangest of all, to take straight jobs. Communes, a tremendous amount of personal effort at best, broke up, sometimes with bitterness. Our weekly dinners ended after some enjoyable years. Most of us were getting busier. Worse, the husband of one friend was distraught that we weren't "really relating deeply" and demanded that we all go away together for a therapeutic weekend. Adrian and I doubted that the fact that we found him boring could be overcome by an encounter group. Deepest, our dream that we might somehow evolve into a commune had evaporated.

In the spring of '72, Liz and I rode my motorcycle through rural Marin County and stopped to watch a Little League baseball game in a rustic field. The parents of the Point Reyes Station team were hip— stylishly rebel clothes, men in ponytails, women in granny dresses or cut-off shorts or some other latest hippie fashion (or non-fashion). Before the game, they smiled and laughed, mellow, occasionally nipping on a joint. The Nicasio parents, many drinking Bud, were farmers and ranchers—burley men in blue work-shirts, with gun-racks in their pickup trucks; the women were hardy, pioneer-looking.

The Nicasio kids were up first. Whatever the kids did—often strike out—their parents called encouragement, cheered, while spending much of their time talking and laughing with each other. They did the same when their kids were in the field, no matter how poorly, or, occasionally how well, their kids fielded. When the Point Reyes kids batted, their fathers turned intense and fierce, hovering on each pitch, shouting instructions: "Keep your eye on the ball!" "Level swing!" "Follow through!" By the second inning, the Point Reyes dads were yelling orders at their kids in the field too: "Get in front of the ball!" "Two hands! Catch it with two hands!" "Down on grounders! Charge it!"

Plus ça change. Hippie had been a wonderful opening, but the vision had atrophied, or perhaps had never included how to live as a grown-up.

By 1973, I'd burned out with Legal Services. The Nixon Supreme Court wasn't going to allow reform through law. Radical political movements had been shattered. Welfare Rights groups withered, as the most astute members got jobs. The Panthers had been smashed by the police and their own self-destructiveness. And whatever community there might be in East Oakland, I couldn't connect to it. From the sea of clients, I almost never received a word of thanks, no matter what I managed to accomplish. Sure, I understood why. From a client's eyes, I was just another part of the white system to be manipulated. Still, it compounded my weariness.

Most of all, I was fed up with the processes of lawyering: filing court papers, dreaming up arguments, drafting interrogatories, winning occasional "victories" that vanished, and, especially, fighting. A few years earlier, I'd vibrated to the Rolling Stones "Street Fighting Man" or the Doobie Brothers "We're taking it to the Streets." Now I felt drawn to the Beatles "Revolution" rejecting "minds that hate." Or The Youngbloods, "Love is but a song we sing, fear's the way we die … Try to love one another right now." Lyrics of hope. Crosby, Stills and Nash's moving "Teach Your Children" concluded, "We can live in peace." My rage felt destructive. Why was I so often angry?

What next? Three years earlier, in 1970, while still with Cathy, I'd tried part-time law teaching, civil procedure and a seminar in poverty law, at a reasonably prestigious local law school. Shortly after I'd accepted the job, Cathy had invited me to join her and some friends camping on a beach in Guaymas, Mexico, for the same week as my first classes. Without hesitation or reflection, I'd chosen to join her. Adrian had agreed to cover for me. Some cover. "Your teacher is by the ocean in Baja," he'd told the students.

Not that it mattered. As the semester wore on, I accepted that I had no calling to be a law teacher. I enjoyed discussions with students, but had little intellectual interest in "the law" (except as a tool for social change) and no passion for legal scholarship. And grades? A detested part of the competitive system I wanted to escape. "I got plenty of letters," I told my classes, echoing Chico Marx. "Everyone gets at least a B; anyone who asks for an A gets one."

In spring of '73, while doing some legal research at Cal's Boalt Hall Law School, I visited a Legal Services colleague who'd become an adjunct professor. He sat fretting in a cubbyhole office with a tiny window, his desk awash with papers. I could feel nervous energy-tension pulsate off him. I left, walking outside into a lusciously beautiful day, on my way to make love with Liz in the afternoon. My chest radiated joy. I was out— goodbye to career, status, dead processes.

I can't recall moments of grand perception—no acid insights here—but being an almost-hippie had somehow taught me that most all of life is process, not results. Process being what you are actually doing, and how you feel while doing it. If the process wasn't satisfying, it was almost certain that the results would not be worth the cost. Satisfying didn't exclusively mean fun, though there better be plenty of that. But struggle was also included. "Men are only free when they are doing what the deepest self likes," D. H. Lawrence declared. With a satisfying process, struggles were enhancing, not debilitating.

In June 1973 I quit Legal Services and set off to live in Ireland with Liz. I had no idea what kind of job I wanted when I returned, but at least I knew I was not a crusader or a social worker. What I wanted from work was enough money to live in basic comfort. That was going to be a struggle; I'd have to hustle. Luckily, I lived in a rich country, and I was privileged—that Law Review credential should help.

Being an almost-hippie turned out not to be an identity, but the tumultuous, irrevocable start down a path less traveled. "You contain enough," Walt Whitman urged, "Why don't you let it all out then?" Great idea, Walt. Live my passions. Don't let earning a living consume my time. And let out my intransigence. Forget teaching law—just take the summer off, period. Farewell to deep parts of U.S. culture I couldn't abide, from competition to Puritanism. Without the hippie culture, I would not have had the courage to begin to discover what I had to let out. A heroic man—Thoreau, Whitman—can stand alone, outside his society. I'm no hero. I needed that hippie world breathing change and encouragement. I needed my almost-hippie friends, fellow seekers struggling to live authentically, who wanted out (at least for a while). "Yes," Adrian observed, some years later, about our life at Legal Services, "on-the-job therapy was where it was at."

Yeah, we were fortunate. As my father dryly noted during one of my rants against The Establishment, "Well, it's not every government that would pay you to fight it." Now I can make a lengthy list of my good fortunes then, ranging from finding my home, Berkeley, to eating inexpensively at a lively new restaurant, Chez Panisse (revolutions happened where we least expected them), to making many of my still-closest friends.

Not to be nostalgic about the 60s. Beyond my personal torments and confusions, being conscious of the U.S. crime of the Vietnam War was not fun. And I was a lousy prophet. We obviously failed to create a new society. Instead, house prices and rents soared. Yeah, I quip now, I should have been buying real estate instead of trying to overthrow the system. Or marijuana: our '60s faith that in 25 years it would seem ludicrous that smoking weed had once been a crime vastly misjudged the perseverance of puritan America. Nor did my vision of our future include Ronald Reagan becoming President, or investment bankers becoming cultural heroes to hordes of suddenly-appearing Yuppies.

What I'd discovered as an almost-hippie was not sustaining clarity but a core vision of freedom. Certainties would always swirl, dissolve, and require restructuring. My demons remained cunning, not exterminated by acid trips. I remained haunted by a demon snarling that I'd failed to focus my energies on one process—financially successful artist was appealing. I wrestled for years before beginning to accept that I was O.K. having no clear vision, that living my passions meant unleashing a herd of turtles.

Rejecting the work ethic proved to be another of life's trick bags. I'd linked the work ethic with money-making careers. Working part time I managed to make enough money to get buy, so why did I remain so busy? My struggles to balance my activity ethic with some time for calm and peace remain ongoing.

Love seemed to spiral through endless uncertainties. With Liz, I'd begun by telling her the truth, and three years later lied to her about having an affair—as she did to me. Through our long, wretched break-up, I struggled yet again to understand how to love, how to move beyond my toxic mix of desire and emotional cowardice. After we ended, I added another struggle, against my demons' new fears that love must end in disaster. Mix all that with doubts about self-love, and I needed help again—this time from a therapist.

Even my certainties about competition grew more complex. Competition was fine, as well as essential, when I played street basketball. O.K., but that did not require that I saw life in terms of "winning" and "losing."

As I was leaving my almost-hippie life in the middle '70s, I knew I was irrevocably changed. I meant to live passionately, doing what I love. I had learned that freedom wasn't about dropping out, but dropping in.

Big deal, condemning voices attacked. All your "authenticity," and love of "processes" is just a cover for selfishness. So what if your politics remain left-wing? You won't actually do anything to help. You're just going to take and not give back.

I'm with Thoreau, my intransigence growled back: "I did not come into the world to change it, but to live in it, be it well or ill." Still, I also nurtured the vague hope that following my passions could lead to contributions I couldn't anticipate. A few days before leaving for Ireland, I'd walked out of my ground-floor apartment one evening. As usual, I'd left the living room lights on so that my stained glass windows glowed radiant-colored light out towards the street, often busy with people walking to the shopping district a few houses away. A conventionally dressed middle-aged couple, probably headed for the burgeoning Berkeley Rep Theater, paused, and the woman asked me, "Did you make those windows?" I said I had. "I just want to tell you how much pleasure you've brought us over the years. We always park on this street so we can look at your art."

Jerry Garcia surely got it right when he sang, "what a long strange trip it's been." Buddha's ten thousand joys and ten thousand sorrows. It's also been a whole lot of fun.

[1997]

BERKELEY IN 2000

What's Berkeley up to now? When I moved here from Manhattan in 1967, Berkeley was a center of the "Movement," young radicals fomenting social revolution. That Movement evaporated, but it decisively influenced the development of a distinctive Berkeley culture. At the core of that culture is: Live Your Dreams—you've got permission.

That's dreams, plural. While many Berkeleyans would love to be able to focus most of their energies on a single, central passion—perhaps becoming a great and financially prosperous artist—few are graced with clear vision of one calling. So most pursue several dreams simultaneously. Rarely do those dreams include making megabucks or stardom. If you want that why live here, when there's Manhattan or L. A.? Not that Berkeleyans lack ambition. Escape requires ambition.

Of course there are many Berkeleys, and to define "its" culture simplifies. The majority population is white, but there's considerable ethnic/racial diversity. A welfare family's Berkeley is unlikely to overlap much with the Berkeley of a family living in a elegant hills home. Still, Berkeley does have a dominant culture, one that shapes the city, culturally, economically and politically.

One widely-shared dream is living your creativity. "There are lots of people here who make their living in the arts of all kinds—writings, music, fine arts, dance—Berkeley's just crammed with them," says David Lance Goines, well-known poster artist and 1964 Free Speech activist. Local culture does not enforce a rigid division between a few "real" artists (paid professionals) and the rest (at best, appreciators). Many Berkeley artists, though not well paid, or paid at all, are passionate and serious, not amateurs, with the disdain that word implies. Their works vary widely, from the concrete—pottery, poetry, weavings, paintings, stained glass—to performance—dance, theater, tai-chi, music—to horticulture or cooking. All this creativity can produce surprising and interesting conversation: the white guy at the Y talking with passionate knowledge about Nigerian music; the older paralegal who's an expert Flamenco dancer; the lawyer telling his office-mates about sculpture techniques.

Living creatively, on top of just living, surely keeps most Berkeleyans busy. A woman bustling from her pottery studio to pick up her child at a day-care center before her anti-nuclear affinity group meeting described herself as "in my midlife hyper-active phase." How to find balance, let alone peace? One musician/therapist/family man counsels, "The secret of a successful middle age is: Don't Overbook."

Whatever your other creative impulses, self-development is a given. "You can be anything you want to be in Berkeley," a local writer observed, "as long as you're Always Growing." Some grow as true scholars, pursing knowledge solely from passion. The near-infinity of the subjects from a sample of my friends include the history of Paris, the making of olive oil, American poetry, hawks' flights, modern physics, and languages, from Spanish to Russian. Then there's spiritual development: numerous forms of religion, including various types of Buddhism and several different Jewish Renewal groups and synagogues, as well as a wide variety of meditation schools and methods. Then there's group-identity development, including drawing from feminism, or LGBT (lesbian/gay/bisexual/transgender) or ethnic/cultural roots. And of course there's therapy-aided development. As with any aspect of self-discovery, therapy can sink into self-absorption, or even absurdity. I once overheard a man ask a friend, "Do you think I should ask my therapist if Jane can see my psychic?" But for many Berkeleyans, therapy broadens and opens, aiding them to live more from their cores, less tormented by their demons.

The most Californian component of Berkeley culture is health. Most Berkeleyans are fit. Many have developed their own unique health regimes, drawing from many sources: from aerobic and weight workouts to yoga, tai-chi, or martial arts to sports; from acupuncture to massage to nutrition; from readings to using healers, ranging from (very) alternative to western doctors.

Many traditional forms of self-destruction, from sloth to alcoholism, are out. No one smokes—well, except some under thirty. Drug consumption seems down compared to the experimental 60s, but that may be me revealing my age. Psychedelics—grass, magic mushrooms, LSD, Ecstasy (descendant of MDA) retain appeal to younger seekers and stoners. Currently, the preferred drugs of my generation are wine and caffeine, perhaps supplemented by an occasional joint. Certainly there's no anti-drug hysteria; the City Council voted to bar drug testing of city employees.

What about sexual freedom? Not much now for the '60s generation, whatever the young folks are doing. With the horror of AIDS added to earlier, often disastrous attempts at open marriage or abolishing jealousy, older Berkeleyans have pulled back. When a gay friend was asked how he was dealing with sex, he laughingly replied, "Just like straight people—monogamy and fantasy."

One core dream is living authentically—well, trying to. The alienation buck stops here. No more bullshit. When you reduce living authentically to words, you get homilies: " "Be honest," "Know thyself," "Get in touch with your feelings." What trick-bags they turn out to be in life.

Take raising kids: a friend, surveying a local street fair attended by many gray-haired parents dressed almost as funkily as they had been thirty years earlier, observed, "The difference between the '90s and the '60s is that kids have replaced dogs." How are parents to be authentic with their kids? What to tell them about drugs? How to respond when they say "You took WHAT?" Authenticity with children becomes another juggling act, including coping with the unanticipated. An ex-Catholic father suggested to his teenage son that they should have a talk about sex. "Sure Dad," the boy replied. "What do you want to know?"

And from this you make a living?

Ah, money—always a problem. Back in 1969, a radical lawyer asked, "Why is it that no matter what we start out talking about, by midnight the subject is—'If Only We Were Independently Wealthy?'" The fantasy may be a trust fund, but the dream is some economic freedom.

So where does the money come from?

Not from corporate-straight jobs, which hold little more appeal than they did in the '60s. Few Berkeley women were enticed by that branch of feminism which proclaimed the traditional male work world as a place for fulfillment. Instead of conventional careers, Berkeleyans carve out economic niches, developing jobs that, hopefully, draw on some of their passion, definitely pay their bills, and allow them to pursue other dreams. It's all sorta small-time: no corporate takeovers here; no stretch limos either.

Well, not relentlessly small time. At one end of the niche spectrum are those who've prospered grandly from doing what they love—well-known writers, a famous sports agent, successful publishers and restauranteurs, even a movie mogul. And, of course, there are the cunning, like the now-wealthy personal injury lawyer who was meeting ambulance drivers during his '60s Legal Services days while his colleagues were attending Black Panther breakfasts. But the cunning are not dominant. More Berkeleyans suffer from what one friend defined as his "money dyslexia."

What's surprising, for a population with a deserved reputation as left-wingers, is how many entrepreneurial niches Berkeleyans have created. A few well-loved collectives—a cheese store, a bakery—survive from the 60s, but communal ownership hasn't proved to be the wave of the future. Instead it's individual entrepeneurship. Here's a quick list from some of my friends: skylight maker, fabric designer, prison consultant, private French teacher, real estate agent, masseuse, graphic designer, freelance editor, psychologist, house inspector, sex worker, book marketing consultant, and various artists—painters, potters, film makers, dancers, musicians, authors. Many who work for institutions have also created their own niches: midwife at a hospital, community college movement teacher for older adults, director of a program to aid the homeless. One entrepenurial sub-category is composed of former ex-academics, collectively sometimes referred to as "Ph.D. carpenters." When I bought a home several years ago, my house inspector and my real estate agent, both long-time friends, each had a Cal. Ph.D. in English. Our house painter, a man of Buddhist serenity, had a Cal. Ph.D. in Rhetoric.

Some Berkeleyans occupy traditional small business niches: local merchant, general practice doctor, home-town lawyer. One Berkeley attorney remarked, "They can carve on my tombstone, 'At Least He Beat the Commute.'"

Most dramatically, entrepreneurs have created many thriving local industries. Take publishing: three decades ago Berkeley had very few publishers; now it's home to a lively community of many, covering a gamut from cookbooks to self-help law to novels and poetry. Most started out as cottage businesses, literally run out of someone's living room or attic. Bakeries offer a similar story. A generation ago, a couple of culinary pioneers started baking and selling bread. Now the city is a bread-making Mecca with ten or fifteen superb bakeries, and Berkeleyans debate who makes the best Challah, baguettes, or bagels.

Some militants are disappointed with Berkeley's niche economics. How can it be applied to an assembly line, or the third world? Not easily, though it does offer some pointers. A few Berkeley businesses have open books—any employee can learn what any other worker, including the C.E.O., earns. Most local businesses offer relaxed working conditions, not corporate authoritarianism. Still the economic dream has not turned out to be collective sharing, but individual escape. Sauve qui peut. [Save yourself]

More pressing is the question of whether niche economics can continue to sustain Berkeley. Niches aren't infinite. The '60s generation struggled to create many. Members of younger generations face even more difficult struggles to create new ones. Equally discouraging is the steep cost of housing in Berkeley. Only the affluent can even dream of buying a house. Available rentals are as scarce, and almost as expensive, as in Manhattan. While alternative forms of housing, like communal living or co-housing, exist, they are far from plentiful.

Realistically, house prices alone dictate that Berkeley will eventually become a place for prosperous strivers, albeit a city with an artsy ambience, sort of a Greenwich Village West. Still, for now, attend any street fair or political rally, see all those energized bohemians, funky family folks, tie-died Deadheads, weirdos, hip-hop teenagers, dancing octogenarians, and you feel traces of hope: somehow Berkeley culture will evolve, not dwindle.

Certainly it's hard to imagine Berkeley as a Republican city. Whatever their political differences, most Berkeleyans fit within the label "progressive." Only a tiny minority are revolutionaries, but the majority takes pride in the culture's heritage of anti-establishment political idealism. Most agree with the region's popular former congressman Ron Dellums, that Berkeley [and the Bay area] "is an island of political sanity.... We are right and we have always been right."

Berkeleyans decry the growing U.S. gap between rich and poor, although few are confident they know the blueprint to achieve economic justice. Many wouldn't mind soaking the very rich, especially rich corporations—but, hey, no threats to home ownership. While a smattering of true believers adhere to dogmas, far more Berkeleyans are activists for a cause, not an ideology. They organize, petition, demonstrate, raise money, lobby. No need to list pages of causes; they run the progressive spectrum, including anti-nuclear efforts, peace work, including peace between Israelis and Palestinians, the environment, and cultural activities. Other activists work in more individual ways: tutoring low-income students; helping a Central American refugee get a job; assisting homeless people to find housing. Though the majority of Cal students are generally not activist, they are not invariably politically passive either. Student mass protests successfully halted abolition of the Ethnic Studies Department and students pushed for U. C. divestment from Apartheid South Africa. At the end of the activism scale is giving money. "If I won't do anything else," one donor noted, "I can at least be a liberal."

Activists contribute to the stimulatingly unpredictability of Berkeley life. The muscled weight lifter getting dressed next to me at the gym reveals he's going to work in a construction brigade in Nicaragua for three months. An elderly, respectable-looking woman on a movie line recounts her decades of civil disobedience arrests. I'm reminded that some Berkeleyans continue to "live their politics," and I remember, at least briefly, that I'm privileged to live so well; karma indicates I should give back.

City politics is progressive, sometimes controversially so. The City Council adopted a resolution calling for the cessation of U.S. bombing in Afghanistan "as soon as possible." Some years ago, there was a bitterly contested referendum over what position the U.S. should take regarding U. S. aid for Israeli West-Bank settlements. Further back, the City Council once voted to conclude a separate peace treaty with Vietnam.

Whatever the value of Berkeley's occasional attempts at foreign policy, domestically the city has a proud tradition of risk-taking innovation. It was the first northern school district to fully integrate its schools, establishing a busing program that has worked, although the results have not been utopian. The first police civilian review board was set up here. More city firsts: banning styrofoam fast food packaging; putting two-ways radios in police cars (a while ago); sponsoring a city booth at the elite S.F. Fancy Food & Confection Show. City voters approved a special tax assessment to put BART, the subway system, underground, rather than noisily above ground, as it is in other East Bay cities.

Another Berkeley first was making all sidewalks wheelchair accessible. The city has become a center for disabled people, who've provided me with unanticipated blessings. One rainy afternoon, wandering through existence with my inner light dim, I noticed a man stoically moving his wheelchair forward by keeping the metal rod attached to his head in contact with the electric button on the wheelchair arm. He exuded inspiration. If he can struggle on, I awakened, surely I can.

Of course, Berkeley remains a city with many conflicts and problems. Sometimes, after fierce ideological struggles, a consensus emerges that proves viable. Many Berkeleyans, including many merchants, became disturbed by street panhandlers, particularly the numerous assertive mendicants on Telegraph Ave, the bustling main street by the U.C. campus. How to balance free speech with freedom from being hassled? Solution: outlaw "aggressive panhandling"—and some were aggressive to beyond threatening—and allow civilized soliciting. But other times, despite years of well-intentioned efforts, difficulties remain. The Berkeley Police Department, integrated in every way, is well-trained, and respected, at least in middle-class neighborhoods. But black teenager drivers report that they still get pulled over here, as elsewhere, for "DWB—driving while black."

The dream of racial integration has been realized in the Berkeley's public life, but class/economics keeps most Berkeley whites and blacks apart. Neighborhoods tend to be black or white or in gentrified transition. Adults of different races do mix at times, usually quite amicably, at a job, in athletics, at a dance concert, or other ways. But in my generation, blacks and whites who are good friends usually formed those friendships decades ago, when life was more fluid. Now, somehow, deep friendships across racial lines are made less often. Nothing intentional, of course—that's just how it's worked out. Perhaps the racial divide will be bridged more by the younger generation, at least those who went to Berkeley public schools. Friendships there do cross racial lines. But how long-lasting will those friendships be? Can blacks and white become closer without basic economic change?

The dream of integration survives in Berkeley's public schools, which have many minority students, including a significant percentage from poor families. While some affluent parents opt to send their kids to private schools, enough middle class kids attend the public schools so that they remain integrated. Berkeley High—chaotic, dynamic—is considered by kids of all races and classes to be a hip place, though not easy. With four thousand students, kids can be overwhelmed. But many students find the range and intensity of classes fascinating, and Berkeley High continues to send numerous students to elite colleges, a crucial real-world test. However, minority students receive significantly lower grades and test scores than whites. Many minority students don't graduate from high school. The school system has made numerous attempts to remedy these problems, with frustrating results.

Some problems have proved to be near-impervious to city efforts, and require national solutions. With its tolerant culture and its comfortable climate (it never snows, and rarely gets over eighty-five degrees), Berkeley has many homeless people. Both the city and private groups provide some shelters and assistance, but not enough. Only national efforts could enable all to have adequate housing. Although even if money for new housing for the homeless was available, where to put it? Few are pushing for any in their neighborhood.

Berkeley's alleged political flaws, such as "political correctness," defined as a humorless over-sensitivity to supposed slights or intolerance of non-progressive views, do not infest the City deeply. Occasionally political correctness pops up, as when the Berkeley Rep announced it would produce "The Good Person of Setzun." And while Berkeley certainly has some rowdy radicals who yearn to shout down those they oppose, most Berkeleyans, who delight in discussion and debate, would relish an intelligent argument with a conservative.

Berkeley's real political flaws lie elsewhere. Super-moralists twitch to lecture others on the "correct" position about anything. Akin to these spiritual policemen is the "ain't-it-awful" brigade, glum spirits bemoaning the imminent collapse of the world because of capitalism/poisons/nuclear war/global warming /imperialism/destruction of the ozone layer/racism/whatever. Imminent exhaustion of gasoline supplies has been quietly dropped from the list. In a diluted version, I've participated in a number of dinners where we decried injustice and oppression, while enjoying another meal of gourmet food and exquisite wine.

More commonly, though, Berkeleyans' political grumbling expresses frustrated dreaming, not whining. They don't listen to us. Economic inequality in the U.S. grows worse yearly. The homeless are mentioned by neither Democrats nor Republicans. The federal government relentlessly pursues the wasteful and destructive war on drugs. The U.S. remains far, far more conservative and uptight than Berkeleyans' visions of a just society.

Political Berkeley is a potent symbol for irate conservatives. A Wall Street Journal article mocked that, "In the funky streets of Berkeley, it's forever the 60's...." David Horowitz attacked the city as a "'pseudo-environment'—a place governed by a fictional version of reality." A Forbes magazine article decried Berkeley's "bizarre social experiments—a kind of inadvertent yuppie populism...This is hardly a dictatorship of the proletariat. Call it rather a dictatorship of a narrow middle-class point of view." A column from the *Wall Street Journal* spoke of "municipal Marxism" in Berkeley, which has a "dingy Third Worldish aura that coincides with its politics." Here's the scoop from Ken Auletta: "In Berkeley, a Marxist government is alive and well." David Kirp scorned student anti-apartheid demonstrations as "morally compelling as a panty raid."

What's the appeal of Berkeley bashing? Hardly the truth. Marxist? Try buying a house here. "Dingy Third Worldish"—the home of Alice Waters' world-renowned restaurant, Chez Panisse? The reality is that some conservatives need a revolutionary demon in the U.S., and Berkeley is the best they can come up with. Occasionally, the same delusional image is presented positively. Kate Braverman wrote, "I am a brick-throwing survivor of the 60s, and there is some part of me that will be forever Berkeley."

Well, it is true that throughout the Reagan-Bush era, and now Bush again, Berkeleyans refuse to accept that greed-is-good. A '90s *S.F. Chronicle* editorial solemnly chastised that Berkeley was still "clinging steadfastly to many causes which have long been out of fashion." Bad enough when it was kids protesting, but when grown-ups keep it up— that's infuriating.

Protesting can be one temporary manifestation of the faded Berkeley dream of community. That community is sought here, locally, not in sophisticated San Francisco. Of course, most Berkeleyans love that big City—who doesn't? But Berkeley's forms of community seldom race into the fast lane. As one local artist put it, "We're either out working, in our studios working, or doing our laundry. We don't fit those stereotypes people have about artists. In the city they're younger, more with it, on edge." Similarly, few Berkeleyans dress-for-success or sport hip clothes. Style, or anti-style, emphasizes comfort: T-shirts, loose blouses, sneakers, funky pants, Levi's. Women may wear makeup, but almost never high heels. The nervous, excited energies and stresses of a big city aren't exuded here. There's no urban downtown; the most Berkeley manages is a couple of ten-story buildings. Yet while it's no place for adrenaline junkies, Berkeley is not a small town. You can be anonymous here if you chose.

Most Berkeleyans hunger more for connection than anonymity. Beyond personal intimacy, they seek connections in numerous ways, from new age spiritual groups (The Jewish "Aquarian Minyan," The Zen Center) to ongoing private classes (free universities, private teachers) to reading groups, dance groups, poker gangs, new mothers' groups, adopting new mothers' groups, Jewish adopting new mothers' groups.

One connection is in-group humor. A prominent sign in one coffee house states, "No talking to imaginary people." Bumper stickers proclaim, "Powerlessness Corrupts Too," or "Intimidate Authority," or "It's Still Not Weird Enough For Me." A battered VW bus sports "fin de siécle" meticulously painted in large white script on its sides.

Another connection is love of books. "In the life of the mind," declared Andy Ross, of Cody's bookstore, "Berkeley is preeminent." Independent bookstores struggle, but most have survived. The City has the highest take-out rate of library books per capita of any city in California. When local branch libraries were threatened with severely restricted hours after the passage of anti-tax Prop 13, Berekleyans overwhelming approved new property taxes to keep their libraries open.

Bookstore literary talks are frequent. Readings by local authors are usually well attended. An appearance by someone of wider renown, say Alan Ginsberg or Toni Morrison, is as glamorous as life here gets. (If you can't park at Walnut Square, somebody big is reading at Black Oak Books.) Readings by literary lions offer a triple delight: the stimulation of hearing and seeing the writer, the pleasures of encountering friends, and the satisfaction of living in a town where, say, Carlos Fuentes or Edna O'Brien reads on a weekday evening. But even readings have their perils. Beyond possible trouble finding a seat, you may encounter a Berkeley intellectual obsessive, haranguing his interminable, pseudo-brilliant theory the moment the speaker asks for questions.

Love of good food is another bond. Soon after the 60s radical fervor crested, Berkeley became a food lover's delight—fine restaurants, superb groceries. This inspired wisecracks about the "gourmet ghetto" or the next era in Berkeley being "post-croissant." Some nouveaux-puritans apparently believed that decline of character inevitably accompanies being a gourmet. But this sternness held little appeal to most Berkeleyans. After all, who berates the Italians for loving pasta or the French for patronizing their neighborhood boulangerie/patisserie?

When buying food, Berkeleayans favor fresh, often organic. Many Berkeley neighborhoods have their own little shopping districts, a bit like France. No malls here, and very few chain stores. Instead, separate stores for vegetables, bread, cheese, fish, meat, wine, health food, as well as bakeries featuring imaginative and caloric desserts.

Decades ago, an appointee of then-Governor Jerry Brown (his first time around) asked me what changes I believed should be made in California. "More sidewalk cafés," I answered. Berkeley's long had some fine ones, and many more have blossomed recently. Most are often jammed, by older Berkeleyans as well as by U.C. students.

The University itself contributes little to Berkeley community. The campus does provide entertainments, from cultural events to sports, including a football team loses with regularity. ("It's good to raise your kids as Cal fans," my old Legal Services boss declared. "Gets 'em ready for life. Can you imagine being raised a USC fan?") Most importantly, the school continues to draw bright, seeking students to Berkeley. But faculty members, by and large, stick closely to their own world. The administration's major role, when it contributes anything, is as villain. From the Free Speech Movement to refusing to advocate divestment during the apartheid struggle to maintaining Lawrence Livermore Laboratory's research on nuclear weapons and Star Wars, the administration serves as the local proxy for the military-industrial establishment (or what Lawrence Ferlinghetti labeled the "military-entertainment complex").

People's Park is a classic of the administration as villain. It's hometown chauvinism to assume that all literate Americans know the history of the Park, so here's a brief summary. In the mid-60s, the University bought and tore down several adjacent houses, four blocks from campus, and then, unresolved what to build, left the land vacant. In the spring of 1969, a few radicals spontaneously began turning the still-empty lot into a park. Within days, hundreds, then thousands, were involved: hippies and housewives, long-hairs and straights, revolutionaries and students. Digging, sodding, hauling, planning; planting flowers, seedlings, trees, grass seed, bushes, vegetables. A couple of weeks of magically shared vision, as anyone who participated will confirm today.

Under right-wing political pressure, the University sent in cops at night to seize control of the land. The next day, after a campus rally, a crowd moved to retake the park. The struggle escalated rapidly until

Governor Reagan, ordering in the National Guard, declared, in words never forgiven in Berkeley, "If it takes a blood bath, let's get it over with." Thousands of troops occupied the city. Barbed wire and machine guns surrounded the Park. Battle-dressed police guffawed as others ripped up flowers and trees.

The result was a stalemate. For years the land remained unused, behind fences. Then the administration's political support withered. The Berkeley City Council and the Democratic governor urged that the land be used as a park. The county sheriff indicated that if the administration sought to build on the land, and required deputy sheriffs to keep order, the administration would pay their cost. And one night some folks ripped down the fence, and People's Park was reborn.

The macadam western end of the park became used as an ersatz parking lot. In 1979 the administration suddenly erected a massive fence around the parking lot. Astonishingly, within hours several thousand people surged to the park and tore the fence down. Then they proceeded to tear up the macadam as well, pick-axes flailing, eventually extending the park to the full length of the lot.

For another decade the land remained a park with legal ownership in limbo. It became a place occupied mostly by homeless, hoboes, drifters and low-level drug dealers. Though the place could feel seedy, or even threatening, flowers were watered and nurtured, free meals distributed, and the Park survived, without any official assistance.

Finally, twenty years after the Park was born, the U.C. Chancellor reluctantly signed an agreement with Berkeley's Mayor which preserved the land as a park. The land is now well-maintained, still mostly by volunteers and homeless people, students, basketball players and other Berkelyans co-exist there. But the administration has not given up. A few years ago, a newly-appointed U.C. Chancellor spoke of the pressing need to build student dorms in the Park. He rapidly learned that the Park is an essential component of Berkeley culture.

Though I'm a Berkeley booster, it's no paradise, and certainly no bohemian paradise. The few dance halls are generally so mobbed you feel like you're dancing on a rush hour subway. Quite a few neighborhood activists still see bars—there aren't many—as a prohibitionist's vision of noise and trouble. And the town closes up early. Only a few restaurants serve past ten. A local actress observed, "The perfect life would be to spend your days in Berkeley and your nights in Manhattan."

"Men are free when they belong to a living, organic, believing community," D. H. Lawrence proclaimed. Berkeley remains far from Lawrence's dream. Few residents have roots here—parents, siblings, childhood friends, generally all live far away. The friendships that are the bedrock of Berkeley don't mesh into an organic, coherent society, but are as diffuse and fluid as clouds. A would-be social climber couldn't find a ladder.

There's certainly little of that fantasy society I dreamt of in my youth, a blend of early Greenwich Village, the Deux Maggots in Paris, and Impressionists in cafés. As writer Leonard Michaels noted, "There are people in Berkeley who are very much concerned with literature... [and]...I think there is always the hope of a literary community here... [but]...I don't have any sense, however that there is what I would take to be a true literary community." Indeed, this is not a city with "scenes"— no art scene, no dance scene, not even much of a political/protest scene any more.

Occasionally, though, public events remind Berkeleyans that they do share in a loose community. A concert by Pete Seeger, Ronnie Gilbert, Holly Near and Arlo Guthrie drew ten thousand, old to middle aged to young, sharing the joy of musicians who've fought the good fight. As the music ended, one elderly activist called out to me, "We've still got better music than the bad guys."

With all its limits, Berkeley culture remains vital and Berkeleyans continue to pursue turning dreams into realities. The demon of alienation has been caged, if not slain. As one East-coast refugee put it, "It's a comfort to be surrounded by people who reveal they're as strange as I know I am." Or, as a romantic friend observed, "Berkeleyans can become extraordinary ordinary people."

[2001]

LESSONS IN LOVE

Early in adolescence, I became certain that the core of life was passionate love. I can't recall how I knew that—intuition?—but I believed in
romantic magic, not that I had a glimmer what love was or how to find it.

An Amherst freshman in 1957, shy with women, I was alone at a Mt.
Holyoke mixer, awash with pretty girls and suave upperclassmen, when I
saw her sitting across the floor. Inexplicably, I walked to her and bowed
slightly. "Hello, I'm Denis. I've been assigned by the Social Committee to
be your escort for the evening." She laughed. "You're the most attractive,
intelligent woman here, so the Committee selected me, the most desirable man, to be with you."

"Well," Kate laughed merrily, "I guess it's out of our hands."

It was certainly out of mine.

We dated for months. Talked—families, stories, hopes. Laughed—
first time I'd genuinely laughed with a date. Two book lovers and dreamers, we danced tenderly to Johnny Mathis' "The Twelfth of Never" and
made out. I never examined the deep stirrings I felt for her. Whatever
the mix might have been—swirls of desire, tenderness, fear she'd leave,
warmth—I'd incorporated my family's Irish-American habit of denial. I
wasn't even aware that I could look inside. I never mentioned "love" to
her, nor did she to me.

Months later, she left me for an Amherst Junior, a handsome guy
with a car. Although acting indifferent, I must have felt some pain, but
my awesomely-unconscious denial skills smothered it.

But we weren't over. During the next year and a half we reunited, parted, and were together again as our sophomore years were ending, when she tearfully announced that she would be transferring next fall to the University of Kansas, in her home state. We both cried.

The following spring she visited Mt. Holyoke and called me. We met for one passionate evening. Near the end, we revealed that we'd deeply missed each other and then she sighed sadly. "But maybe it's better. I always knew it wouldn't work out."

"Work out?" A new concept.

"Yes ... you're a Catholic."

"A Catholic?" Already an Ex-Catholic, that religion seemed no more significant than my shoe size.

"I always knew we wouldn't get married ... because ... my parents ... they just couldn't take it if I married a Catholic."

Uh ho, I'd missed something. Love apparently was not simply magic that would engulf me and The Woman. However, Kate's lesson that I had no comprehension of complexities of love did not nudge me to explore my romantic feelings or try to communicate them.

When I was sixteen Dad had called me into his study and announced that we should have a talk, a rare event. We sat silently in mutual embarrassment until he announced that he knew I was getting older, and would be thinking about sex soon. (Soon?) "I want to tell you something about love and sex." He paused. I looked at him, interest overriding my awkwardness. "About marriage," he perhaps smiled. "Remember, whoever you marry, you'll have to talk to her at breakfast for fifty years."

An astounding notion.

"And love. You really can love a woman. It's not just sex. I remember my brother Steve saying 'That's like kissing a woman after you've fucked her.' He was wrong. If you love a woman, you do want to kiss her after you've made love with her. Maybe not as ardently, but you kiss her ... because you love her."

We never discussed love again, and I never forgot his teaching: love really existed.

Throughout college, I didn't discover many other clues to what love was. My English-major friends loved to talk (day and night) but I don't recall talks about love or passion. I sought the truths of life in novels, but those which spoke directly to me were tales of loveless, money-making males: Marquand, O'Hara, Fitzgerald, Lewis, *The Man in The Gray Flannel Suit*. Romantic love was not delved into as part of the English curriculum, even when we read Lawrence or Shakespeare's sonnets.

By my senior year, I'd learned, to my astonishment, that I could be appealing to women. Tall, lean, reasonably attractive, I was high energy, with an Irish wit. Only years later did I realize that probably my most appealing quality was that I was curious and liked to listen as well as talk, so I asked a woman I was dating about herself. I liked women—specifically, Lisa, a gorgeous redhead, artist, and Smith senior. Through our last college year, in a haze of enchantment we talked, laughed, kissed passionately, explored each other's bodies, danced sensuously to Jimmy Reed. Both mildly bohemian rebels, she dreamt of sculpting, me of books. Thrilling at her image when we were apart, I'd feel surges of warmth from my heart. Neither told the other we were "in love," but I knew I was close to it.

Occasionally, she was busy on a weekend. I didn't ask why. It didn't matter. We were moving closer and closer to declared love. Besides, her departures enabled me occasionally date Betsy, my crush from last year, now back at Mt. Holyoke after several months off for a mysterious liver disease. (In reality, a suicide attempt, I learned later.) How could I feel the at-least-near love I had for Lisa and still go out with another woman? Not a question I pondered, although some friends noted that mine was not noble behavior.

Senior prom. Lisa and I at last slept naked together, made love. The next day the warm spring air felt as if we could float on it. She twirled and danced down a street, youthful Aphrodite, her long red hair flowing, trees seeming to bend with her. We talked about going to Manhattan after college. She'd already spent a weekend at my home, meeting my parents. Our magic would continue.

A week later she told me she was getting married to her prep-school love. "It's what I've always wanted." But we both still wanted each other too. We met, cried, hinted at eloping. Uh oh. I knew what that meant: marriage, kids soon, responsibilities, necktie-jobs—ME in the Gray Flannel Suit. No, I would not become a grown-up yet. Alone, I cried more, turned angry, staggered through days with a sharp ache in my chest. We met one last time, cried more, hugged, and parted. So I received my initial lesson of love shattering into heartbreak, pain as sung in blues songs. I hurt all summer.

Working in Manhattan (occupation: "employee"), I became hooked on glamour—flashy beauty, flashing wit. Michelle had it. Better, we loved the same books and movies, as well as partying and talking. Best, she wanted me. We made love on our second date.

A bohemian Californian, Michelle had smoked dope, been an actress, and divorced at twenty. She didn't want to talk about her marriage. I quickly ceased asking questions. I didn't know if I "loved" her but we'd been going out almost three years and the subject of marriage started coming up. I hadn't raised it. Stalling, I hoped for more years free from being a grown up. Negotiations ensued. Pressed, I surrendered to what I later dubbed the "three-year rule." If you went out with a woman for three years, and she wanted to marry you (and of course she did or why would she have wasted three prime years on you?) you were obligated to go along. Anyway, I wanted to get married sometime and who else could I marry?

By 1969, I was a long-haired, semi-radical lawyer working for the poor in Oakland Legal Services, and content with Michelle, who'd resumed being an actress. Sure sex was no longer sizzling, but didn't that come with marriage? Then Michelle devastated me by announcing she no longer loved me and was leaving. Alone, I felt pains in my chest as if a heated steel band had been placed inside me and someone was maliciously tightening it. Tormented by loneliness, I was incapable of learning anything.

Weeks later, I paced by the phone, seeking the courage to call Kaitlin, the witty statuesque blond I'd encountered at the non-profit she worked for trying to reform Oakland public schools. Picking up the phone, I shook with fear and put it down, Surely she had more desirable men pursuing her, perhaps some debonair journalist with a sports car. Sporadically, over more weeks, I tried and failed to make the call, until a mysterious bubble of Do-It surged inside me. She answered! She said she'd be delighted to go out! We went for drinks in San Francisco and soared through an evening of laughter and talk.

A few days later my Legal Services colleague Adrian fixed me up with Helen, a Ph.D. student in English at Stanford. Slender and alluring, she vibrated intensity like a taut, glowing wire. We shared rebellious spirits, hating the Vietnam War, drawn to the counterculture. Deepest, we shared a passion for books. With her I could be the real me, no longer buried under my public self of radical lawyer.

Within two months I was enmeshed with each of them, and each seemed to care for me. Life became too speedy and thrilling a whirl for me to probe if I could use the word "love" to cover the flood of intense, gnarled feelings coursing through me. Making love with Kaitlin felt ecstatic. As did making love with Helen. But alone I'd feel tormented over my still-secret miseries over Michelle, or shivers of fear about my withholdings from Helen and Kaitlin, or occasional terror that I was careening to disaster. Lesson: I could be with and feel deeply drawn to two women simultaneously.

Seven months after we met, Helen abruptly married her thesis adviser. "I never knew where I stood with you," she wrote. Shocked, I felt renewed devastation. She, my demons howled, had been my real soul mate, lost by my cowardice.

I continued with Kaitlin but couldn't pull free of Michelle, who flitted randomly back into my life. I told myself I was **married,** which meant you stuck it out; there'd never been a divorce in my family. Some flickers in my soul knew that dark, needy desperation drove me to cling to Michelle; my grim endurance could not be love, but our marriage ground on.

At a theater party, I took my first acid trip—the poor man's psychiatrist. Terrified, pressed against a tree, more alone than I'd ever conceived was possible, I shuddered in the void of knowing almost nothing as true. Love? I hated Michelle. A darker wave washed over me: I hated my body. I hated myself.

Shocks waves from that trip-epiphany propelled me to change— beginning to work out regularly, seeing a therapist. Struggling to pay attention to what I was "feeling," I fumbled for self-love, so banal to state, and such an onion-peeling process to try to live. Thirty years of denial and repressed self-hatred couldn't be exorcised in a month. Love, I began to see, required intimacy, and that required courage. I had long discussions about love with worldly Adrian. "People have needs," he shrugged. And beyond that, I pushed. "Trust," he replied. He is obviously right, I gnawed myself. Real magic requires trust. And trust requires telling the truth.

Within a couple of months, I left Michelle and moved in with Rick, a Berkeley actor friend, and his sixteen-year-old actress girl friend, Brenda, a budding flower. Kaitlin and I voyaged to Guaymas, Mexico with some of her friends, including her college roommate, Suki, a beautiful, butterfly soul. Days of bliss, except when I was haunted by the fear that something remained very wrong with me.

I became truthful with Kaitlin, who remained loving as I waffled with her. Somehow, I didn't feel full magic, but believing in magic seemed flawed. Then a friend introduced me to Liz, a stunning Cal English student, a shimmering, somehow a bit ominous, hummingbird, aflame with skewed brilliance and sensuality, hungering, like me, to live authentically. Although a feminist, she drew some cold female glances for her provocative dressing. Her mind and spirit fascinated me. Our conversations, the best kind, reached where neither of us could go alone. Lovemaking was wilder, more adventuring, than I'd ever lived before. I vowed to tell her my truths, including about my demons. She told me truths: she'd had a baby (given up for adoption) when she was sixteen; she'd had many lovers; her life could become despairing and confusing.

One spring evening we agreed we'd walk to meet each other on the street near my apartment. Yards apart, we were both seized by a mystical energy field that drew us together as if we were magnetized. We hugged and laughed, stunned with joy. Magic had enveloped us. We both knew we'd fallen in love. I didn't worry if that magic didn't include understanding of love. Floating through days, I felt classic lover's delights: the world was grand; my love was a dream-made-real. Together, we shared euphoria, feeling deep love-making merging.

I was hooked. Sadly, I told Kaitlin that I loved Liz. "I wish we'd talked," Kaitlin answered.

Liz soon moved in with me. She taught me the pleasures of frequent hugging, kissing, snuggling. We shared more soul secrets, examining our dreams, fantasies, and dark sides. We read, hiked, explored, laughed. And we agreed that we'd talk if one of us felt something wrong between us, or in either of us.

"What about monogamy?" I posed, feeling suddenly brave. "I'm not monogamous by nature."

"What does that mean?" she replied.

"Ah, …. it means …. Well, you know…"

"No, I mean what are you going to do about it?"

"I don't know. Nothing now. If it comes up, we'll have to deal with it."

"Yes, we will," she said emphatically. "And I'm not monogamous either."

I heard only what I'd told her.

Months later, Kaitlin's friend Suki, butterfly-radiant as ever, began working in my Legal Services office. She brought me a note from Kaitlin asking me how I was. Kaitlin and I met. "It took me a while," she said, "but I figured if a man doesn't want me, that's his problem." We evolved to friends.

Suki had been with Jules for over two years. Jules insisted on non-monogamy, which no longer upset Suki. "I know he won't leave me," she said "and I like my freedom. I used to worry that I was letting Women down, not policing my man, but I realized if someone's upset by that, it's her issue."

A year later, Suki and I, both drawn to art, began hiring a model and drawing regularly at my and Liz's apartment. Months later, Suki joined me in a weekly wine tasting class in San Francisco. Riding in and back, we talked about love, what we'd learned. "Love is a feeling," Suki said. "Connections, warmth flowing from your heart—All in the present. It's not for getting you anything."

Liz and I would be leaving in five months to live for a year in Ireland. Suki and I began discussing what love could be when you knew it would end. Wouldn't it be pure because you couldn't have expectations? You'd have only the love you created and shared in the moment—which could be magnificent. After a week's vacation, I returned to get a call from her, asking about the next wine-tasting class. I felt a thrill. Something in her voice? Nah, I told myself, you're inventing. (Later, I realized that whenever I had that feeling I was almost never inventing.)

Returning from the City, we parked outside her house. Without speaking, we looked directly at each other, understood that we'd become lovers that night, and began laughing. We made love with exquisite tenderness, smiling joyously. I got home late and told Liz that a bunch of us had gone out partying after the wine class.

Once or twice a week, Suki and I reveled in intimacy and passion, When she described how she saw me, I thrilled to hear her present what I secretly thought my best self. One sunny weekday, we set off on my motorcycle and stopped at a traffic light. Suddenly, she exclaimed, "There's Jules!" and shouted greetings. He called back to us, telling her he'd see her on Friday. A bit more evolved than me, who continued telling Liz I was out drinking with one male friend or another, and would be home late. I didn't feel comfortable lying to her—but I didn't feel disturbingly bad either. After all, I'd warned her that I wasn't monogamous. I definitely didn't want to end with Suki before I left, and I dreaded confronting Liz about my affair, at least until we were away. Most importantly, this couldn't threaten our future. Suki and I were truly only lovers for now, until I left. She'd remain with Jules. I would tell Liz about Suki, as we drove across the country ... well, surely once we were in Ireland.

Adrian hosted a monster good-bye party for me and Liz. Stoned and slightly drunk, I stood alone in the middle of the hubbub and suddenly knew—me who was rarely intuitive—that Liz and I had betrayed each other. Adrian noticed my stricken face and led me outside. Liz was on the front steps, talking to Peter, one of my old friends. "Get out of my life," I snarled at her. Shocked, she ran to me, crying, demanding to know what was the matter with me. As we walked up the street, I insisted things were disastrous; she responded that I'd become crazy. Suddenly, I knew. "This is never going to work," I declared, "if we don't tell each other the truth. I've been sleeping with Suki." She stared at me, looking desperate. "I knew you were sleeping with someone," she moaned. "I've been sleeping with Peter." Two days and many denials later, she admitted she'd slept with five others while we'd lived together, including one where she admitted it'd been sick. Very sick, I tormented myself.

Karma had caught up to me, with lessons galore: 1) I'd rationalized my affair with Suki because Liz knew I was non-monogamous, as if that excused me from revealing when I actually was making love with another woman; 2) I'd unconsciously assumed that a woman I loved would never be as deceptive as me, let alone more so; 3) I'd believed that my deceptions weren't meant to harm, so no disastrous repercussions would follow; 4) maybe I couldn't be loved for who I truly was, if that included wanting to be in love with more than one woman at the same time. 5) The sharpest lesson was that lying was a mistake for me, an inept liar who believes he will get away with it. If I wanted magic, I was going to have to learn to tell the whole truth.

Later, I realized I'd also learned another, better lesson—Suki's teaching about what love was. She was right: love was a feeling.

After three tortured months in Ireland, Liz and I returned to separate apartments in Berkeley. She insisted I was still her man, but the more I probed for her core, the more tormented I became. All these wonderful qualities, but what was her essence? Adrian observed that we were beginning to learn that everything is filtered through your soul. Over more painful months, I sadly concluded that Liz's' soul was very lost. But though we tried to break up, we'd see each other on some pretext and be writhing in sexual ecstasy within hours. A distressing lesson: Sex could remain fabulous, even as the embers of love dwindled to extinction.

When I finally left Liz, I promised myself that at last I'd be capable of loving. No more deceit, no more emotional balloon payments. I would look inside myself, and reveal the truth. And I'd try to see a woman's soul before falling in love with her. Well, however adept I proved at that, I'd let her see into mine. The only thing lacking was Ms. Right, who proved elusive. Solace was involvement with some wonderful women, often more than one during the same time. I didn't lie, although I didn't always volunteer unasked-for details. Adrian noted, "It's easy to be honest if you don't care." When I told Kaitlin that I wasn't hiding my romantic entanglements, she replied, "You bastard, now it's their problem."

Over years, I'd randomly encountered Brenda, progressing as an actress and now in full young-woman blossom. I'd developed a crush on her, drawn to her sparkle and superb sense of humor. But she preferred me to remain a friend. We went to an occasional dinner or rock concert, once even for a friend's weekend party/extravaganza. Growing comfortable with each other, we spoke spontaneously and candidly. Then, after an intoxicatingly intimate dinner, we returned to my apartment and suddenly, she hugged me intensely. I looked at her face, close to mine, and we kissed. We made love. Blam! I felt feelings that seemed like love—tenderness, a rush of warmth, as if our spirits touched. Definitely magic—but I was wary of magic. As for love, my doubts seemed pervasive. Several weeks later Adrian remarked, "You've been seeing Brenda a lot lately. Ever think of living together?" I laughed. "No way. She's fourteen years younger than me. And an actress. Not a chance."

She and I were in my apartment, looking out at a rainy night. "I thought today about us living together," Brenda said softly, "but I knew right away it was silly."

"Yeah, it wouldn't work," I felt clear.

"I thought you'd say that. It's a relief."

"True—although I wish it could work." I was suddenly clear about that.

"I do too...." We were silent.

I laughed slightly. "Well, would it have to be silly?"

Our faces were very close. "Maybe it wouldn't be..." she smiled.

A shock of belief and desire coursed through me. We looked into each other's eyes and our hopes felt tangible. How thrilling it could be to live together. We looked even deeper at each other. I felt waves of what I knew was love. Maybe we had really connected. We held each other and kissed with yearning. Soon, we'd agreed that she would move in. I asked if she wanted to go out and celebrate. "No," she smiled, "I want to stay home."

Telling Kaitlin, I said, "I can't see what I have to lose." "Just time," she shrugged. But time was something I was prepared to be extravagant with. Opening to love with Brenda was a gamble. Whether we'd deepen to lasting love or not, I loved Brenda now. Yes, she was young and, having grown up in Berkeley, restless to explore other worlds. If we broke up, I vowed that I'd try to recover faster than the year plus Michelle and Liz had each cost me. While we were together, I'd live what I'd learned about love, from telling the truth to feeling love to telling her I loved her.

I stayed in love with Brenda until she abruptly left, nine months later, for Hollywood and another man. I felt far more lacerated than I could have anticipated. Sinking into torpor, resuming smoking, sleeping little, I sought recovery advice from Kaitlin, Liz and Adrian. You need to feel the pain, they agreed. That I could do. Also my first run in the Bay to Breakers Race was now only five weeks away and I'd trained for the race over a year. I willed myself to resume working out, which stimulated healing. Deeper, I was nourished by knowing that that I had truly loved; I hadn't failed. As E. M. Forster wrote about lovers, "the process of creation is itself an achievement."

More years passed: infatuations, escapades, affairs, wild women, wonderful women. A Legal Services friend moved back to Berkeley and asked Adrian how my love life was. "Multiple," he answered. "Oh good," she replied, "that's how he likes it." True, but still, sometimes when alone, I'd ache with yearning for intimacy and enduring love, perhaps listening to one of my secret songs, the Moody Blues pining, "I'm looking for someone to change my life. I'm looking for a miracle to happen."

My sister and I discussed what I now knew I wanted. Glamour was no longer important, though beauty, brains, a sense of humor, and love of reading remained so. Also now sanity was vital, as was a good soul. And someone who'd been through love a couple of times, "pre-shrunk." Plus someone supported herself. Plus ... "Ah, I see how it works" she cut in. "As you get older and the pickings get slimmer, your demands get higher."

Forty-two years old, I was at a party and saw a dark-haired, beautiful woman, dancing alone. I joined her. After two dates Rachel and I had discovered we shared much: both loving to laugh and rebels from the '60s, we insisted that money-earning wouldn't dominate our lives, preferring to live (comfortably) on the margins. A dancer inseparable from her dance, she was Jewish, intense, passionate, a fellow reader, wanted kids, as well as being attracted to my spirit, wit and body (fortunately for me, her type).

Who can determine how much of falling in love is timing? Certainly we were both ready. She'd been divorced for over a year, and had already had enough of single life. Drawn to her sincerity and liveliness, I felt sparks of hope. Maybe …

Weeks later, lying in front of my fireplace after having literally made/ love, our faces inches apart, we looked directly into each other's eyes. Thrills expanded through my body. I felt … I knew … I had seen into her depths. She was fine, all the way through her soul. We'd connected. We both felt it. Wow! So falling in love was magic after all.

Staying in love proved more difficult. Her ex-husband returned, wanting her back after rejecting her months before. Brenda, definitely still in full flower, returned from Hollywood and told me she'd realized she wanted me back. I told her that she was (just) too late. "No! You Love Me!" she exclaimed in certainty, not anger. Turmoil, tears. "Why is life so much like a soap opera," Brenda asked, "except it's nothing like it?" The decisive reality was that Rachel and I wanted, needed, to continue together. After a couple of crazy, sometimes anguished months sorting out entanglements, we soared into Stage One, which we later defined as, "laughing and making love all the time." When I proposed a backpacking trip, she replied she'd loved to. I called Adrian to borrow his tent. "Wow," he said, "You really got it all, didn't you."

Falling in love was a euphoric drug, but we both knew we'd have to evolve to Stage Two—Real Life, keeping magic alive. New terrain for me. Forster had educated me that, "The heart signs no documents." Maintaining love required attention, honesty, and probably luck. We promised to tell the truth and follow feelings. Neither of us was instinctively inclined to "processing." "Do I have to?" one could query when the other announced, "We need to talk." But we both knew we did have to.

We struggled over "Commitment." Why, I insisted, would I promise to stick around no matter how bad it got? Noting that commitment was also the term applied to involuntary incarceration of mental patients, I insisted that I wasn't monogamous. She insisted on it, having experimented with open marriage and concluding it was disastrous for her.

"Love is the crooked thing. There is nobody wise enough to find out all that is in it." Yeats got that right. The tale of how we managed to keep magic/love alive would require a novelist: passion, tragedies, conflicts, opening hearts, angers, laughter, fights, understanding, joys, good fortune. Agreement on big things: We both love physical activity and travel, don't define success in terms of money/career, need a lover with many independent passions. Agreement on little things that could become big things if we disagreed: we're both tidy, share cooking and shopping, prefer to keep our finances separate. Meanwhile AIDS rendered non-monogamy dangerous, if not deadly. Besides, I was far from deluged with temptation. And trying to "process" an affair would destroy our magic and terminate being together. So non-monogamy was left officially unresolved, but moot.

After years living with and loving (most of the time) Rachel, I realized I'd evolved into feeling a commitment, without ever having "made" one, the commitment of wanting to continue, to stay together. Living it feels far more enhancing than confining. Not that it can't chafe. Dailiness grinds at magic. We have to create structures for encouraging the continuation (or return) of magic. And what a drag it having to "communicate" can be. As one lover put it, "If he really loved me, he'd know what I was thinking." And what discouragement when talking doesn't bring harmony but clarifies differences. Then there's her flaws. And mine. Depressing, all that magic can't eliminate. How mundane that the therapy-folks are right when they talk about the "work" necessary to stay in love, "dealing with your stuff." Right but limited. Because no "work" can guarantee magic, only remove barriers to it. Only by dwelling in magic often enough, living the gift of magic, as Rachel and I fortunately have, can love continue, evolving and enduring.

[2005]

DRAGGED TO PARIS

Moving to Paris would be a catastrophe. The city was foreign and far away and I'd have no friends. Fourteen years old, I dreaded being yanked away from my jock buddies. But in 1954 my Dad got a one-year Marshall Plan job introducing quality control to European industry, so we left suburban New Jersey—Dad, Mom, seven months pregnant, and six kids, ranging from me to a one-year old. We traveled second class on the French ocean-liner, the *Liberté*. The State Department would have paid for first class, but frugal Mom applied her money-saving principals to federal spending too, so she would not squander government money on luxury.

In Paris, we all stayed in two rooms in a modest hotel in the 16th. Mom, I later learned, was coping with one of the most difficult times of her life, looking for a new home in addition to all her other tasks while Dad was away working. I timidly poked into the whirl of this big city—people, unintelligible language, traffic, noise. Numb as much as stunned, I worried about the school I'd attend, the English-speaking American Community School of Paris (ACS). Happily, I discovered one redeeming feature of Paris, the *International Herald Tribune*, where I followed my heroes, the N.Y. Giants, as they marched to winning the Pennant and then, astoundingly, swept the World Series against the favored Indians. But even victory was bittersweet. I wasn't at home to watch it on black and white TV, nor able to exalt over Yankee fans.

Two weeks after arrival we moved to our new home, a large house with a clay tennis court in Croissy-sur-Seine, several miles northwest of Paris. My sister Joanne, brother Steve and I began attending ACS, housed in a small, run-down mansion near the Bois de Bolounge, with about 25 students per grade. Within days, I'd identified the cool guys in my class— a gang of four, surprisingly not athletes but Parisian sophisticates. Each was witty and owned a motorcycle. They spoke French, went to billiard halls and cafés, apparently drank wine and beer, and talked knowingly about St. Germaine de Près and Sidney Bechet's jazz. I'd always been popular with guys, but this group did not welcome me, early confirmation that I'd be miserable in Paris.

I'd been at school less than a month when one of the cool guys, Bobby, small, stocky and loud, accosted me and declared that we would fight. He didn't announce a reason. Terrified, I knew I'd have to fight. Though athletic, I was tall and skinny and had never been in a fight, but I couldn't be branded a "chicken."

A few days later, we fought in a large school-hallway coat closet, surrounded by a group of guys, certainly not invited by me. Bobby and I eyed each other, then he moved towards me. Leaping at him, I grabbed his head in a headlock as we fell. Wrestling on the floor, he fought to free his head from my arms. I held on with far more force than I knew I possessed. Struggling, he screamed for me to let him go and fight fair, but he couldn't escape. Suddenly, he announced that the fight was over, a tie. I instantly agreed. He never challenged me again.

To get to school, I walked a mile to Chatou and then took a train to Paris' Gare St. Lazare. Occasionally, I'd walk the other way, to Bougival, crossing a bridge over the Seine. Mom told me that it was the same bridge that Monet and Renior, painters I vaguely knew of, had painted. From Bougival, I'd take a bus to Paris. By either route, once arriving in Paris, I'd then take the metro to school. Rush-hour metros were jammed with French workers, weathered, rough men, dressed in worn blue shirts and blue pants. Often they smelled strongly, from the garlic many chewed, or from the hand-rolled unlit cigarettes dangling from their mouths. The men seemed strange but also appealing, somehow radiating a "Don't

Tread on Me" attitude I'd never sensed from the commuter men in my hometown.

Paris was gray, with soot-coated buildings and shabby streets. Astonishingly, many suit-wearing men were so poor they rode bicycles or motor scooters to work. Cars were scarce, and often old, cranky, or, like the bizarre Deux Cheveaux Citroen, sounded like a dying sewing machine. Clothes of French boys were dull, sometimes near shabby. Nobody had cool button-down shirts or decent sneakers or, what I somehow learned French kids yearned for, Levis.

Croissy too was poor, though it had some large houses, as well as many potato fields. The town's one mangy shopping street of impoverished little stores was named rue General Leclerc. I never asked why they would name a street after General Electric. Nor did I express my horror after learning that the wooden horse head above a store meant the store sold horsemeat that French people ate. Oddly, stores closed from noon to three, or maybe even four. Most all houses had high walls around them, not suburban lawns. There were people in town, Mom reported, who didn't speak to others because of bitter feelings from the War.

Mom, in one of her letters to friends, wrote: "As usual, Denis' chief concerns are his friends, sports, his standing in school and his social life." But except for sports, I remained unhappy and left out, hiding my secret crush on a beautiful popular girl, Linda. Still, I had made friends with a couple of new kids in my class, and developed a modest after-school social life of trips to the American Embassy cafeteria. Open to all (at least, all Americans) the cafeteria provided tables where kids could gather, chat and consume milkshakes, sodas, or hamburgers, briefly feeling back home.

My sister Catherine was born in November. With a new baby, six other children, and a frequently-absent husband, Mom reluctantly concluded that she could use help, especially as help was inexpensive. Two sisters in their twenties, recently arrived from the countryside, moved into our house. Mom found them invaluable—cheerful, competent, child-loving. They accompanied Mom shopping, where she frugally continued to buy cheap, if not the cheapest, meats, vegetables, fruits.

After a few weeks, the sisters announced that they would leave. Mom, shocked, asked them what was wrong. One replied that Mom could feed her family as she wished, but the sisters were French, and could not continue to eat bad meals. Mom reluctantly agreed to buy them food adequate to their tastes. So Mom shopped for food on two levels: continued frugality for her family, and French for her *bonnes*. After a few weeks Mom realized: This is nuts—I feed my family worse than my help. So family food was upgraded, and Mom began to learn French cooking.

Confirming French culinary values was the family with two young kids who lived in the cramped apartment over our carriage-house garage. The wife told Mom that they spent over 50% of their income on food. Astonished, Mom asked how they could possibly choose to spend so much. "You have to eat!" the wife replied.

So my youngest siblings grew up with fine meals, often French, and good wine, and never knew the food-as-fuel meals of Mom's Irish-American heritage. Over future decades, whenever I returned home, I'd delight in the gourmet meals Mom prepared.

French cooking or not, Steve and I yearned for peanut butter—real, old-fashioned, with-nuts peanut butter. We couldn't find it anywhere in Paris. For some bureaucratic reason my father didn't qualify for privileges at the huge army PX, with its rows of peanut butter jars. Then, somehow, in February, we learned that a fancy store on the Right Bank (Fouchon's?) carried American peanut butter. Spending from our savings, we bought out the supply, perhaps twenty-four jars. Drawing on my earnings from past summers of caddying, I understood for the first time that saving might be desirable, not a duty thrust upon me.

Mom and I drove past the café Deux Magots (meaning either "a hoard of money" or "a Chinese porcelain figure"). I liked the name—calling a café after maggots was outrageous. Instinctively, I loved Paris cafés. My suburban hometown didn't have a real restaurant, let alone a café. Paris cafés exuded a mystically inviting spirit—full of adults at ease, talking, laughing, reading, or just sitting outside, relaxing, observing. Learning that many painters and writers hung out in left-bank cafés, I spun vague, romantic visions of the freedom and fun these bohemians lived—surely a better life than having to wear a suit and tie and go to an office. I never imagined what these artists actually did when not at cafés. Except I was sure they had fun.

ACS basketball tryouts were held in October. I'd long loved basketball, but in grade school had been permanently branded as not first rank. But here, no one knew. Not only did I make the team, I became one of the two stars. Learning to play and move as part of a team was pure joy—and I made more friends.

Our school didn't have a gym, so we practiced and played our games in various *Lycées* (French high schools). During basketball season, I often walked through different sections of Paris. Meanwhile, I absorbed sights of Paris from other travels, from peanut butter hunts to museum explorations led by Mom. By winter, I knew the Seine, the Eiffel Tower, the Champs Elysées and the Étoile. I could manage the metro system, though I couldn't fathom why they had first and second-class cars. Providing better cars for the wealthy couldn't be right. That wasn't how the New York City subways worked.

It was late February, or early March, after practice. Ambling in the glow of post-athletics I was heading to the nearest metro station. Halting near the Seine, I raised my head, and looked, suddenly in awe at the city around me: beautiful, majestic buildings, all in harmony; golden late afternoon light glowed on windows and sparkled on the river. Paris was glorious, elegant magic, a vast open-air museum. Like Paul on the road to Damascus, I became an instant, total convert.

I began to learn. Society: The black-clad, sour old women taking tickets in the metro or fiercely collecting some pittance when you occupied a chair in the *Tuileries* were World War I widows, meagerly supported in their old age by the French government. Politics: a Prime Minister named Mendes-France ended a war in some remote place called Vietnam. But he'd made himself a laughingstock in France by urging the French to drink more milk and reduce their consumption of wine. I'd yet to have my first alcoholic drink and loved milk, but I approved of adults dedicated to wine drinking, again instinctively voting for bohemian living against puritan sobriety. I even began to learn French. We had a required French class daily, with a fine teacher. Though I couldn't understand Parisian conversations, I managed to communicate with storekeepers or subway ticket sellers. Without awareness, I fell in love with the sounds of the French language.

Not that I was precocious. Mom described us two in the Jeu de Paume, her looking at her favorite Impressionist painters, while I, "dressed in sneakers, Levis, and a red and blue basketball jacket, read a copy of Time." Mom continued, "As we said all along, it will be a wonderful thing for our children to be exposed to all the advantages of French culture."

Some Parisians were gruff or haughty to me, an American. Stupid Frogs, I'd mutter, having learned that insult at school. But I also became increasingly aware of boorish American tourists. Once on a Paris bus, I mentally cringed as some Americans shouted louder and louder in English at a bus driver, who placidly shrugged. Finally, one of the Americans approached me and barked, "You're American aren't you. Tell this guy what we want." I looked puzzled at the man and replied, "Pardon, je ne parle pas anglais."

Trips in the city became adventures. Basketball season ended and I was free after school. Sporadically, I'd take a metro to some part of the city I didn't know, and then get on a bus with an open standing area in the back. Maneuvering myself to a railing—I'd learned some useful skills on those rush-hour metros—I'd watch portions of Paris go by. Enthralled, I'd get off, wander, and eventually ask someone where the nearest metro station was (always not too far away) and head towards the Gare. Timidly, I began to sample Parisian treats. I sat in a café, ordered a soda, and no one pointed or laughed at me. Patisseries offered sumptuous éclairs. With Spring, Paris became more beautiful: stately trees budded leaves; graceful buildings rose on a human scale, not domineering like Manhattan's ferocious skyscrapers; the Seine, the soul of the city, flowed gently.

Much of Parisian life remained puzzling. Why, to play basketball in an official *Lycée* league, did I have to obtain an identity card, which required submitting six photos, as well as a statement of my grandfathers' birthplaces, to some Parisian bureaucrat? Why was the date always included when "Defense d' Afficher, loi du 29 Juillet, 1881," was painted on building walls to warn against posting advertisements? Why were

Arabs often treated with contempt, worse than Negroes had been back in New Jersey?

Still, much broke through. Passion! Couples, mostly young but not always, kissed intensely, on streets, in parks, on benches. Even students at my school sometimes hugged and kissed. Sights I'd surely never seen in my suburb. I was in puberty; romantic passion—not that I knew anything about it except it involved kissing—was thrilling. Amazingly, public passion was also acceptable. "French priests certainly don't seem concerned with sins of the flesh," Dad chuckled. Raised American-Irish-Catholic, I'd attended Sunday school, where I'd been warned by nuns against "near occasions of sin" (anything that could possibly lead to sex). Priests and nuns had assured me that Catholicism was universal and identical everywhere. Though not at all religious, I'd believed that. Paris became my first dose of religious relativism, an awakening that Catholics could believe very different notions about God and God's rules.

Liberté surged inside me. On a glorious spring afternoon I sat in the train home and glanced at my (cheap) wristwatch. Suddenly, I loathed the watch; it felt like a chain, imposing a tyranny of precise time. Why chose to be so constricted? Impulsively I took the watch off and threw it out the train window.

On a beautiful May morning, my sister Joanne and I walked to the bus stop in Bougival. I knew that another bus that stopped there went to Versailles, where our family had gone once. "Let's play hooky and go to Versailles," I spontaneously urged. We did, though neither of us had ever played hooky before. Few people were at Versailles except staff. We rented a rowboat, and idled on the water for hours, ecstatic in our sunshine-drenched freedom.

During basketball season, Dutch, our coach as well as Latin teacher, had frequently mentioned our most recent game, often complimenting me, in our next class. Surely, Linda, sitting near me, would be impressed and … But she never seemed to notice, even when we reached the quarter-finals of some Parisian championship before losing. Nor did she attend the basketball banquet at the end of the season, where I received the only athletic letter of my life—a big red "A."

I'd dreamed for weeks of taking Linda to the prom. Finally, I dared to linger by the front hedge after school, until she walked out alone. I popped in front of her and asked to go with me. She erupted with laughter, and walked away. Stabbed, I fought back tears, suffering my initial education of love as pain.

We went to Normandy for the summer, where I had an awakening of some costs of Liberté. On a family trip to Omaha Beach, I encountered strewn remnants from D Day—ship carcasses in the water, twisted metal and shattered wood on the beach, and shell-pocked, often surprisingly intact, remains of concrete German pillboxes high on the bluffs. Steve and I struggled up a hill to one pillbox. How could any American soldier have made it up here while Germans above were firing machine guns at him? I was awed, even humbled. I'd seen many World War II movies, but reality was of a different order—frightening, and impressive.

For all my glimmerings of freedom in Paris, when I returned to New Jersey in the fall, I mostly reverted to being the same adolescent I'd been before Paris—a bit of a rebel, but basically conventional, and repressed. Underneath though, dreams of Liberté percolated. I yearned for a life of passion and freedom, which to me meant becoming a bohemian, hanging out in coffeehouses with a sexy girl friend dressed in black and staying up late passionately discussing art. Only much later did I realize that genuine artists spent much time alone, creating.

Slowly, over future years, I came to understand my good fortune in being dragged to Paris. Forced from the cocoon of my suburb, I had begun to awake. I could defend myself if I had to fight. I used that headlock in two other fights and drew on my sense that I could protect myself to avoid some others. And certainly, after Omaha beach, war could never be glamorous. Surprisingly, back in New Jersey, I began to dabble with oil paints. Further, my buddies didn't have to define me athletically or any other way. I played some freshman basketball in college, and in my seventies still shoot baskets.

Some awakenings took longer to cohere. I had to live through more heartbreaks before beginning to see I knew nothing about love. And only when I reached law school did I realize that I wanted to be able to speak French adequately, taking my first class in it after ACS. Since then,

I've continued studying French, sufficiently so that I can now speak Français with French friends. Cultural understandings also emerged only over years: realizing that the Eisenhower affluence I'd grown up with was a blessing, not a state of nature; perceiving that French civilization was wise to place food—good meals and wine—at its core.

Most all of the awakenings I first experienced in Paris have held (though I've proved to be weak in the savings department). I love bohemian freedom, and still don't wear a watch. I earn my living as a writer. In my thirties, a passion for painting emerged. Taking classes, joining drawing groups, I explored painting. But plagued by one of my demons—I awoke to their existence well after that year in Paris—I struggled for years to accept that I could paint simply because I love to. Now I've had an art studio for over three decades. And when Naomi and I were buying a home, we agreed that it had to be within walking distance of a café. It is.

Most magically, my life-long love of Paris has held—the walker's Paris, the café-sitter's Paris, the museum Paris, the lover's Paris, the Paris available to all. The Paris I've returned to as often as I could, the endlessly fascinating city.

[2001] (2012)

SIXTEEN THINGS I LOVE ABOUT THE FRENCH (AND A FEW I DON'T)

The French are different from Americans. Vive la différence. There's much about France for an American to love. My love started as a high-school student in 1954, living for a year in Croissy-sur-Seine outside Paris, while my father worked for the Marshall Plan. Attending the American Community School near the Bois de Bolougne, I played on the basketball team against French teams, which meant traveling through the City to various lycée gyms. Slowly, the beauty of Paris sank in. Deeper, I felt intuitively drawn to sidewalks cafés full of energetically talking people. And I was joyously stunned seeing men and women passionately kissing in public

Over the following sixty years I've returned to France often. During four decades, I was an occasional hotel-occupying tourist, usually in Paris. Then, in twelve different summers (from 1997 to 2013) my mate Naomi and I exchanged our house in Berkeley for roughly a month for a French family's home: Twice in Paris; four times in different coastal towns in Brittany; twice in towns outside Montpellier; and once each in Bellecombe-en Bauge in the Savoie mountains above Lake Annecy, and in Nice, and in the Pays Basque, and in St. Chamas, a small town forty miles northwest of Marseille. Each exchange has been a dream. We've made friends we meet whenever we can when we return to France. We've learned to speak French well enough to carry on conversations, from politics to books to the personal, without using English. My love of France and the French has deepened, although I've developed some dislikes too. I'll start with some likes.

1) **Their passion for their language.** The French love of their language is astonishing and impressive. A devout reader as well as a talker and a writer, I'm naturally interested in language. French friends have taught me how deep concern for language can be.

In Bellecombe in 1999, we became friends with Bob and Mado, an older couple who'd moved there from Lyon more than 20 years before. During most of our subsequent French home exchanges we visited them for a coupe of days. If I were forced to define Bob and Mado in terms of class, I'd say that they were working class and very classy. One afternoon at their house they disagreed over the proper usage of a French word. Each held strongly to his or her opinion. Within moments, each had pulled out his or her large, heavy French dictionary, vigorously arguing their view. I can't recall the word, nor how the dispute was resolved, but I'll always remember the fervor each brought to precise understanding of French.

To many French, speaking and understanding their language well is a vital component of living. They concur with quiet pride when I declare that French is the most beautiful of languages. Mado explained that some French language rules exist because otherwise spoken words would have an unpleasant sound. Language is so important to the French that many major politicians write books to demonstrate their graceful verbal skills and literary abilities. An inarticulate, word-fumbling President is inconceivable in France.

Knowing the French passion for their language, I appreciate friends, as well as an occasional shopkeeper or bartender, who correct my French. They know I understand that's it's a compliment for them to correct me. I speak French well enough so they believe that I, like all lovers of their language, must want to do it as well as possible.

2) **They can be intensely romantic.** We've heard the myth: The French are Lovers. Here's one tale about that. In Brittany I asked a couple we'd become friends with how they met. He was a high-ranking employee) in the National Finance Department. She was perhaps fifteen younger

than him. They'd been happily married for over twenty years. Chuckling at my question, they paused, then nodded agreement that he could tell us. "She hadn't paid her television tax. [In France, you must pay a yearly property tax each TV.] She'd been called by the tax people, and then sent a couple of letters. "Threw them away," she laughed. "So," he continued, "It was kicked up to me. I wrote her a stern letter—You better pay the tax or else…. blah, blah … or call me. So she called me…" He paused, looking loving at her, "and I fell in love with her voice. … I told her that she needed to come to my office so we could discuss this personally."

Hard to imagine an IRS agent telling a similar story.

3) **Sidewalk Cafés.** The New Jersey suburb I was raised in didn't even have a restaurant, let alone a sidewalk café. The Parisian café magic I first absorbed as a teenager still enthralls. Sitting outside at a café, sipping a grand crème (roughly, a cappuccino), reading or watching people pass, remains one of the most satisfying of French pleasures. And once you've ordered, you can stay as long as you like.

Cafés serve as gathering places, not solely a place to consume coffee. Parisians have their favorites, usually in their neighborhood. One classic café type is the flâneur. "Flâner," the verb, is inadequately translated as "to lounge, saunter, stroll, loaf." A flâneur (male) or a flâneuse (female) is a city creature who delights in the pleasures of ambling through urban streets, talking, looking, laughing, enjoying and, of course, partaking of café life. As does the flâneur's spiritual kin, the bon vivant.

4) **French cuisine.** The delights of French cooking are hardly secret. French domestic cooking is usually a living tradition. Recipes are passed down for generations. Cooking well is an egalitarian pleasure, available to all (except, perhaps, the most poor). You don't need to be rich. Family dinners, or the big Sunday lunch, are times for gathering, enjoying conversation and eating/drinking with pleasure. No rushing.

A culture that puts eating well at its center has done something very right. Eating well means, to use the now-standard phrase, "living in the present." Enjoying a meal is being alive to your actual existence, taking time to nourish yourself and feel the pleasures you have by doing so.

Before my family lived in France, my frugal, Irish-American mother regarded food as essentially fuel. In France, she continued to spend as little as possible on food. A French family of four—two young children—lived in the tiny second-story flat over the garage of our Croissy house. France was still post-World-War-II poor; the husband had a demanding job and didn't earn much. My mother was astonished when she learned that the wife often bought more expensive food than Mom did. Discussing this with the wife, Mom grew more astonished when told that the family spent over 50% of their income on food. "How can you spend so much?" Mom asked, as politely as she could. Now the other woman was astonished, "But you have to eat," she proclaimed—meaning eat well.

Eating well starts with shopping well—buying fresh baguettes or other bread daily, and frequent visits to other local stores, perhaps a fromagerie (cheese) patisserie (desserts), boucherie (meat) poissonier (fish) or to a traitteur, roughly a high-end, to-go delicatessen, offering treats like lapin à la moutarde (rabbit in mustard sauce) or celerie remoulade, all prepared by the proprietor. Each stop commences with friendly personal exchanges of greetings—by name if you're known; if you're a stranger, it's "Bonjour Monsieur," "Bonjour Madame."

There's more food shopping at neighborhood open-air street markets. Some Paris areas have open markets most days, offering everything from fresh vegetables to meat and fish to Moroccan or to Arab dishes to exotic spices. Some markets are immense, like the one in Paris' Belleville district. Other street markets range from mid-size to small. But every Parisian neighborhood has at least one.

Then there's supermarkets. Some purists might bemoan supermarkets' competition with neighborhood stores, but most French seem happy with the combination. After W.W.II, the small-store lobby prevented supermarkets from opening in France. The fight to finally allow them was lead by a priest, distressed by the high prices poor people had to pay because of the small stores' monopoly over food distribution. Eventually, supermarkets arrived. Some actually are super, offering bountiful choices, from delicious patés to fresh vegetables and fruits to meat and fish, and a patisserie and a vast cheese selection.

French meals, whether at home or in a restaurant, are normally healthy as wall as delicious. While some traditional French haute cuisine remains rich in cream and butter, the culinary trend is distinctly towards less fattening food. Portions are modest by American standards. You leave a restaurant meal feeling satisfied, not stuffed. Traditionalists are understandably troubled by the increase in fast-food joints and the weight gain that they lead to. Joe Bové became a hero to many French for leading the well-publicized dismemberment of a planned McDonalds near Montpellier. Yet despite some ominous signs that French food culture is waning, my sense is that it is so deeply entrenched that it will last and evolve.

I want to note two particular French-food favorites.

5) **French Cheese with Red Wine.** Charles DeGaulle famously observed, "How can anyone be expected to govern a country that has 325 cheeses?" Or perhaps the number was 355—I've seen several different numbers with that quote. They do surely have LOTS of varieties of delicious cheese. During our first French home exchange, our Parisian family introduced me to the tradition of a cheese course after the main meal. Talk about a duck to water. Then Bob further educated me on the necessity of eating cheese. "Un repas sans fromage," Bob proclaimed, "est comme un jour sans soleil." [A meal without cheese is like a day without sunshine.] Moreover, he preached, I must drink red wine (never white) with cheese.

6) **Profiteroles.** The queen of desserts (not the king, because the noun is feminine). Nothing low-calorie here: Ice cream in delicate pastry puffs, topped with warm chocolate sauce and whipped cream—an ideal combination of indulgence, elegance, and sweet. Their popularity has now reached the U.S., where you find them occasionally on restaurant menus. They taste almost as good as they do in France.

7) **The Land.** Geographically, France is blessed. The country is beautiful and varied—coasts on the Atlantic and Mediterranean, mountains of the Alps, the Pyrenees and the Massive Central, lush farmland and gorgeous rivers. There must be ugly parts of France, but I haven't seen them. All of our exchange regions, as well as other areas I've travelled in, including Normandy, the Loire Valley, the Dordgne, and Strasbourg, have been delightful, not only beautiful but with some lesser known but very appealing elements.

First, they have no poison oak or ivy—a boon for lovers of hiking in mountains, through woods, or on other less-traveled outdoor routes.

Secondly, there are coastal walking paths on most of the ocean coastlines of France. Unlike the U.S., where "private property" rights foreclose walking on almost all ocean-front land, in France you can stroll by the sea for miles on "sentier côtiers," coastal paths accessible to all. The paths were originally "chemins des douaniers," custom-inspectors' paths. The right of the King, or Napoleon, or the Republic, to prevent smuggling overrode private ownership.

Modern France retains this tradition, reinforced by a more recent law, "la loi de 1976 sur la servitude littorale." Roughly three to five yards of the edge of coastal land is held as public right-of-way. Behind that land is private, whether fields, farms, houses, or immense walls of rich estates. Occasionally, for whatever mysterious reasons, private owners or businesses have been allowed to creep to the edge of the land, forcing the sentier to briefly turn interior. But this is the exception.

Friends told us that the finest hour of Mitterand's socialist rule in the 1980s was when a government minister personally drove a bulldozer into an access-blocking wall Brigitte Bardot had erected on her sea-front land in the Riviera. The minister got his publicity, workers finished the job, and the point was made. THIS land is our land.

8) **The French refuse to give up their vacations.** The French regard their four or five week summer vacation, and a couple of more weeks during the year, as an essential component of Liberté. Several friends have revealed their fear that "Globalization" is in reality a cover for the imposition of American workaholism. French stubbornness about their vacations can create hassles, as the majority proves every year by insisting on taking their vacations in August, despite all attempts to persuade them to vacation at less crowded times. Anyway, let Americans boast about how long and hard they work and take only a week or two off a year. The French will continue to opt for, and fight for if need be, a saner balance.

9) **They don't have a lawyer-and-insurance-ridden personal-injury accident system.** No insurance company hobgoblins or kill-joy lawyers deciding you can't play here or swim there or do whatever because of possible liability or lawsuits. Kids bounce merrily on public trampolines. Cities sponsor street parties without massive insurance

costs. Their accident-compensation system is simple. As our American friend Mark, who owns a home in Brittany put it, "If you get hurt they'll take care of you and if you die they'll bury you."

10) **They have sane gun laws.** There's no NRA in France. No powerful gun-lobby insists that individual possession of machine guns is a core right of Liberté.

11) **Government support of public events.** French governments, national and local, pay for spectacular collective, communal events that would be highly unlikely to get public funding in the U.S. One prime example is Paris Plage, a "beach" created in August every summer on the highway on the Right Bank of the Seine. For a month, all car traffic ceases on three miles of this major Parisian thoroughfare. Temporarily replacing the highway are tons of sand, palm trees, beach chairs, cafes, water-sprays, food purveyors, and many other treats. Originally a one-year project, the Plage was a spectacular success, loved by Parisiens and visitors. So the Plage became an annual event. Each year, new treats are added or varied: more water-sprays and fountains, a swimming pool, a climbing wall for kids. There's dancing and Tai Chi classes and strolling entertainers, and much, much more. And always the pleasures of strolling by the Seine—at a "beach"—with thousands of other amblers.

And it's FREE!

Of course, France is not paradise. Here are some flaws that particularly trouble me.

The rigidity of the education system. The French education system is state-centralized and tightly-controlled—with often-distressing results. Here's one example.

Michelle, a granddaughter of Bob and Mado, profoundly wanted to become a doctor. An excellent student, compassionate and humorous, she would have made a fine médecin. There is one yearly national exam for entrance into French medical schools. Roughly ten percent of the applicants pass. The percentage is controlled to prevent over-competition (as the government and practicing doctors define it). Michelle did not succeed the first time, although she came close. Applicants can only take the exam twice. She did not pass the next year either. Her dream of becoming a doctor was dead. There are no other ways possible to go to medical school in France. In the U.S., with its diversity of medical schools and entrance requirements, she would undoubtedly have been able to live her medical dream.

The lack of an entrepeneurial tradition. It's far more difficult to start a new small business in France than it is in the U.S. A young computer programmer spoke of his admiration of Silicon Valley, bemoaning the impossibility of he and some colleagues creating their own business in France. They would not be able to obtain any start-up financing or loans from banks or the government or venture capital firms. Unless, he added you had connections ("branché) or were a graduate of a prestigious Parisian university (called the "Grandes Écoles"). So while corporate business may prosper in France, many potential small entrepenuerial businesses never get a chance. One result is the country's persistently high unemployment rate.

Racism. The riots in poor ghettos in 2005 manifested a reality that troubles many French—the country's failure to cope with its immigrant/Arab/black population. As a teenager in Paris, I was shocked by the dismissal, even contempt, some French openly displayed to Arabs. Decades later, overt racism may have diminished, but the core problem has grown. France now has millions of non-white citizens and residents. Most are poor; unemployment runs 30% or higher. Many non-whites are housed in shoddy apartment buildings in dreary suburbs, out of sight from central cities. French friends tell me that little has been proposed by French political leaders to try to ameliorate these problems. Well, at least rabidly-anti-American French intellectuals (yes, some remain) can no longer smugly sneer at U.S. racism, and prattle on about how they've always welcomed black American jazz musicians.

The Government's Adherence to Nuclear Power. A large percentage of French energy comes from nuclear power. The state bureaucracy is heavily committed to nuclear energy and resistant to exploring other options. As a result, France is far behind other European countries, Germany for one, in the development of alternate energy sources, from wind to solar.

I can't end negatively. Back to things I love.

12) **What French Women Can Do With a Scarf.** They can wear one in hundreds of ways, each time looking elegant, or dashing, or whatever

is the desired effect. Scarfs are a key component of French women's flair for style, a flair that doesn't diminish with aging. As many gray-haired French women demonstrate, older women can remain beautiful.

13) **Joie de Vivre.** Love of living, delight in conversation, an interested, curious mind. a ready sense of humor. Finishing a delicious homemade dinner, Bob quipped, "Ah, une autre repas que Thatcher n'aurait pas." [Ah, another meal Thatcher won't have.] And happily, most French people I know admire the openness and adventurousness they find in Americans. So we join in their joie de vivre and merry times are had.

The Glories of France. The French love their "gloire." Historically, gloire was often seen in military terms (think Napoleon, Louis the XIV's wars). Fortunately, gloire has many saner manifestations. Here are three favorites:

14) **French Painters.** One of France's greatest gifts to world culture. The Impressionists, and so many others: Millet, Delacroix, Ingres, Bonnard, Redon, David, Daumier, Lorain, Corot, on and on. The ultimate, to me, is Monet's Water Lilies (Les Nymphéas) in the Orangerie— paintings astonishingly rich and varied, a work of absolute genius. Once, examining them up close I observed, "Amazing. Monet painted the greatest abstract painting ever, long before anyone else conceived of the concept." And the greatest abstract painting ever is only one great aspect of Les Nymphéas.

15) **French Writers.** Another gift to world culture. Those I've read in English include François Villon, Voltaire, Molière, Baudelaire, Montaigne, Collette, Balzac, Mme. De Sévigné, Hugo, Flaubert, Dumas, Maupassant, Zola, Rimbaud, Proust, Irène Némirovsky, Simenon, Simone de Beauvoir, and Romain Gary. And in French, thanks to my French class: Pagnol, La Fontaine, Camus, J. M. G. Le Clézio, George Sand, and others.

16) **Paris.** One more Hurrah for the City of Light, endlessly fascinating, with far too many charms to list favorites. Hemingway got it right, "Paris is a moveable feast."

Vive la France.

[2006] [2014]

FOREVER WILD

Little Adirondack towns like Old Forge are touched by the wildness of the Park around them, those lands protected by the New York Constitution as "forever wild." Whatever my New Jersey suburban hometown offered, it surely wasn't wild. But happily, for over fifty summers, since my parents purchased a camp (local for summerhouse) on Old Forge Pond when I was seven, I've lived Adirondack wildness, unfettered freedoms, that my soul craved.

When I was a little kid, everything about our place felt wild: mysterious, liberating, calling out for exploration. The camp itself, originally built as a small hunting cabin in the '20s, had evolved into a melange of oddly-shaped rooms. Latticed wood cabinets, built into corners of the living room, held exotic china, old oak boxes, and numerous other treasures. On the porch, two ancient canvas-covered seats swayed from creaky metal springs. Two birch-bark birdhouses decorated the inside porch wall. Long before I had any idea what a "work of art" was, I felt the magic some unknown artist infused in those creations.

Outside, dirt steps led up a steep hill, through ferns and trees, to the road. No lawns here. Down from the camp, past more trees and ferns, was the ultimate magic, the lake (technically, Old Forge Pond). Our massive two-story boathouse jutted out into the water. The rough upstairs room became my base for adventures.

At the water's edge was a trail leading up past an ersatz lighthouse to the channel, the mile-long link to First Lake of the Fulton Chain of Lakes. The trail began two houses from us, at Rivette's Boat Livery, a hodge-podge of rickety buildings and docks crammed with boats, motors, papers, old cans, oil rags, gas pumps and innumerable unfathomable objects. Rivette's was also the starting point for the romantic mail boat, with a captain who actually delivered mail up through Fourth Lake.

My father was a college math professor and quality-control consultant. Even with three kids to support, he managed to pry much of the summer free. In June we'd set off in our old Ford, luggage piled high on the roof, for the long drive over backcountry roads, past Burma-Shave signs in farmers' fields. Finally, eight or ten hours later, we'd arrive and receive our first reward—our annual Knotty Pine Restaurant dinner, a mushroom hamburger on toast. (I haven't ordered one in decades, to preserve the perfect hamburger of my memories.) Then back in the car for the familiar drive down old-fashioned Main Street, turning the last corner and—Shazam!—the pond and channel stretched before us, a shimmering vision of joy. I can't recall a single rainy day arrival, though surely it can't always have been sunny.

No school! Summer stretched before me long as a lifetime. Age seven, I learned to swim in a class at the town beach, and met Jack, my first best friend. Daily, we adventured, often exploring in the nature around us: searching in old quarries, watching water gush over the pond dam, hunting frogs in swampy ponds, investigating the water-logged remnants of ancient railroad tracks. Even the economic catastrophe, for the townspeople, of the Second World War aided our exploits. One result of the wartime dearth of tourists was a number of abandoned, decaying houses for us to creep through.

Above all, adventure meant water: jumping and diving off our dock; swimming to the wartime cork float my father had salvaged; loafing and splashing on inner tubes; fishing—catches of bullheads and undersized sun fish; exploring marshes, water lilies, reeds. Or a jaunt to the beach, building minnow traps and encountering other town kids, some tough and contentious.

On the water, I discovered the magic of boats. With the camp came a beautiful wood canoe, a sail-canoe, and a Sponson, a large wood rowboat with balsa-wood pontoons, designed so that the boat was impossible to tip over. Very true, and we surely tried. The Sponson could be fitted with our two-and-a-half-horsepower outboard motor. I'd wind a rope around the flywheel, yank and yank, then usually yank and yank more, and eventually—sometimes—the motor sputtered to life. Free on the water! No age limit to drive, no license required.

Jack taught me to navigate the narrow channel, how to maneuver by its unmarked obstacles—rocks dangerously close to the surface, sunken logs and tree stumps, unexplained ruins, shallow spots. Steering through, I was Mark Twain, man (OK, boy) of the river, masterly avoiding peril. We'd stop at the uninhabited sand bar halfway up the channel, or, if we felt really adventurous, journey a couple of hours further to the islands of First Lake—Dog Island, or the much larger Treasure Island, with remnants of what had obviously been a grand camp.

I entered adolescence. Our family had grown to six kids, then seven. We drove up in a battered '46 Packard limousine, zipping over that marvel of the Eisenhower years, the New York Thruway. Our camp had been improved too, including a refrigerator replacing the ancient icebox. Most excitingly, a porch now extended out over the water from the second story of the boathouse. The porch was designed and built by Charly Day, an old Adirondack guide my father seemed to revere (and he was not a man prone to reverence). Charly, I absorbed even through the fog of puberty, was different from men I saw back home. Taciturn and independent, he sure didn't wear a tie. With perhaps a high school education, he constructed a porch that floats over the lake, supported only by three slender slanting beams. Though it seems held up mostly by some woodsman's magic, it has survived for decades.

My father built two small bedrooms upstairs in the boathouse for me and my brother. My room had just enough space for an old bed, an older dresser, a small table and a lamp. It was heaven. No one to police me and Jack into bed. If alone, I'd usually read long past midnight. Mornings I'd wake up alive with happiness, serenaded by the sounds of water lapping against the dock.

The sailboat canoe had rotted. I rarely used the outboard anymore; it was so slow. I dreamt of a ten-horse Mercury. (I can still see it. Bright deep green casing. My first lust.) Elegant Chris-Crafts, beauties of wood, grace and speed, were beyond my dreams, as they were clearly beyond my parents' finances. Chris-Crafts were for the wealthy in their stately camps on Fourth Lake, or shielded in the Adirondack League Club.

Fortunately, some of these wealthy provided me with an income. I began to caddy when I was ten. Each summer I worked my way towards the top: A Steady— regular, almost-daily caddying for the same two golfers. Out by nine, in by one, no more waiting for the mythical "big party from Rocky Point" that Eddy, the Pro, daily promised us would momentarily arrive.

Hanging out on the caddy porch, I discovered new wildness, learning rudimentary gambling, pitch (a primitive form of poker), and coin tossing. Or I'd follow Jack down to a genuine old swimming hole in the Moose River. Occasionally, I got to be a real outlaw, when Eddie heard a rumor that a state labor inspector was passing through. It was illegal for anyone under fourteen to caddy. Eddy'd give the warning and we'd scatter into the woods, like Robin Hood's merry men, until danger was past.

Caddying eighteen holes double (a bag on each shoulder) for a decent tipper paid five dollars, occasionally six from a real sport. Thirty-six double meant at least ten dollars, and exhaustion. Soon I was functionally rich, living my first taste of wildness as extravagance. Sauntering into Miller's soda fountain, I'd squander money on two large cherry cokes. Occasionally, Jack and I declared a comics' day and each bought fifty or more comic books. Then an orgy of reading, hour after hour indoors gorging comics, until our eyes blurred and we could no longer distinguish the Green Lantern from Batman and we'd stagger outside as if we'd spent days in a cave.

Caddying was a free man's work. Lacking a steady, I could take a day off whenever I wanted. Spontaneously, I'd decide to sleep late, then perhaps loaf on the porch, or adventure with Jack. Mobile on our bikes, we explored trails he'd discovered in the woods, or created secret club-houses on a mountainside or in a cave. Other times we'd meander along route 28, perhaps stopping at Croft's Wonder?Land (Croft put the "?" in the title), a shambles of picnic tables, "live bait," souvenir shacks, an old ice house and a jar for donations for "Croft's Trip To Florida."

Sometimes nature would surprise us: an immense flock of goldfinches filling the sky as we walked through grasslands; astoundingly plentiful wild raspberries surrounding us as we hiked on McCauley mountain; the enticing early morning aroma of freshly baking bread coming from the D & D grocery.

Jack was blooming. He'd become a passionate photographer, had constructed his own darkroom, and taught me about f-stops, hypo, enlargers. He continued to lead me to adventures, from deeper woods explorations to building robots to making gunpowder and bombs.

Changes were nipping me. As I phased out of caddying, it was being phased out by electric golf carts. Jack and I began to see less of each other, though I was watching when his homemade rocket blasted over a thousand feet into the air. Old Forge was changing too. The town beach was fenced in and no longer free. The channel had been dredged and tamed. New camps closed off the sand bar. Fewer and fewer guests arrived at the dwindling number of majestic old hotels. Money now came to town from middle class families, vacationing in cars and staying in motels or rented camps.

Even as a self-absorbed teenager, I noticed some bad changes. Putrid septic tanks overflowed by the late August. The water lilies were gone, replaced by icky seaweed. But I was preoccupied with new mysteries: popularity and girls. I hung out with the guys who gathered outside the drug store on Busy Corner. Mercifully free from the rigid hierarchy of my high school, I experimented with inventing myself, mostly trying to look cool, occasionally half-consciously groping towards being authentic.

Jack had a new job, at the Enchanted Forest, and a car. A car like no car anyone had ever seen. Hotter than any other car, of course. A Ford sculpted as if it were a spacecraft, with all sorts of special Jack touches. The front dash looked like something from a jet plane: rows of dials, little red knobs and switches, meters. No door handles on the outside; you pressed a chrome strip at a secret place, a circuit connected and the door popped open.

Through Jack, I got a job at the Forest. A couple of summers later, I became one of its parking lot attendants, and made a new best friend, Bob, who taught me the lucrative art of extracting tips from customers in exchange for putting a bumper sign on their cars. Then finally—and it sure seemed long coming—I was eighteen, the legal drinking age then in upstate New York. Wildness became bars, going "up the line" to Inlet nightlife. My parking lot affluence allowed indulging in high-stakes poker games, as well as buying a round of drinks or ordering champagne. The remaining hotels employed many college girls away from home and curious. I lived my first glimmers that passion wasn't only in D. H. Lawrence, nor freedom just a word from civics classes, as I encountered people who seemed truly untamed: drifters, card sharps, adventurers, honkytonk piano players, women who wintered as ski-bums well before that term was invented.

Years later, I remarked to my father that somehow, even in those years, I'd absorbed a love of nature. "Even though you were only in it walking from your car to a bar," he noted. True for the nights, but daytime I worked outdoors. Driving our new 35 horsepower outboard motor through morning mist, I commuted over the pond. In the parking lot, I lived with the weather, learning some of its signs: when a wind suddenly rose and curled tree leaves from the bottom, it would rain soon.

Adirondack wildness drew me far more than any career I could imagine, so I returned to the parking lot after graduating from college. After Labor Day, I joined Bob in living and bartending in a grand and decaying hotel, and partying with drifters and hustlers, wild men and women, most of whom lived in cheap housing the area offered. Outside, I saw the wildness of fall colors and lakes void of people. Then cold arrived, wildness was turning harsh, and I left.

I got a job in Manhattan, nine-to-five. I described my occupation as "employee." Now wildness was any escape from routine. I felt unchained just sitting on our boathouse porch, and developed a deep appreciation for my father's refusal to have a telephone in our camp. To reach us you had to phone Rivette's; Frank would send someone to get us, if he thought the call warranted it. (Once, as a teenager, walking through the livery building, I heard Frank bark into the phone "Clifford? Nope. Not here. Try Appleton's Garage," and he hung up. I asked Frank who that was. "Oh, just somebody from the State Department," he growled.)

I managed to get to our camp only a couple of times a summer. Entering town, I'd note approvingly what remained unchanged, and bemoan what "progress" had occurred: the parking lot was now paved and lined, and attendants had been abolished; more hotels were closed; the mail boat had been discontinued. Even our living room cabinets had been removed. But once on the boathouse porch, a soothing natural- ness returned: laughing with family or friends; reading (the ideal place to finally read *War and Peace);* lots of just rocking and watching—clouds drifting over the pond, swallows and bats at dusk, peach and magenta sunsets. Moments of bliss. "Why do I ever go back?" I cried at the end of a July 4th weekend.

Then I moved to California and sadly announced the end of my Adirondack wildness. Wrong. We began to have family reunions at our camp. Wildness now became me and my now-adult siblings free to unleash our animal energies—whirling through swimming, basket- ball, running, tennis, golf, climbing nearby mountains, canoeing, hiking. Nights were for our newly-developed sport of "porching"—hanging out on our boathouse porch, exercising our Irish wit, with occasional open- ings towards intimacy.

I continue to return every summer. Much of the funky wildness I loved as a kid survives: the birdhouses, swings, the boathouse porch, our Sponson and canoe. Some years ago we paid an Adirondack craftsman to strip decades of paint and grime from the canoe, and its wood now gleams like a functional museum piece. My bedroom remains heaven. We still find wild raspberries. Even the mailboat returned.

I haven't seen Jack for two decades. Some years ago though, I did encounter his mother. She told me Jack worked in the New Mexico des- ert as head of advance testing for a U.S. car manufacturer. He regularly refused promotions to Detroit, because that meant a desk job, and he insisted on driving real cars.

There've been losses. Rivette's boathouse burned down, replaced by an oversized eyesore. Croft's was replaced by a "mini-mall." Almost all the wide-porch houses on Main Street have been reduced to tourist shops. Our float finally rotted, despite all my father's care. The last grand hotel was sold to make way for expensive condos. Housing is scare and expensive—no more cheap rents for marginal adventurers. And acid rain threatens to destroy all life in the lakes.

Despite the losses, there's also been real progress in Old Forge. The painting show I recall seeing hung outdoors on chicken wire has evolved into a thriving Arts Center. Water skiing is banned from the pond, and those pesky jet skis are limited to five miles per hour. Around the pond, a sewer line replaced septic tanks. Up the lake, rigorous inspections ensure that the remaining septic tanks work. The lake water is cleaner than when I was a kid. Water lilies have reappeared, and ducks now frequent the pond.

Most of all, the beauty and magic of the lake remain. Our camp, especially the boathouse porch, has become my place for Time Out—reflection, introspection, looking inside at my own wildness, trying again to distinguish liberating impulses from my demons.

Outside, my Adirondack wildness now includes time in unspoiled wilderness. Decades ago, Sierra backpacking trips taught that I need and love to be in wild nature. Like Thoreau, I'm restored by the "mysterious and unexplainable ... the tonic of nature." That's all around me in Old Forge: swimming in the pristine waters of an uninhabited lake; climbing a nearby mountain or venturing to one of the high peaks; paddling a canoe down the middle branch of the Moose River; the cries of a loon; a hike on a new trail. A few hours retreat into the woods brings serenity, a gift from the Adirondacks that remain forever wild.

[1989]

CLIFFORD'S MAXIMS

As I've laughed, learned, labored, and loved through sixty-five years of life, some experiences have cohered, or congealed, into maxims. I offer them, and some maxims of friends, for whatever cheer they may provide.

First, self-explanatory maxims

- Excess in Moderation.
- Life is a series of lessons you get no chance to apply.
- The only time I approach enlightenment is the first three days after recovering from an illness.
- Be good to your feet—they connect you to the earth.
- Never buy margarine.
- Feminism revealed that both sexes want the double standard.
- Success is probably an illusion, but failure is very real.
- If it really matters, it can't be measured.
- Many people seem quite sane, until you look at their love life.
- Time is God's money.
- Intelligence is the servant, not the master, of the soul.
- Support your neighborhood artist.
- There's always more room at the bottom.
- It's difficult to believe you can be loved for who you know you really are.
- In my mind, I'm always an hour behind.
- I never get depressed. I go straight to despair.

- Happiness is when the person you love is coming home but isn't there yet.

<u>Second, with a bit (or more) of explication</u>

- Shrimp seldom last long.

First discovered while watching actors eat at a theater party, but true at any celebration.

- When in anguish and doubt, do the dishes.

Moving water is healing.

- The hard way is not necessarily the wise way.

First discovered during college, when I took a demanding and boring bio-chem class, because it was harder than the other required option, Evolution, and harder meant a better education. Unfortunately, the easy way isn't necessarily the wise way either.

- You can't win a fight with a crazy person.

As my ex-wife taught me, decades ago.

- I'll never marry her again.

What I learned about marriage from my ex-wife.

- In details there are truths.

Particularly if you want truths about a person's life. The crux is discovering the right details, not merely any details. "Exactitude is not truth," Matisse.

- First, you must put out energy to honor the appropriate gods.

I discovered this beyond-rational law decades ago, while fruitlessly searching for an apartment in Manhattan. After weeks of drudging effort, I was walking to the subway to go to work when I fortuitously saw a guy putting up a for-rent sign in an apartment window. I soon rented the apartment. My efforts had sufficiently appeased the apartment-house gods so that they provided me with a good place.

- I'll spend any amount of money on something, as long as it doesn't last.

Not for the penny-saved-is-a-penny-earned crowd, this maxim is for those who share my passions for travel, excellent meals, good wine, great women, entertaining, and fine seats at performances. Frugality is for buying possessions, except books, and perhaps arts works and CDs.

- Over the age of fifty, living to the fullest requires the wise use of drugs.

And nobody can determine what's wise for you but you. Quite a range of choices: prescription drugs, supplements, herbs, legal and illegal intoxicants. My Berkeley doctor informs me that quoting this maxim has soothed the anxieties of numerous Berkeleyans who needed a prescription drug but worried over creating impurities in their bodies. [One former-hippie friend observed, "Remember when we took drugs for fun?"]

Third, maxims from friends

- Every generalization I've made in my life has been based on a sample no larger than seven. *(Steve A.)*
- Everything is filtered through your soul. *(Dick D., on human complexity)*
- In medicine as in life, we all have a lot of sympathy for something that's acute and very little for something that's chronic. *(My doctor)*
- The secret of a successful middle age is: Don't overbook." *(David R.)*
- It doesn't take much to get me excited, but a whole lot to keep me satisfied. *(Naomi P.)*
- Growing up is giving up. *(Jack B., my college freshman roommate)*
- Neurosis: an unreasonable response to a reasonable fear. *(Hayden C.)*
- Why should I pay attention to you, when you can pay attention to me? *(My brother Steve on the Clifford family dynamic.)*
- Tip well, and cheat on your taxes. *(anonymous)*
- Money married is money earned. *(Tom F.)*
- Wining beats losing. *(Motto of my poker group)*

And finally, as the French put it, "Si j'avais seulement su" [If I'd only known] … would I have made no mistakes? Or learned nothing?

[2004]

A MORE MODEST PROPOSAL
(UPDATING JONATHAN SWIFT)

Those courageous Washington officials—President Bush, Vice-President Cheney, Administration leaders, members of Congress—who created or support or voted for the Iraq war are melancholy and hamstrung by a grave lack of Constitutional power. They have no authority to compel their own children to go fight—so their children don't. Our warrior-leaders are understandably embarrassed, even ashamed, about their children's cowardly shirking. Indeed, our leaders' pain is so deep none dare talk of it.

A simple Constitutional Amendment can end our leaders' impotence. Draft-age children of war leaders must be compelled to fight. Specifically, the Amendment should provide:

"Upon entry of the United States into a war, all draft-age children of:
(1) The President and Vice-President
(2) All Executive Administration Officials confirmed by the Senate
(3) Any member of Congress who votes for the war shall immediately be drafted into the U.S. military for term of no less than two years."

After this Amendment is adopted, those federal officials who support and prosecute a war can cheerfully point to their own children's lives (or deaths) as symbolic of America's noble purpose and willingness to sacrifice. The parents can at last stand with FDR, Lincoln, Robert E.

Lee, and other great Americans whose children actually fought in wars their parents led.

Aside from the joys of combat in exotic foreign lands, our leaders' children will reap other benefits. They'll have the broadening experience of living and working with people from the poorer classes of the U.S, whom they probably missed during their young lives of privilege. They may learn a new language, or other skills that could serve them well in later careers, from prison guard to bomb detector. Another great advantage, for those leaders' children who become officers (and survive) would be learning valuable leadership skills, in a true "School of Hard Knocks." Further, having served valiantly in combat, their military credentials would be immune from attack if they later entered the political arena.

Of course, there are some minor details to be resolved. How is "war" defined? Whenever our soldiers are being shot at seems a sensible definition, but in our Democracy all citizens should have the right to participate in defining so crucial a term. Next, suppose a war leader had no draft-age children, but did have draft-age grandchildren; should they be called? Again, let our citizens decide.

What about mere supporters of the war? Simply because they have no power in Washington, should older supporters be denied the ability to force their children to fight? Some might argue that supporting the war is minor compared to organizing and leading it, or voting for it in Congress, so supporters' children should be exempt from this new Amendment. But the pain war supporters suffer over their cowardly children is no less than our leaders feel. Perhaps, following the Great American Political Tradition, a compromise is desirable here. Give older war supporters a choice. If they choose to, they could force their draft-age children into the military. Children of parents who chose not to do this would remain civilians.

But what about draft-age kids themselves, whatever their parents think or do? If a draft-age kid supports the war, shouldn't she or he be compelled to fight it? A wise policy, surely, yet outside the purview of this Amendment. The intent of this Amendment is solely to give parents the power to put their children where their mouths are. Once the Great

Advantages of this Amendment are proved in life and death, perhaps its rationale can be extended to other war supporters.

The highest Importance of this Amendment is the effect it would have on our enemies. The dedicated commitment of our leaders, willing to sacrifice their own children for the High Ideals of the U.S., must surely terrify all our foes, and appreciably shorten our wars. Equally important, our leaders could feel real pride in their children, knowing that their values had been passed on.

[2004]

SHORT STORIES

THE PARKING LOT

A new '58 Buick raced into the lot. A good omen—fast drivers were usually good tippers. With the flourish of a traffic cop in Florence, I waved the car up to Rob. With a yet more-courtly wave, he motioned the driver to the one vacant slot near the entrance. "We've been saving this place for you all day," Rob grinned, as he deciphered the license plate's county code. "We heard you were coming. You're the people from Rochester."

The driver laughed, as drivers usually did to Rob's opening gambits. "Welcome to the Enchanted Woods," Rob greeted, his tanned face exuding youthful friendliness. "Would you like a bumper sign on your car sir?"

"A what?"

"A bumper sign!" Rob proudly displayed the green and yellow cardboard sign emblazoned with the Wood's name.

The man guffawed. "You put one of those signs on my car and I'll anathematize you."

"You'll what?"

The man was out of the car, leading his family towards the admission gate, before he hollered back "Anathematize you!"

It was the first time I'd seen someone handle Rob. Of course sometimes a stiff simply ignored him, refusing to fork over a tip no matter what his ploys. And occasionally others said no, they didn't want a sign. At this, Rob might smile and reply, "I don't have one on my car, either." But this guy bested Rob at his own game.

"Wasn't he great!" Rob exclaimed with delight. "What's anathematize?"

"A fancy word for curse—like a witch's curse."

"Anathematize ... a-nath-e-ma-tize," he memorized. He loved ornate words. "Ain't people strange," he chuckled.

It was almost five. Traffic had slowed. Leaning against a car, Rob and I basked in late afternoon sun. Across the narrow upstate New York highway were the ruins of a glamorous 20's hotel. Just below that was the lake. On the other side of the shimmering water rose gentle mountains, little more than hills.

I'd been working in the lot for three weeks. Our job was to direct cars to orderly parking, and wire a sign to each bumper. Paid the minimum wage ($1.05 per hour), we were permitted to take tips. A lot of tips, Rob was educating me, could be made, if you hustled.

When I'd been assigned to work with Rob, I worried that he might be superior, aloof. I hardly knew him, and he was twenty, a year older than me. He was undoubtedly cool, lithe and athletic, six feet tall, with blond hair, slate blue eyes, and an aura of movie-star handsome. But he was friendly from the start, showing me how to wire signs on different bumpers, and instructing me on the art of extracting tips, an art he was certainly gifted in. "Hey," he laughed, "Why shouldn't I live like a prince? I am one."

Me, I didn't know what I was. When a grownup asked, "What are you going to do with your English degree?" I'd sometimes quip, "Oh, become a minor poet." But bravado didn't alter my fear that earning a living meant becoming a slave in a necktie. My father, like most fathers I knew, did something he didn't like much in an office, and was often grumpy at home. It was distressingly easy to list what I would not do— just about everything. Business was obviously out. I'd learned that by reading, from *The Organization Man* to Sinclair Lewis, as well as from seeing all those weary men in my suburban hometown sag home from commuter buses. Law? Mouthpiece for corporations or ambulance chaser? Advertising? Spend my life making up lies about soap?

I could see only one out—become an English professor. I felt no calling to teach, and was certainly no scholar, but I'd have to get a Ph.D. Some future. In a college honors class, a professor queried me whether a poem was properly classifiable as "gothic" or "romantic." "What difference does that make?" I snarled back. "I want to know if it's any good." He peered disdainfully at me, then warned, "You're going to have to know how to make this kind of distinction when you get to graduate school." Great—after years of doctoral drudgery, I could write trivial articles and grub for tenure, angling for security and summers off. In Old Moose, the remote Adirondack town where my parents had inherited a funky summer cabin, unfocused dreamers angled for work on the county highway crew: decent pay, security, an undemanding job. Maybe, I'd joke to my English major friends, I should try for the highway crew myself, with the proviso that I got summers off.

I had to come up with something. No career meant money broke you. Since high school, my demons tormented me that I'd fail, ending up an alcoholic like Uncle Michael.

I'd begun my career search by caddying for a few summers, then started at the Enchanted Woods as a part-time toilet cleaner and had ascended to posing as a costumed Robin Hood. Now I'd risen to parking lot attendant. Daily, hundreds of cars arrived at the wide macadam lot. Rob and I alternated making our pitch. Rob's standard opening was a welcome oozing charm. The driver would nod back greetings and Rob would pounce "Would you like a bumper sign on your car, sir?" His tone shifted, still friendly, but simultaneously signaling that the sign would cost.

"Ah ... yeah ... I guess ... How much?"

"There's no charge. You can tip if you like."

"Oh sure." Expansive now that it was only going to cost a quarter. "Slap one on."

In those Eisenhower years, most drivers truly wanted a sign—as a souvenir, or for the kids, or, most of all, to show their neighbors that they'd had a real vacation, gone somewhere. What people want, Rob taught me, they'll pay for—maybe reluctantly, but pay they will. With an immigrant's vitality, he strove to make sure that no one who took a sign escaped paying. After convincing our boss to buy us uniforms, he located white pants with inordinately deep front pockets, which we loaded with nickels at the start of the day. When we ran to an incoming car, we sounded like a moving cash register. "Gets 'em thinking," he smiled, his intense eyes narrowing in appreciation of his cunning. For prospects who wavered, he had a ready supply of encouraging lines. The sign was useless? "Oh no, it keeps the bugs off your bumper." The wires could harm the car? "Oh no, we use special anti-rust resistant wires." So reassuring was his manner that I never heard anyone catch the literal meaning of that phrase.

Occasionally, during slow periods, we'd both work the next car, perhaps offering a serenade, complete with mock Al Jolson gestures, to accompany the music that broadcast from the park's loudspeakers (I still know all the lyrics to "Never Smile at a Crocodile"). Or, if I seemed to be having trouble extracting money, he'd saunter by, ostentatiously flipping a half-dollar, and calling out, "Half a buck tip on that last one."

Before I returned to college that Fall, my father had a rare talk with me. Worried about my future, he queried if I was drifting, and wasn't preparing myself for what I called "the hard cruel world." I joked that I wanted to find a career offering the parking lot's delights: working without supervision, outside in summer sun (when it rained, we loafed, sheltered inside the park), meeting people, making enough money so I was functionally rich, and having someone like Rob to talk with.

The next summer, Rob and I resumed our dialogue. Among our favorite topics was the wisdom we derived from the parking lot. "People are either sports or stiffs," Rob declared. "Sports ... they know how to live. Big. They have fun. They tip. Now your stiffs—look at 'em. Those stupid sun hats and their mousy little faces. Held in. And cheap! Why they won't even pay a measly quarter for the bumper sign they want ... You know," he mused, "I don't think sports have more money than stiffs. They got spirit. Stiffs are afraid. They expect life will go wrong and get them, so it does. They'll never have enough money to have any fun."

What about people who didn't want a sign, I asked. We agreed that they too could be divided into sports and stiffs (also dubbed "Zorros" by Rob). The few representatives of the rich we encountered were surely stiffs. They'd peer warily from their Imperial or Cadillac, as if they'd arrived for a tour of Harlem, and disdain anything as vulgar as a bumper sign. Their groomed children, freed from boarding camp for a day, seemed as muffled and joyless as their parents. On the other hand, sports with taste simply didn't want a sign, no flaw in itself. A few sports even tossed us tips in exchange for keeping a sign off their bumpers. But whether they wanted a sign or not, sports laughed with us, enjoying life rather than regarding it as threatening.

Stiffs were worse than moral symbols; they were threats to our prosperity, so we enforced our morality. Rob long ago devised effective counters for most feints a stiff might try.

Stiff, "Oh a little free publicity, huh."

Rob, "Free? Who said anything about free?"

Or, Stiff, "A sign. Yeah, the kids mighty like it."

Rob, "The kids gonna pay for it?"

If a driver simply said "Yeah, put the sign on," our craft was waking him to his obligation to tip. Often, all it took was a little forcefulness.

"There you go sir," Rob announced loudly. "The sign is on your car."

"Oh ... ah ... (fake surprise) ... is there a charge?"

"No, but you can tip ... "

If a stiff didn't respond to Rob's voice or other initial prods, he would escalate, looming by the driver's door, barring easy escape. Rob's arms were folded; his eyes, radiating expectancy, bored into the driver's face. Most stiffs cracked under those pressures.

Occasionally a persistent stiff ignored all of Rob's efforts, determinedly avoiding his glare, and slithered away. "Arg!" Rob might scream, dropping his handful of signs and wires, clutching his stomach, moaning, staggering, falling to his knees, to the astonished amusement of arriving customers. "Zorro got me! Stabbed me through the heart. I'm dying ... dying ... no money ... no money for the kids' food."

Even during the summers, I sometimes questioned our parking lot morality. It didn't seem to have anything to do with the High Art, Literature Division, apparently believed in by the few college teachers I admired. Wasn't it serious attention to literary and moral complexity that was going to free me? Was our code mere hedonism, without depth? Once I broached these questions to Rob. He laughed, slapped my back and exclaimed, "Ah, it's all part of the rich pageantry of life."

I learned my odd trade well, but Rob remained the master. We'd keep rough score during the day of what we were making, reporting how we'd done on the latest cars. Slowly, inevitably, he'd pull ahead, picking up a half-dollar to my twenty cents, a quarter to my nothing. I can't recall a single day I was sure I made more money than he did.

Not that it mattered. I was making hundreds a week, freeing me from the cramped finances of a scholarship student. And Rob and I had become friends. I was intrigued with his certainties, so different from the witty pessimism I lived with in college. (My roommate would mutter, while grinding out another paper, "Growing up is giving up.") "First," Rob proclaimed, "you gotta have money. No money, no freedom. Man, if I was back in Poland, we'd all be fighting over potatoes."

He was equally sure about love. "When I fall in love and get married, that's it." This from a man who courted most of the beauties in the North Country, often several simultaneously.

"How about messing around?" I provoked.

"Ah ... Who can tell?" he conceded. "You know how we men are," he winked, "animals ... But when you're married, it's family." As always, he spoke of family as sacred, his tone implying he'd kill to protect his parents, older brother or two younger sisters, none of whom he seemed close to.

How could he be so confident, I wondered, that someday he would naturally, truly settle down? I couldn't imagine him as a station-wagon-driving daddy. The day before he'd suddenly hollered, "We are the mountain people! Free!" and threw up his arms, like a triumphant runner crossing the finish line. But it never occurred to me to risk probing him about his marital certainties. Instead, I asked him what his wife would be like. "She'll be beautiful and ... I'll know when I find her. I'll run the business and she'll run the house."

Despite my parking lot riches, when I returned to college my demons resumed their attacks about my future, or lack of it. Surely money wouldn't always come so easily. Then what? Failure, despair. But then another summer arrived and I returned to the parking lot and smothered my demons with prosperity and adventures. When Arnold Palmer came to town for a golf exhibition, he somehow wound up with Rob, playing pool and drinking at Rob's cabin until four in the morning. When Rob reported a trotting horse race was fixed, it was, at 40 to 1.

Rob was, of course, a ladies man, gifted with the allure of the wicked. When he spoke of the book he was going to write, "Mother's Big Mistake: I Let My Daughter Work in the Adirondacks," coeds who worked in the resort hotels sensed with a thrill that he wasn't kidding.

At an Adirondack boosters' banquet, a call came from the loud-speaker: "Will the owner of a 1959 Thunderbird, License number YA233 please move it. It is blocking the driveway." Rob rose, ostentatiously muttered, "Damn!" and succeeded in impressing the waitress who had, until then, been cool to his charms. Rob yanked out his car keys, walked out the front door, doubled back to the bar and waited until the real owner moved the car before returning.

One evening we met two good-looking girls at our favorite bar and made dates for the next night. When the evening arrived, we were both a little weary, and the hotel they worked at was far away, so we decided to skip it. We were sitting in the bar, around 9:30, when I saw the two girls walk in, obviously furious. I nudged Rob. He turned with deliberate slowness as they marched up to us. "Where were you?" he demanded accusingly.

"Where were we? Where were you?"

"We were there," he proclaimed, "at eight. On the dot!"

I glanced away. The girls were silenced as their anger swirled with confusion, then each spoke.

"You were there?" "Where?"

"In the main building!"

"We got to the lobby just a couple of minutes after eight."

"I do not wait," he informed them.

"Well ... god ... you could have called us ... or warned us."

Within minutes, Rob had everyone apologizing. He graciously admitted that perhaps he was too demanding, insisting on such punctiliousness.

One evening, talking about our encounters with women, he observed, "You know, right away we start to compete, especially if one's better looking than the other. We each try to shine, hog attention, and subtly put the other down. Right?" I'd never admitted that, even to myself, but it was true. "That's stupid," he went on. "We ain't in love with them. Why fight? You know what we need?"

"More women?"

"A non-aggression pact!" he explained gleefully. "No more attacks. We help each other. We'll take turns or something. You start with some girl. I ask her to dance, and instead of trying to steal her, I talk about wonderful you—yes, you are fun and all that, but underneath you're actually very sensitive, kind, vulnerable."

Secretly, I was terrified of any woman I was attracted to, and certainly willing to try any ploy that might increase my ability to hide those fears. To my astonishment then, and chagrin now, our pact proved to be rather effective.

Rob speedily won over my mother, usually an Irish skeptic. "How," she laughed, "can I dislike someone who swaggers in here and says, 'My basic virtue is sincerity and my basic goal is humility'?" He'd whirl into our kitchen, raise her arm with an easy grace no other twenty year old would dare attempt, let alone pull off, and declare, "Mrs. Corbett, good to see you again. You look wonderful. Yellow suits you." Or, "You've changed your hair." His praise was always accurate and his warmth genuine. Deftest of all, his mock-courtly style enabled her to feel comfortably included in his play.

"Oh yes," she told me, "he's a charmer. You can't help but like him, but ... I hate to say it ... I don't think he'll bear up well." I paid attention because I'd learned that her evaluations of people were generally acute. "He may make a lot of money—although I wouldn't be surprised if he lost it all. But when his charm and cunning aren't enough ... " She shook her head. "I pity the woman he marries. She's liable to have an alcoholic on her hands."

I was silent, unable to disagree. I'd heard many stories, some from her, of people who'd been broken by life. Except for a vague concept labeled "character," I had no vision what it took to make it.

When I graduated from college, the only thing I was sure I wanted to do was work one last summer with Rob. So while most of my friends awaited graduate school or law school, I returned to my land of lakes, sun and pleasures. My father remarked he'd raised the best-educated parking lot attendant in the country.

Rob and I were together almost continuously. Mostly we worked or partied, but occasionally we were quieter, and spoke with some candor. I described how my heart had been stabbed by my college ex-love. Revealing that he was actually a year younger than me, he said he had never been to college, despite the Syracuse U. windbreaker he often wore. He confided that he valued having a friend who was an Ivy League graduate, and a reader, admiring how I struggled through Gide's *Straight Is The Gate* at lunchtime. We continued to avoid topics like sex, or our futures. If that troubled Rob, he surely never hinted at it to me. I didn't even notice what we avoided.

My last summer was ending. With youthful melancholy I savored the beauty of the Adirondacks, sitting on our boathouse porch, gazing at a lingering sunset, or watching the colors of the lake. In the parking lot late one afternoon I was dreamily transfixed by the elegance of clouds overhead, while the park's loudspeakers serenaded me with "Faraway Places." Days drifted by until Labor Day came. Sadly, I acknowledged the end.

Then, as my parents packed to leave, I realized that I had nothing to return to. Why not stay on? Rob was.

We got bartending jobs and living quarters at the Grand Moose Lodge, a magnificent old hotel declining into impoverished decadence. We worked conventions and chased ladies and adventure, often playing high stakes poker with a 300-pound bouncer, woodsmen who got by somehow, and Charlie Coop, who ran a bar in Utica and was found murdered (supposedly by the Mafia) in the bottom of a well that winter. At work, Rob continued my education. Upstairs, in the Lounge, I delivered drinks to a convention of tie-wearing executives, who called in loud voices for "a double shot of Jack Daniels," or "the best Canadian Whiskey you've got." Downstairs, Rob poured 'em all cheap blended whiskey. "They can't tell," he assured me. Without exception, the men sipped their over-priced booze with apparent delight.

Autumn worked magic. The mountains blazed luminous intensity, leaves of gold, vibrant orange, luscious red, rich magenta, royal purple. The summer vacationers were gone and their cabins closed. Away from the hotel, all human noises ceased. Rob and I discovered a mutual love of wandering. In the woods we spotted deer, raccoons, once a red fox. Walking at the water's edge, we heard waves lap against docks and the cries of flocks of migrating birds. We didn't work days, so once we were up and had staggered off the last night's excesses, we'd usually idle around the lake, perhaps taking out a boat and drifting, both of us silent, listening to the lake sounds and feeling fall winds, with their message of poignancy, gust against our faces.

Winter came early. No more conventions, only the locals digging in for another bout of eking out a living in freezing snow. Time for us to leave, neither of us knowing for what. Rob expressed vague notions of traveling west. I'd go to Manhattan, maybe get into publishing; I'd long admired Maxwell Perkins.

Rob drove me to the highway. Uncomfortable with our feelings upon parting, neither of us spoke until he stopped the car. "Good bye," his voice trembled. "It's all been great." I agreed. Uncharacteristically, he hugged me. We looked directly at each other, held for a few seconds, smiled, and then I got out, promising to be in touch.

Thumb out, I stood hitch hiking, trying to absorb the sights of my last moments free in the woods, and feeling hopeful. So what if I had no career? I could always hustle, or hook up with someone who could. Life would be an adventure.

Years passed. I sent Rob a couple of Christmas cards at his parents' address, but never heard from him. I only saw him in a recurrent dream. I am—at whatever my current age—back in the North Country, and meet Rob, who hasn't aged at all. Somehow, we're back working in the parking lot. It's always a Sunday, our most lucrative day. Together again, we laugh and run in radiant sunshine, pocketing money, free and untroubled.

Then my family had a reunion in Old Moose. I asked around about Rob. Yes, over the past few years he and his family came to his cabin occasionally. Family? Yes, he was married, had four kids, and ran a prosperous restaurant/bar in Syracuse. I called, and was told he was vacationing somewhere near Lake Placid. No, they couldn't give out a number. They'd pass on my message, if he called. When I drove by his parents' old cabin, it was closed. Sadly, I conceded we weren't destined to meet.

My brother and I went out for drinks at the Old Moose Lodge, now in terminal decay, soon to be converted into condominiums. We were busy reminiscing when Rob and an attractive blond woman entered, talking intimately, almost solemnly. His face bore worry-lines, but otherwise he was as fit and handsome as twenty years before. I called to him. He turned, registered astonishment, then whooped with delight, and ran to us. We laughed and hugged, then he introduced his wife, Evelyn. As we launched into the joys of reunion, he surreptitiously slipped a twenty from a huge roll of bills buried in his sweatshirt pocket and paid for a round of drinks.

For the next few days Rob and I lived adult echoes of our youthful friendship. I met his four ebullient children and began to know Evelyn, who was not what I would have predicted. Reflective, a reader, she certainly didn't appear to be dominated by her husband. Rob and I often stayed up late, trying to sum up the joys, copings and sorrows of two decades. He'd created a prosperous restaurant, where singles, young families, and older working men all co-existed. Now he was restless, pondering moving to Florida, trying for a bigger league. He had never smoked dope (well, once, he admitted), taken acid, felt involved in "the 60's", been divorced, or visited what had become my home, California. He wanted to hear about all of it.

Often we talked about our parking lot days, ranging from nostalgia for our wild times to what we now realized we'd given each other. Thanking him for showing me I could hustle, I said I remained impressed that he'd always earned more tips than I had. He laughed with surprise. "You believed that? I thought you were usually making more than me, so I had to exaggerate to keep up."

Long past midnight, we talked about basics—love, money, family, trust—learning that though we'd lived very different lives, we'd learned many of the same lessons. I described my continuing battles with my demons, and copings with money. "Yeah, I've sure got my demons," he revealed. "And money ... money's only part of it," he spoke softly, and I knew he was talking to himself as much as to me. Then he looked directly at me, and I felt a trust we'd never known was possible during our summers together. "Evelyn ... we've had hard times. Some very hard times. Something happens to her when she has a kid. After ... after each one, she sort of broke down. Last time she had to stay in a ... hospital ...

for a few months … God!" he laughed "Me, the king sport, with three kids and a new baby, scurrying around the house, cooking dinner, changing diapers, hiring baby-sitters, and visiting Evelyn,... hoping ... waiting. It was rough."

"She's O.K. now?"

"Yeah, she's fine." A fondness came to his eyes. "She's tough."

Did you ever think of splitting up?"

"No ... uh ... well ... yeah, a couple of times. She has too. I haven't always been an angel," he chuckled. "I have weak flesh. But abandon my kids? Never ... No." He sighed. "I used to get afraid - what happens if she never gets any better? A martyr I ain't. Nah, I knew what I had to do." He shook his head. "It's been real bad at times ... but I still love Evelyn. And I sure love my kids."

I puzzled silently over the mysteries of connection and continuance, then touched his hand. "That makes you lucky," I told him.

"Lucky?" he challenged, bemused at the inadequacy of applying that word to his life, then suddenly he laughed. "Yeah," he said, grinning to include me, once again, in his world. "I've always been lucky."

[1991]

THE RIGHT THING

"There really are facts," Kelly instructed Adrian, "genuine facts. That's one thing I learned from Judge McCann. We need a sympathetic plaintiff—not one with four different fathers for her kids."

"I like learning from an expert," Adrian dead-panned.

"Right," Kelly laughed. "I just lost big in the Ninth Circuit. That's how to become an expert: Be the first one to lose big."

"I want to know how to get there," Adrian replied, hinting at the intimidation he felt in front of judges. He intended to master being a courtroom lawyer, but during his year In Florida Legal Services, there'd been no one who could teach him litigation. In the months since he'd moved west in mid-1968 to work in a large poverty law office in East Oakland, Kelly had guided him in preparing a major lawsuit against Governor Reagan's new welfare "overpayment" regulation: If a family was paid too much under the complex payment schedule of the Welfare Department, the state could "reduce the grant to zero"—give the family nothing for two months, even if the family had done nothing wrong and had no idea a mistake had been made.

The two men walked out of their shabby storefront office, onto the bleak ordinariness of 46th Avenue. Pale lemon-yellow light filtered through incoming fog. Three black men, leaning against the doorway of the Fish Market across the street that served various illicit purposes, appraised them coolly. Abruptly, Kelly asked Adrian why he'd gone to law school.

Adrian glanced wryly at Kelly. "I didn't want to write a Ph.D. thesis."
Kelly felt another spark of kinship. "Same reason I went."

Working together, the two had discovered many affinities. Both rebels and romantics, in their late twenties, of Celtic ancestry, they sought a life both meaningful and exciting. Adrian was a slender man, just under six feet. His arched nose and curly red hair set off an angular face, alive with vitality and smiles. Yet even when most energetic, he retained traces of watchfulness, his blue-green eyes observant. Kelly was slightly over six feet, lean, with the dark hair, blue eyes, and the volatile temperament of the black-Irish. Each had grown up in East Coast suburbs and gone to Ivy League schools. Both had "done well," a Fulbright for Adrian, Law Review for Kelly, and had developed a similar persona, valuing wit and quickness of mind. Their doubts about "success" had been sharpened by the same authors and books, Sinclair Lewis, Marquand, O'Hara, *The Organization Man*, *The Man in the Gray Flannel Suit*, depicting the stifling fate awaiting them as corporate career slaves.

As they approached their cars—Adrian's Porsche convertible, Kelly's battered VW bug—Kelly, as nervous as if he was calling for a date, asked Adrian what he was doing that night.

"Nothing. Want to come over for dinner?" Adrian knew that Kelly remained tormented by his wife Ronnie's abrupt abandonment of him, months earlier.

"Ah ... um ... ah ... sure, I'd love it." Kelly was awed by Adrian's bachelor self-sufficiency. Women flowed through Adrian's life. When he gave a dinner for seven, it was a feast of exquisitely prepared crab quiche, ham with glazed-orange sauce, tiny artichokes in lemon butter, spinach and bacon salad, fine wine and dessert of fresh fruit in melted chocolate, accompanied by suitably strong dope. Most impressive to Kelly, Adrian neither had a date nor seemed to miss one.

Adrian lived in a light-filled four-room apartment on a tree-shaded Berkeley street. Preparing dinner, he whistled, pleased that he had a role to play with Kelly, and wasn't the junior associate he often felt at work. Kelly wandered through the apartment. The walls and much of the furniture were white. A few small pictures, knickknacks, and plants were tasteful arranged in corners and shelves. The place exuded a spirit of controlled independence.

Chatting after dinner, Adrian mentioned the "straight world."

"I won't do it!" Kelly erupted, as if ominous bullies threatened to drag him into a three-piece suit that night.

"You're not doing it now," Adrian soothed. During college, he'd feared that he'd end up living his mother's dream for him, a distinguished Manhattan lawyer, trapped with a family in a Park Avenue apartment. But now he believed he could choose his path in life, and perhaps his fate. "We're doing fine."

"There's a difference between procrastination and escape."

Adrian produced a joint. Stoned, he floated, feeling at ease, peaceful. One hit cast Kelly swirling, fears biting him, screaming doom of loneliness. Then he braved asking Adrian what had happened to Marlene, the woman who'd accompanied him across the country.

Adrian shrugged. "Wasn't meant to be."

Kelly sat silently, feeling that he knew little about love. He'd believed it was magic that, somehow, came over you. Now the truth seemed to be that it was often a tangled, dark business. He sighed, lying back on the couch. Adrian turned on the TV and they watched the news. False-humored men with razor cut hair babbled blandly about grotesque events as if they were explaining something. "Very weird," Kelly muttered.

"The thing about dope," Adrian said, "is that you learn you don't believe in what you're supposed to believe in." He shut off the TV and put on a Billie Holliday record. Each took another hit from the joint.

"Adrian," Kelly asked." Do you like living alone?"

"Yes ... There are times I'd like a warm body here every night but you know, when you live with a woman, you never get to finish a book." He shrugged. "Not that finding a warm body is much trouble in Berkeley."

"Don't you mind the loneliness?" Kelly pushed.

"Ah ... yeah ... but I like to make my own decisions." Adrian smiled encouragement. "Once you realize that a lot of life is passing time well, it gets easier."

"I don't want to be alone," Kelly announced.

"Love lasting forever," Adrian chuckled. "No, I think it's like the lines in that rug." He pointed at the oriental rug on his floor. "They come together for a while, blend, then separate."

I won't find out tonight, Kelly realized, how he's come to believe that. Since he hadn't read *Of Human Bondage*, he was correct.

Adrian poured more effort into his lawsuit: further research, pondering, rewriting, then grinding critiques of his complaint and legal brief with Kelly. Meanwhile both were trying to cope with the torrent of change they'd plunged into. Twenty-five, thirty, sometimes over forty clients a day brought their miseries to the East Oakland office: welfare hassles, evictions, unemployment denials, discrimination, debts, car breakdowns, beatings, scams. Beyond clients' cases, the two men established relationships with a nascent welfare rights organization, attended Black Panther breakfasts, and forged an alliance with the leader of the East Oakland Panthers, Fred Benston.

Energy and change swirled around them: The Vietnam War, the Anti-War Movement, "Power to the People," Feminism, Black Power; the Grateful Dead and Jefferson Airplane, Hippies, "Turn on, Tune in, Drop Out," LSD. The two speculated on the meaning of all this churning, marched against the war, explored the Bay area, and returned five days a week to work in the ghetto and discuss the merits of big cases versus individual service work, how to locate the "Community" and the importance of resisting the urge to be leaders, the elitist error of whites in the civil rights movement. They felt at the center of their age.

After several more rewrites than Adrian thought necessary, Kelly agreed Adrian's case was ready. But they still hadn't found a viable plaintiff. Several more weeks passed, then a woman arrived at their office distraught that "The Welfare" had cut her off although she'd done nothing wrong. For two days, her three kids had eaten only beans. Now she had no more food and no money for food. Adrian checked. Her story held. The Department had stopped payment solely because of its previous budget miscalculations, which she had no way of knowing about. He and Kelly worked a frantic day and evening, turning her reality into a written declaration. "This is it!" Kelly shouted. "Make that judge cry."

Adrian had always loved theater. Now his cast was himself as the star, a stern federal judge, a bailiff, a court reporter, the Assistant Attorney General, Mr. Baxter, as the villain. "Do you have your rule 65 declaration?" the judge demanded. Adrian loved his crisp feeling of competence as he handed the original to the clerk. Mr. Baxter fulminated against federal interference in what was clearly a local matter. Adrian countered that federal law clearly prohibited this type of arbitrary punishment. The judge nodded agreement, than barked at Mr. Baxter, "Have you read the woman's declaration? Do you contest it?" Mr. Baxter couldn't. The theater became magic. The judge scrawled his name on Adrian's temporary restraining order. The next morning's San Francisco Chronicle bore headlines: "Judge Halts Reagan Welfare Cutback."

With his love of ceremony, Adrian had become the office leader of birthday parties, holidays, celebrations. About twenty people milled around in the secretaries' room, waiting for the stragglers to arrive so they could all set off for Adrian's victory celebration. Passing time, Opal urged Adrian to think of something really funny for the upcoming April Fool's Day.

Oh," he drawled, "just tell someone you love them."

Whatever Adrian told them, Kelly was impressed that he got them. "How do you do it?" Kelly asked one evening as they drove out to teach a welfare rights class in the Tassafaranga Housing Project.

Adrian felt an impulse to tell Kelly some truth, and a simultaneous delight realizing that was what he wanted. "I started training in prep school. We only got free during vacations. So I got to be an expert in the fast rush."

"And Fran?"

"I told her over this weekend ... I don't want to get involved." He grinned, somewhere between embarrassment and amusement. "We're older Kelly. They fall in love so easily now."

"You don't believe much in love, do you?"

He flicked Kelly an austere look. "People have needs."

Adrian had expected to be alone since he was a teenager. So much in his life had felt like a conspiracy to make him wary: the treacheries of prep school; the mean vagaries of his stepfather, a man who'd growl "Should that window be more open?" and berate Adrian if he didn't guess the desired response; the fears and pressures of Princeton, or worse, law school.

Their East Oakland office talk grew drenched with angers and frustrations. Nixon and the Vietnam War raged on, apparently impervious to protests. Antiwar demonstrations turned violent. The Weathermen were planting bombs. Gays fought cops at the Stonewall bar. Hard-core radicals proclaimed they were "Taking it to the Streets," or planned "From Protest to Resistance." Revolutionaries bought guns, took target practice. Kelly passed an uncomfortable but uneventful night in the Panther headquarters; they hoped to deter police raids by the announced presence inside their office of white attorneys.

Finally wearying of his lonely misery, Kelly dared ask a woman for a date. Soon, to his astonishment, he was enmeshed with an entanglement of lovers, learning that the "sexual revolution" included him. With lovers, Kelly instinctively hid what he risked discussing with Adrian: Why had he been so tormented when Ronnie left him? What did love actually require? Adrian spoke of inner peace, and, above all, trust.

"Trust?" Kelly laughed. "We Irish never heard of it."

"Saying what you feel," Adrian mused. "Giving up control. For that, you really have to trust."

Adrian had lived so long nurturing a dream of having a real friend, an equal, that he sometimes still felt astonished to now have one, a revelation that astonished Kelly, who'd always valued friends and made them easily. Adrian admired Kelly's seekings, from wrestling with the meaning of his work to drug-and-shrink aided stumblings towards understanding his emotions. The two often adventured together, sometimes on recently acquired motorcycles, other times delighting in conversations soaring to where neither could reach alone.

Cautiously, Adrian revealed some darker feelings to Kelly. Lifting his normal control, he'd mutter a telling observation about an office colleague, or define the stability of an unhappy marriage by observing, "A hysteric needs an obsessive." Revealing that he knew his capacity for self-hatred, as Kelly was discovering his own, Adrian observed, "If my soul dies, it'll be my coldness that killed it."

They had fights. Adrian learned Kelly's brusqueness could turn mean and that his truth-pursuing could be gnawing, obsessive. Kelly learned that there was something deeply secretive about Adrian. Worse, he could be cavalier about work. "Look at this mess," Opal angrily told Kelly. "You know Adrian. So charming. 'Oh, I'm not good with these details. Could you just finish the declaration from these notes.' And I can't even read them." Distressed, Kelly acted the boss, sternly instructing Adrian not to palm off work. Adrian snapped a reply and soon Kelly was shouting and Adrian had withdrawn to coldness. The next morning both came to the office as distressed as lovers after an vicious quarrel. As soon as they saw each other, each sighed relief, knowing nothing irrevocable had happened. "We'll work this out," Adrian declared. "Interesting ... it's sure is easier talking about openness than living it."

Society seemed to be erupting: illegal U.S. bombing in Cambodia, students murdered by National Guard troops at Kent State, revolutionaries proclaiming "armed struggle." People quit legal services to move to "back to the land," to live in an ashram or commune, to join some revolutionary group, even for straight jobs.

The stream of clients flowing into their office continued unabated. By the end of a day of seeing new clients, Kelly was usually exhausted. Worse, he increasingly doubted that legal reform could make a real difference. Most of all, he doubted he knew what would make a difference. "I don't know how the world should be run," he told Adrian. "I don't know how to love a woman. I grew up pretty repressed. Thank god I didn't take to being an altar boy... You know, it may be a full-time job to save my own ass."

But soon, Kelly abruptly fell in love with Liz, a flamboyant, sensual Cal English student, shimmering and taut, like a fierce hummingbird. Both joyed in being with Adrian, who was often alone now; only occasionally was a woman passing through his life. Kelly was pleased when Liz and Adrian evinced instinctive connections, including a mutual love of flirting. After a motorcycle ride through the Berkeley hills, Kelly found the two of them enthralled in conversation and looked with pride at Liz, her full round figure sexily revealed in halter top and cutoff Levis. "What are you two talking about?"

"Our wicked ways," Adrian teased. Liz's eyes locked onto Adrian's and vibrated from playfulness to depths, as if to say—you take it anywhere you want, I can handle it. Adrian's winked approval of her provocativeness, while wondering at Kelly's naiveté, thinking that he retained more than a trace of the altar boy.

Liz moved in with Kelly. Discussing monogamy, each told the other they didn't really favor it, believed in "freedom." Neither probed what the other meant. Kelly lived blissfully with Liz for several months, until she began demanding he get divorced at once. "I've told you and told you," he said. "I can't risk it. Ronnie is demanding alimony. Half the judges hate me. Ronnie's an actress. Some Reagan judge would love to stick it to me."

"If you loved me, you'd get a divorce."

Kelly didn't seek a divorce. Liz's occasional rages at Kelly grew more intense, and he continued to love her.

By 1972, courts had rejected most of their major cases. The cases they won produced little long-term results. Governor Reagan and his minions were proving to be formidable welfare foes. They complied with court orders only when facing jail sentences for contempt of court. Then they responded rapidly with another, often also illegal, cut in welfare payments, and the struggle resumed.

The ocean of client woes rolled endlessly on. While Adrian seemed untroubled, Kelly felt increasingly drained, and not just by clients. Why had he ever wanted to be head of the office? He was weary of personality clashes, supervising major cases, visits from Nixon-appointed evaluators, demands from people who asserted they were speaking for the Black Community or the Chicano community.

"What are we doing?" Kelly demanded of Adrian. "Working hard, working hard. Isn't that what we were going to avoid? The only difference between me and a corporate lawyer is that at least he gets paid well for what he does."

"Yeah, but he does horrible work" Adrian countered.

"Well, we're not changing anything."

"But it's such fun to be the good guy. The hero. We ride into town and clean out the bad guys. And we don't have to stay around after that."

"But we don't clean out the bad guys."

"That's not the point. The point is that we get to play the good guys."

"That's nonsense," Kelly growled. "I wanta quit."

"Quit? Aren't you going to be the new Deputy Director!"

"A step up?" Kelly scorned. "To where? I want out! I'm no revolutionary, and I'm certainly not a social worker. I'm a pagan."

Nixon would again be President. McGovern's campaign was doomed. The Panthers were broken. Fred Benston's body was dug out of a grave in the Santa Cruz mountains. How, Kelly wondered, had he ever let his rage blind him to believing that the Establishment might be overthrown or collapse? At a welfare rights meeting Kelly asked the women what they wanted. "Go after our kids' fathers more," they urged. "Make them pay their fair share." They demanded more DAs, more prosecutions. "Probably good ideas," Kelly observed to Adrian afterwards, "but hardly a recipe for revolution."

Liz announced she was thinking of moving out, then cried. Pain seared Kelly's chest. "Don't leave," he pleaded. "I really love you. I'll call Ronnie, try to worked it out." They held each other. "I love you," Liz sobbed. Some days later, Liz got home late, and told Kelly she'd stopped over at Adrian's to talk to him, as she had before. Again, he'd helped. Kelly responded that Adrian was wise.

Kelly had doubts though about agreeing to Adrian's urging that the two go backpacking; Kelly had never done it.

"Hey," Adrian nudged, "You've been the one telling me life is really process, not results. Try it."

"Where to?"

"I'm not sure. Backpacking somewhere in the Sierras. I'll pick up some maps and we can just take off."

"Just take off." The words reverberated in Kelly, reawakening his college dreams of freedom, the thrill he'd felt reading *On the Road*.

With a sweeping bow, Adrian unveiled their camping food—a ham, chicken, candy bars, fruit, eggs, chocolate, beef jerky and two bottles of wine. "Wine?" Kelly queried. He'd thought backpacking required cutting the labels off tea bags.

"You know I like to live well."

In August heat, they drove through the sun-burned Sacramento Valley and browned foothills of the Sierras. Adrian whistled a sorrowful tune. In a dinner near Donner Pass, Adrian gathered in a man with the rugged look of a lumberjack, who jabbed his finger on their topo map. "Paradise Lake. Beautiful. Pretty high up. Shouldn't find too many people there."

An hour later, they tugged on their packs and set off. Glimmers of sunset filtered through the tall pines around them. Silent except for Adrian's sporadic whistling, they hiked up a rising trail. The sky darkened. Trees seemed to loom larger, surrounding them like threats. Adrian stopped, shedding his pack. Kelly quickly followed, stretching his weary back. "When do you think we'll get there?" he sighed.

"Kelly," Adrian gently corrected, "we're already there."

"You mean I won't get a grade for this?"

The next morning Adrian woke early and made a fire. The clear sky was radiant blue. Two hawks swooped far away, then disappeared. The sun-drenched land seemed pungently fresh, like newly baked bread. Kelly woke to sounds of chirping birds. Adrian cooked breakfast of eggs, rolls, and much coffee.

Reeds bent in the wind and glistening ripples coursed over Paradise Lake. White-snow peaks of the Sierra Nevadas jutted in the distance. During the afternoon the two men existed on a small beach, hardly talking. Time, passing as immeasurably as the shift of the sun, slid by. Adrian sat by the water, idly throwing stones. Kelly joined him. Bathed in warm orange-yellow light of early evening, they stretched out on the sand.

"Ah ... I feel peaceful," Adrian announced.

"I didn't know peace existed, until I met you," Kelly complimented.

"And I didn't know what a friend was."

Over dinner, Kelly bemoaned his continued fights with Liz. "But I do love her," he concluded "I really do."

Adrian raised his eyebrow, saying nothing, reminding himself that he'd made it a rule never to get involved between a couple. Odd response, Kelly thought idly. Well, about love, Adrian did have ... call them peculiar ideas.

Cheered by the glow of a fire, they sipped Kaluha and hot chocolate. "Adrian," Kelly felt warmth flood through him, "it's been grand. Being your friend ... We both really are romantics."

"I think we're learning how to make the truth romantic." Adrian placed a hand on Kelly's shoulder; Kelly instinctively remained silent.

"The truth ... " Adrian smiled. "That takes a tremendous amount of trust. I trust you." He paused. "I've wanted to tell you for the longest ... " His voice was soft. "I ... ah ... I'm gay."

As soon as he heard, Kelly knew that he'd somehow known that, subconsciously, for a time, and that it made no difference to their friendship. Adrian didn't even have to ask him to keep it secret. He knew he would, feeling pride that he could.

Adrian described years lived in isolation. "Strange" feelings buried during puberty, secret realities hidden since his first gay sex while on his Fulbright. By the time he was in Duke law school, he was adept in duplicity. As F. Adrian Bennett, he was president of the local chapter of the Law Students Civil Rights Research Council and active on peace marches. As Bill Bouvé, he pursued his passions in Washington bars and bedrooms. "I knew how I'd end up—a sad but wise observer."

Adrian had written his mother that he'd realized he'd moved West to experience his own freedom. Of course he hadn't given her any details. He'd known that something was brewing for gays in San Francisco. Still, he was surprised, then delighted, then an active participant, in what he'd discovered—freedom of the cock. Tumbling in and out of beds, couches, sofas, back rooms, bathhouses. Acts still felonies in Florida. Suddenly, he could live the intensity of his desires. Fascinated with sex and sexual power, he thought occasionally of a line of Sherwood Anderson's: "if I am a creature of carnal lusts I will then live for my lusts." Somehow, living desire had thawed him so he now dreamed of a mate, a yearning he'd buried.

He smiled at Kelly. "For so long I wanted to tell you. All your searching, and I couldn't tell you mine. You must have thought I was standing still ... God, I admire men who are out of the closet ... I'm not ready."

"Scary, huh?" Kelly answered. "Besides ... there must be a part of you that likes living a double life."

Adrian raised his eyebrows with respect at Kelly's acuteness. "True ... but I think it interferes with my real dream—the search for the perfect boy."

Both stoned from strong dope, the two wound down their travels at a Berkeley bar. As Kelly sipped a beer, he suddenly sensed Adrian's vibrations change; an animal aura came over him, a palpable sense of desire. It was subtle; only because of their intimacy, and the dope, did Kelly notice. Without reflection, Kelly knew instinctively what those waves of desire meant. He turned to look at the attractive woman sitting at the end of the bar. His glance landed on a lean blond boy, with an open white shirt and pouty mouth. Kelly laughed aloud. The boy was no more sexual to him than a potato. He glanced back at Adrian, now enthralled with open flirting. "And then," Kelly told Adrian when they left the bar, "I really, finally, got it. No way you chose what you felt in there, what I couldn't feel. 'Sexual preference' isn't the right term at all. It comes before everything. It's born, not made."

Adrian hugged Kelly joyously. "Ah, it's great to be known."

Several weeks later, Adrian was pleasuring in a night alone, perusing a book on architecture, when the phone rang, "I have to talk to you," he heard Kelly's quavering voice demand.

"Sure ... breakfast ... "

"No ... now!" Kelly cut him off.

"I'm sort of tired tonight. Can it wait?"

"NO!" Kelly screamed.

Adrian shivered, a sensation he'd had since childhood when he felt accused. He'd done something terribly wrong. He didn't know it was, but he was evil. Doomed. Then he wrestled his demon to calm, assuring himself that he'd learned that he wasn't doomed.

Kelly arrived, shaking; he'd obviously been crying. "It all came out. Somehow, I knew. Me, who's never intuitive. I told her. She had to tell me the truth. So finally she admitted she'd slept with Ken, her T.A. We cried. Then suddenly I knew she was still lying. She denied it, but I knew. Finally she broke down. Told me about them all."

As Adrian spoke soothingly, Kelly recoiled. "You knew!" he attacked. Liz had revealed that she'd told Adrian months before about her affairs. "Why didn't you tell me?"

"I felt ... bad about it. But Liz swore me to secrecy before we talked ... and you had enough clues. She showed up here one night, crazed, blurting things out, crying. I promised her that I wouldn't tell."

"You promised ... " Kelly felt emptiness, not betrayal.

"I didn't know ... I thought ... " Adrian fumbled for the words and charm to make it right. Kelly glared at him, and he felt knifed. He leaned over, sighing. "I'm ... I'm sorry."

Kelly released a mournful chuckle. "Well, that's something."

"I am. I was wrong. It ... it wasn't you I identified with," he said with a sad sharpness. "It was Liz. We both like sexual power ... and I've been as lost as she was."

Kelly suddenly sensed that the truth here could be very dark indeed. "Adrian, did you sleep with her?"

"No." Adrian trembled inside. He knew Kelly's code of male honor: You never sleep with a buddy's girl. Kelly had once described walking across the street to avoid saying hello to a girl who'd dumped his best friend months before. Adrian felt fear stab him, a clenching in his stomach. But he knew he had to tell Kelly all. He wasn't sure why he knew that, he just knew it. How did I get here, Adrian grasped, while Kelly looked at him with a strange mixture of expressions. Adrian had thought that there were big dramatic moments to life, when great choices were made. But his life wasn't working out that way. Somehow, you came out somewhere, and the only choice you seemed to have was self-betrayal or not. His life was an accretion; he'd tried to choose his path, and suddenly there was no going back and he'd chosen to eliminate the option of going back.

"Kelly ... I almost did sleep with her. One night when she was over we started fiddling around on the couch. She was on the prowl ... I lay there ... and ... I just didn't. I guess even I knew it was wrong."

Kelly sat stunned, suspicious that Adrian might be lying, and knowing that he'd be mistrustful of Adrian for a long time.

Adrian saw confusion and mistrust surge in Kelly's eyes, and felt sharper fear. See, a voice ranted in his head. I warned you. Keep your fucking mouth shut. Screw that, another voice surged out, rolling over his demon. You don't live like that anymore. He'd told the truth. Kelly would see that, surely. It would be all right. It'd take time, but it'd be all right.

He felt a sudden pang. If he lost Kelly ... then he felt a wave of calm flood through him, and he knew that in some deep way, it was already all right. He'd done the right thing. At last, some mocking voiced teased, as he stood up to hug Kelly.

[1993]

A SENSE OF ACCOMPLISHMENT

Thank god, Patrick thought, there were still men in the Adirondacks who could do things right, as the tree fell precisely in the narrow space between the main house and branches of a large pine.

The workers gone, Patrick began chopping the tree into firewood. He considered calling Kelly, the eldest of his seven children, who'd arrived two days ago from California for the family summer reunion. Ah, let him alone, Patrick decided, feeling a stab of something—rancor, disappointment, whatever; he wasn't one to interrupt a job to analyze what he felt. He'd assured Mary that he wouldn't fight with the kids this summer. Kelly, a dreamer, was perhaps the most reluctant of any of his kids to help with chores. When Kelly was young and told to do something, he had invariably responded "Right now?" Patrick joked that's what they should carve on Kelly's tombstone.

Patrick, who disdained power tools, grabbed an axe. Dressed in his favorite clothes, paint-spattered brown pants and a worn flannel shirt with the sleeves cut short, he resumed chopping. He loved swinging the axe, the muscles of his lean, strong arms clenching, tensing, then absorbing the satisfying crunch as he smashed the axe head in. Working rhythmically, he sweated in the sunlight filtering through the leaves of oaks and tall pines. After he'd split the tree into firewood, he took a moment's satisfaction in his work before the next task, storing the wood in the old cement ice shed behind the main house, sixty feet uphill.

Kelly, luxuriating in summer freedom, was noshing and reading the New York Times, when he heard his mother's voice. "Kelly," Mary called "Honest Abe the woodsman needs your help."

"Sure, Mom," Kelly replied. He'd promised himself he'd cooperate with his father's inevitable calls for assistance. No fights this time.

Kelly thought that as Patrick aged he grew increasingly disturbed by the sight any of his children at rest. The day before, Kelly had been reading *Humbolt's Gift* on the boathouse porch, when Patrick stomped up and declared, "Hey, could you take the garbage up to the road?" Though Kelly saw no reason for urgency, he understood that Patrick meant immediately. "Sure, Dad," he'd responded.

Patrick announced that he'd stack the firewood in the shed, directing Kelly to carry it up. Kelly took the quickest route, following a narrow rain ditch by the side of the house, skirting the white and lime-green ground cover. Militantly cheerful, he whistled as he dropped another armful of wood on the narrow walk between the shed and the camp. "Better not carry so much," Patrick warned. "You could slip." Kelly guessed that Patrick worried that he'd trample the leafy ground cover, and preferred him to take the longer route, up the steps by the other side of the house. But Patrick would never say that. Several years before, Patrick and Katlin, his youngest, had debated which one would drive Kelly the fifty-one miles to the Utica airport the next morning. Kelly sat silently on the porch swing, wondering how the contest would turn out. "Oh no, Katlin, you're only up here for a week, I'm here all summer ..." Patrick soothed. "No Dad," Katlin countered, "you've already had to pick up Stuart and Elizabeth. I'll go." Back and forth they volleyed each nobly willing to sacrifice, until suddenly, on her turn, Katlin paused, looked directly at Patrick and declared, "I WANT to take him." "Oh well ... " Patrick conceded instantly, "If you want to take him. ... ah ... that's fine."

With the next load, Kelly took the same route up as before. "Now be careful!" Patrick warned again, while snarling inside; Kelly should know how to do it right without having to be told.

"I'll be O.K.," Kelly replied cheerfully. "I won't hurt anything."

Like a flash of lightening, black fury exploded through Patrick. "Look," he snapped, "there's no pathway on that side. If you go up that way, take smaller loads."

Kelly, stung, felt old furies rising in him. No, he checked himself. I am not going to play this game. Some years before, Patrick, a successful industrial consultant as well as a math professor at New Jersey's Montclair State College, was to give a speech in San Francisco. Kelly had picked him up at the airport. Driving to the City, Patrick asked Kelly how his work was going. Kelly answered that he was planning to leave Legal Services in the spring, didn't know what he was going to do next. Patrick asked if he ever thought of returning to New York and working for a law firm, a question he'd raised several times during the five years Kelly had been in California. "No," Kelly replied offhandedly, "I never think of it."

Feeling snubbed, Patrick suggested that it might be prudent to consider it. "What? Me in the corporate world?" Kelly laughed. "No, I think not."

"You think everybody who wears a tie's worthless, huh?" Patrick erupted. "Do you think I'm a failure?"

Fuck you, Kelly raged inside, then suddenly remembered: I don't have to do this. He'd defined it as the "red-hot poker theory of conversation." Somebody, so often, his father, laid down a verbal red-hot poker and baited him—I dare you to pick that up. Since his early teens, Kelly invariably had. All those fights with Patrick about Kelly's "attitude," his "disrespect." "Don't talk to me in that tone of voice!" The two of them standing inches apart, both enraged, Patrick's fists clenched, Kelly's eyes glaring mutiny. But neither of them ever pushed to an irrevocable act of violence.

Nope, I ain't picking up the poker this time, Kelly knew, as Patrick trembled with anger in the car. "Sorry," Kelly said quietly, "I didn't mean that. Sorry if I sounded that way."

"Oh you didn't mean it," Patrick fumed. "You think you can tell me that it's all corrupt, after I work to send you to college and law school ... " He raged on. Except for an occasional muted apology, Kelly didn't respond. Deprived of an opponent, Patrick slowly calmed. They drove on in silence until Kelly felt it was safe to start exchanging news.

Gathering his next load of firewood, Kelly decided on accommodation and picked up a smaller armful. Enjoy the process, he reminded himself, slowing to look at the slate blue lake water, the light dappling through the pine trees. Go slow and ... Womp! He stumbled against a root, and a log jammed into his ribs. Yeah, yeah, fucking process indeed, he muttered.

Patrick, pleased that Kelly hadn't disobeyed him, resumed meticulously stacking wood in the shed, grabbing a log from the bunch Kelly had dumped, carrying it inside, wedging it carefully onto the pile, then starting over. Each time Kelly returned with another load, Patrick had completed his task and stood waiting. Returning downhill, Kelly thought in wonder at Patrick's constitution. Almost 70 now, and still smoked two packs of Camels a day, as he had for over 50 years. The man was a living violation of all the health creeds Kelly tried to live. Though Patrick drank coffee after dinner as well as breakfast, Mary reported that he slept as he always had, like the proverbial baby. He loved sweets, and daily consumed a breakfast of bacon and fried eggs. Six feet tall, he maintained his weight at 165 pounds and had a cholesterol count 80 points below Kelly's.

Dropping another armful of firewood, Kelly, recalling his intention to show Patrick affection, complimented "God, you do a lot of work to keep this place, don't you."

"Yes," Patrick snapped, as if he were not being appreciated.

Why does he get so angry, Kelly shook his head as he returned for more wood. He doubted that he would ever be able to plumb his father's complexities, but still, he'd returned this summer, as in the past several summers, with the desire to know him better. No, it's more than desire, he reminded himself. It's need. I want to connect.

Mary was the family storyteller, but occasionally Patrick, soothed by martinis, had spoken about his life to Kelly as they sat together on the boathouse porch in the early evening. Patrick told melancholy stories: his childhood in Bismark, North Dakota, a hard place; his Irish father, sitting defeated on the front porch of his failing restaurant during the 20s, spinning forlorn dreams of new businesses while Patrick's stern mother somehow held the family together; Patrick, the fat kid with the athletic, popular older brother; Patrick's struggles to get through Columbia during the Depression; a job as a Macy's executive trainee, assigned to tell employees they were fired the week before Christmas; quitting two weeks later, searching, and finally landing a teaching job at Montclair State, having to hide the fact that he was a Catholic—they didn't want any "Micks."

And out of all that, Kelly knew, came a man with a fierceness in him, with a passion to succeed, now listed in *Who's Who*. A pioneer of industrial Quality Control, he had a gift for translating statistics into functional product-testing realities that could be used by supervisors, managers, assembly-line workers. Kelly had seen him give a couple of talks. He was always affable, witty, under control.

Kelly had made a few attempts to explain his life to Patrick. Instinctively, he spoke mostly not of his joys, but his struggles: his disillusions with radical lawyering; his often-disastrous love life; his demons continuing demand that he be successful. Kelly's efforts at candor seemed to discomfort Patrick. Besides, no matter how Kelly tried to soften it, he'd rejected a normal career. So Kelly, uncertain if Patrick found it painful to listen to him or really didn't want to know, retreated to safer topics.

Patrick, knowing Kelly would appreciate a break from carrying wood, greeted him holding two beers. As Kelly drank, Patrick silently suffered a moment's sadness. The summer before, he'd muttered to Kelly, with more than a trace of poignancy, "I'm not sure I understand any of my children." He'd been disappointed when Kelly moved to California, and didn't understand why he'd remained. An editor of the Columbia Law Review and clerk for a federal judge, Kelly could have been a success, but he seemed to want to postpone accepting responsibility forever.

"None of my children have much ambition," Patrick once observed to Kelly, "but you seem to have the least." Kelly shrugged, deciding not to provoke Patrick by replying—Escape is an ambition.

With his four other sons, all now working in corporate finance, Patrick could chat about the stock market, investment strategies—man's talk. Not that Patrick valued money. He and Mary still lived in the large suburban New Jersey home Kelly had grown up in. A year ago, visiting them for a day, Kelly idly asked Patrick what the house was now worth, knowing that it had risen to well into six figures from the sixteen thousand Patrick had paid for it in 1950. Patrick eyed Kelly with a sagacious look and nodded "Oh, it's worth ... forty ... fifty thousand by now." Astounded, Kelly later asked Mary about it. "Oh," she laughed, "your father doesn't have any idea what the house is worth. He's not interested in that at all."

Temporarily ignoring their firewood task, Kelly and Patrick sat quietly together, hearing waves lap against the boathouse dock and wind rustle the trees, until Patrick broke in, "So, how's the book business? Still solvent?"

"Yeah," Kelly answered, "Going well."

They chatted more about jobs, then stood up to return to work. "God, it's beautiful here," Kelly exclaimed. "I love it."

"I do too," Patrick revealed quietly. His land of freedom. Escape from absurdity and tension, the vapidity of teaching, the venality of commerce. For years he'd refused to have a phone at the camp, claiming he couldn't afford one. He felt a wave of fondness for Kelly, the most romantic of his children. Maybe today they'd put in the float. The first day Kelly arrived, Patrick, with an attempt at offhandedness, suggested that perhaps this year they shouldn't bother putting in the float, the cork world war II navy float he'd preserved—scraping, re-canvasing, repainting— since 1947. "What!" Kelly cried, "No! We have to have the float! We've always had the float!"

Patrick laughed. "Some radical you are."

Kelly laughed and carried on. "Mom needs that float to keep the boats out." Anchoring the float 15 feet from their dock protected Mary, who went for two swims daily, from reckless motorboats.

"Well, OK," Patrick replied, as if Kelly had talked him into it.

Kelly watched as Patrick placed the last piece of wood on the pile, then they strolled to sunshine by the side of the house. "Ah," Patrick relaxed, stretching. "Doesn't that give you a sense of accomplishment? "

"No," Kelly replied without reflection, "I'm just glad to get it done."

A flicker of rejection passed over Patrick's face. Kelly, realizing that he'd been insensitive, tried to reach towards Patrick. "Well, I guess, sort of ... there's a sense of taking care of things ... "

"Never mind," Patrick snapped. Work was his identity. It was in the struggles of the job, earning a living, that a man found meaning. Years before, Kelly, during a time of torment so severe he'd sought help from Patrick, asked him what you could truly believe in. "You can do a good job," Patrick replied. A creed Kelly heard from other men. His favorite English professor had told him, "I work very hard. That's one thing you can do with your life." The judge Kelly had clerked for said "They should put on my tombstone: 'He Worked.'" The wife of a senior partner of the Wall Street law firm who employed Kelly one summer told him, "You're all the same. You'll all go to a firm and work hard."

The firewood job done, Patrick rebuilt the wood framing of several front steps, and then took a brief swim. Kelly resumed reading *Humbolt's Gift* on the boathouse porch. It was late afternoon when Patrick hollered that he was ready to put the float in. "I'll get the pulleys," Patrick called. Ach, Kelly thought, how that man loves pulleys—loves any tool, a wedge, hammer, roller, or pulley, as long as it had been invented B.C.

Propped against a wall inside the boathouse, the cork float was rectangular shaped, open in the middle, and heavy. If another brother were available, he and Kelly could bend under the top, lift the float on their backs and inch it to the dock within minutes. But now pulleys were inescapable. Patrick tied two short ropes around one side of the float, and ordered Kelly to hook a pulley on one of the ropes. "Where?" Kelly asked. "Hook it on the side," Patrick snapped. Kelly, unsure whether "side" meant front or back, fumbled with the pulley. "Oh here, I'll do it," Patrick sighed with disgust. Kelly stepped aside, anger overwhelming his sadness at how incapable Patrick was of explaining anything to him.

Struggling to move the float to the edge of the dock, both grew tense. "OK, now attach the rope to the bottom and pull it this way," Patrick commanded. Kelly pulled on the rope. "Not that way!" Patrick exploded, "THIS WAY! Goddam it!"

Fury burst in Kelly at the new infliction of his old grievance, being berated for failing to understand ambiguous work orders. He glared rage at Patrick, who glared it back. As they continued working, Patrick directed Kelly with frenzied urgency, demanding speed and competence, as if they were preparing for an invasion, and every second mattered. "Ok ... now back just a bit ... NOT THAT FAR GODDAMMIT."

"Aw FUCK!" Kelly blew. "Why don't you just calm down and stop that goddam shouting."

"What ... Who ... " Patrick's face tightened with fury, "Who do you think you're talking to! I'm you're father. Don't you dare ... "

"I'm not playing this game anymore," Kelly cut in. He leaned the float against the wall. "We can finish this later," he announced, and walked out.

Patrick, riddled with rage, grabbed a cigarette. Clenching his fists, his jaw trembling, he fought off his desire to chase after Kelly and pummel him. A rush of shakiness surged through him. Thank god Mary was off for a bike ride, and hadn't heard. Then rage returned, and Patrick decided he'd have a martini early. For decades, he'd kept a pitcher of martinis in the icebox. Before dinner, he'd have one glass, sometimes two. He never had a third.

Nestled in his favorite wicker chair on the house porch, Patrick watched grosbeaks feeding in his bird feeders. As he sipped the last drops of alcohol and lit another cigarette, his angers clashed with a wave of remorse. Kelly had been trying. If only he wasn't so damn insulting.

Patrick rummaged for his latest murder-mystery and tried to force himself to read, but his gnawing anger returned. To fend off his rages and despair, to find any peace, he had the strength that came from his and Mary's love, and spending two summer months mostly outdoors, and Catholicism. Mary had always been devout. Publicly, he remained a skeptic, but now he went voluntarily to mass with her every morning. Something about being in church helped against his blackness. Recently, in a rage, he'd prayed, asking The Lord for help. Kneeling down in the small wooden church, head bowed, he heard a voice inside him instruct, "Count Your Blessings," and he was instantly comforted, knowing that he had blessings.

Comfort rarely lasted long. Except in church, Patrick resisted exploring the darkness inside him. Even if he'd wanted to delve into his inner being, how could he have? No one told him that the worst enemy was internal. A loner, he had no friend to confide in. And he'd no more consider a therapist than divorce. His world said Work. A genius can fight through his culture. Other men can flee or remain in it; if they stay, they absorb it like oxygen.

Tossing his book aside, he retreated to the camp's cramped, damp basement. His room of order: nails and screws sorted by exact size into hundred of jars, rows of hammers, screw drivers, files, planes, wrenches, clamps. He dug out rot from one of the heavy wooden winter storm-shashes. Focus at his task vibrated against waves of anger until absorption in the job quieted his demons.

Kelly, upstairs in the boathouse, was smoking a joint. It's hopeless, he thought. He just goads me until I crack. That goddam ... Kelly's demon began to rage. Ranting on, it howled ever fiercer; like all demons, acting out didn't diminish its force, but strengthened it. Then, as the dope hit, familiar waves of anxiety flooded through Kelly, swirling with his anger: you fraud ... you're a coward and a fraud, and you've always known it ... that fucking asshole ... Suddenly, he felt a familiar hurt. It'd taken considerable therapy, from LSD to therapists, to uncover the source of that pain—his longing for his father to love him. And you know part of him hates me, he reminded himself. Just plain hates me. Old lion, young lion. I was the first son, the first child. What's the reverse of an Oedipus complex? He must have hated the way I took Mary from him. I even look like her. He hated me more than the others. Suddenly, Kelly chuckled. Probably true, he thought, but he sure got pissed at them too.

As Kelly crushed out the joint, a floating feeling, an impulse to move away from rages and fears, arose in him and he walked outside to the boathouse porch. Golden late afternoon sun poured on him, on the rippling lake water. Calming, he looked to the sky, white clouds moving languidly overhead. A lone outboard cruised the lake. Anger flowed off him, out to space. He felt a sudden surge of warmth, love for this place he'd always loved. Yeah, he thought, I still need to work on this Dad stuff. The point, he knew, wasn't to demand a perfect, or near-perfect, father. It was to try to see what your father was, and how he'd affected you. He recalled Big Willie, 290 pounds, former pro football player, writer and thinker, locker-room friend. They'd been sitting together in the steam room at the Berkeley Y, listening to some guy whine about how his father had never been sensitive to him, didn't understand him. As Kelly and Big Willie headed towards the showers, Willie muttered "Shit. You mean you HAD a father! And he didn't beat you! And he supported you!"

Kelly flashed to his brother Kelvin's conclusion of a late night porch discussion. "I figure Dad's a bad father, but a good person." That's true, Kelly remembered. And, crucially, whenever one his children were really in trouble, Patrick was loving, a rock. A year out of college, Kelly couldn't find a job in Manhattan. Fired from one publishing company, rejected by others, he was sinking into panic when Patrick called him and said "Let's go up to Old Moose for a few days. Open up early." Neither mentioned that the two of them had never done this before. In their summer camp, Patrick felt a rare ease with Kelly. They joked, talked, rambled. Patrick spoke of his own work struggles, his torments while job-hunting in the Depression. Soothed and loved, Kelly returned to New York with faith that he wouldn't fail.

Patrick somehow knew whenever any of his children had serious money problems. When Kelly was at his most broke after leaving Legal Services, he got a letter from Patrick, a rare event, telling him that if he ever lacked money for food or rent, to let Patrick know and he'd send it. When other of his kids had money troubles, Patrick called them secretly into his study—Mary might think he was spoiling them—and with an embarrassment kindness produced in him, whispered, "Look, ... here" and gave ample money. When Brendan had been hooked on cocaine, Patrick volunteered thousands for a drug clinic.

Kelly thought appreciatively of Patrick's rebel humor: "I teach for three reasons—June, July and August." Mary loved to tell stories of Patrick's prickly wit. At a tedious dinner party, Patrick was finishing his second cup of coffee when a man asked him, "Doesn't that keep you awake?" "It helps," Patrick called back.

Kelly sat in a rocking chair, letting memories flow through him, settling on the one talk he'd had with Patrick about sex. Kelly was sixteen, and had been masturbating and fantasizing for a few years, when Patrick called him into his study. "Son ... " Patrick began in what he hoped a paternal voice sounded like, "I ... I ... I think we should have a ... talk ... You're old enough now ... uhm ... so you should know something about women ... " God, I'd love to, Kelly snickered to himself, keeping his face serious, knowing how painful this was for Patrick. Definitely, Mary had sent him to do it: You Must Do Your Duty and Have a Talk With

Your Son. Kelly prepared himself to listen to pious Catholic nonsense, or maybe some silly birds-and-bees stuff. "I'm ... I'm sure you know something about sex, by now," Patrick continued. Not nearly enough, Kelly joked silently. "But ... I guess what I want to tell you is that sex is connected to love. Or it should be. It's not just mechanical. Years ago, I remember my brother saying 'Oh, that's like kissing a woman after you've fucked her.' But he was wrong. If you love her, you do want to kiss a woman afterwards. Maybe not as ardently as before, but you do. So ... " Patrick shrugged, touched Kelly's shoulder, and their meeting was over.

Remembering how deeply he'd learned that his father believed in love, Kelly sadly pondered Patrick's inability to teach his children. He had a lot to teach, if he'd been able to. And what pleasures, Kelly thought, we all could have gotten from his teachings.

I oughta go apologize, Kelly realized. OK, so I can't really talk with him. But it's crazy for a man over forty to be squabbling with his seventy-year-old father. Let it go. Just then he heard Patrick's tread on the stairs to the porch, and stood up.

"I came down to say I'm sorry," Patrick offered.

"Thanks," Kelly replied. "I was just going up to the house to tell you I was sorry." After their fights during Kelly's adolescence, Patrick frequently was the first to apologize, as if his rages simply were storms that passed.

"I guess we both can still get on each other's nerves somehow," Patrick said.

Kelly felt near shame. "Hey, I really am sorry. I wish I could just stay calm."

"Well, let's just forget it. I guess I just keep forgetting that you're not a kid anymore."

Kelly smiled, while silently wondering—why in the world would you want to treat your kid that way? He walked to Patrick and hugged him. When Kelly had first realized he wanted to hug his father, many years before, Patrick had responded stiffly. But by now he too had learned he could hug, that he liked to hug, and he clasped Kelly strongly.

They sat on the boathouse porch. An orange-gold sun hovered above the low purple mountains to the west. Dusk's stillness enveloped them, as they sat silently, both loving what they saw, and knowing the other loved it.

Clunk, clunk. They heard the sounds of metal beneath them. "Mary," Patrick called out, "is that you?"

"Who else?" She called back in her chipper voice. Unless it was raining, she'd gone out for a row every summer evening for decades, in the eight-foot aluminum rowboat Patrick had given her. Patrick and Kelly watched her row with crisp regular stokes, moving rapidly up the lake.

"She really is remarkable," Kelly said.

A slight sound, perhaps a sigh, escaped Patrick. "I don't know what I ever did to deserve her," he said quietly, leaning against the porch railing, watching until she'd rowed out of sight. Then he thought of some short stories Kelly'd written and sent him, of the California 60s—experiments, drugs, promiscuity, orgies. "You know, Kelly ... I think what makes me feel saddest about your life is that you haven't had anything like that."

Surprised, Kelly felt a pure pang, and looked directly at Patrick and saw empathy in his eyes. "Yeah. It makes me feel the saddest about myself too," he replied.

Kelly broke out a bottle of Grand Marnier. As they sipped drinks, Patrick reminisced about consulting in Europe after World War II, spending weeks away from the family's Paris home. Kelly mentioned he remembered Patrick being gone often when he was young.

"I had to have two jobs. I always had to work hard," Patrick said, his tone aggrieved.

"But you liked to work hard," Kelly observed.

"What choice did I have?" Patrick snapped. "I had all those kids to support."

Kelly mused, then spoke softly, "You know ... I think you would have worked just as hard if you had no kids," he risked, stirred by their apologies, the drinks, glimmers of sunset, impulses in his soul. "Having all those kids gave you an out, gave you a reason to be working so hard all those years, so you never had to resolve why you really did it. And now, your kids mean more to you than anything but Mary."

Looking appraisingly at Kelly, Patrick folded his arms and rocked slowly in his chair. Then he suddenly grinned. "Yeah," he nodded. "I guess that's true."

[1997]

THE BIG GUY

"Slick!" Al enthused, rising from the bar stool. "Man it's good to see you! You are looking lean."

"Trying to stay with it," Kelly smiled, and hugged Al.

"Ah ... Rachael," Al called to a blond cocktail waitress, dressed in a mock-Elizabethan blouse revealing substantial cleavage. She turned, smiling to Al as if he were an old lover. "May I present my friend Kelly," Al bowed decorously. "Rachael plans to go to law school," Al mock-whispered. "I've sworn never to reveal that she had to wear such an outrageous costume."

Rachael laughed, picked up her tray and set off. "Still doesn't take you more than fifteen minutes," Kelly complimented. "Not bad for a guy with gray hair."

"Ah," Al muttered, "to make love to her would be a violation of the Pure Foods Act."

As they'd done for years, the two men settled into their bar-talk: rambling, laughing, quick-moving exchanges of person news, political observations, life philosophy. Suddenly Al became quiet and pensive.

"You OK?" Kelly asked.

"Ah, same old shit," Al muttered. "Going nowhere. I might buy another house," he growled, as if it were a crucifixion. Yanking out a pen, he grabbed a cocktail napkin and wrote on it. "See these numbers," he pointed at the 45 appearing on the napkin. "That's how old I am. By the time they're reversed..." he scribbled a 54, "I better have done it."

139

Knowing that "it" meant Al living all his dreams, Kelly's Irish-American training in reticence held him from offering advice. The two had spoken to each other often of their demon of despair, but not, as Al seemed to be now, while fighting the demon.

"Let's go for a walk," Al announced.

On a cool fogless night, they strolled silently on the Berkeley pier jutting far out into the Bay towards San Francisco, glimmering beyond the blue-black, rolling water.

For years Kelly was always the initiator of their nights out. But this time Al had called him. Kelly knew that Al must have some new trouble, but confidences between them were always volunteered, not probed for.

"Fucking bullshit hassles," Al suddenly exclaimed. "Doctors on me to stop this, start that. Always something. Now … I got a call from Evelyn. The DA's suddenly after her. Wants $76,000 for back welfare. Jesus. Robert's twenty-seven and now the Man wants big money. She's terrified her husband will find out. When they press her, she'll give them me."

As Kelly knew, Al and Evelyn got together in Oakland when Al was seventeen and she nineteen and married to a guy in the navy. While her husband was at sea for months, she got pregnant. Robert was born days before her husband arrived home. Al, a high school dropout, enlisted in the Marines a few weeks later. Evelyn's husband refused to have anything to do with Robert. He'd been raised in the ghetto of West Oakland by Joyce, Al's Grandmother, who'd received welfare payments for Robert until he turned eighteen. Now, nine years after the last payment, the D.A. had suddenly demanded seventy-six thousand dollars from Evelyn for back welfare payments.

"I told her I'll handle it," Al concluded. "I can pay a few grand. But 76 K. That'd more than wipe me out."

"O.K., let me handle it. " Kelly declared; again, being a lawyer would prove useful. "I'll work something out."

"I gotta keep Robert out of it."

"Agreed." Kelly knew Robert was a vulnerable spirit. Though bright, athletic and movie-star handsome, he lacked Al's brass. As a teenager, Robert's favorite book was *Catcher in the Rye*. His form of rebellion had included abstaining from all drugs, and dressing as preppy as he could afford.

"One thing," Al announced. "I gotta pay you,"

"Absolutely not!"

"Man, I have to!"

"Did I pay you for listening to all my grief with ladies? For all those rides to the airport? Let's not do this."

Al sighed, pondering, then smiled. "All right ... Thank you, man." Impulsively, he hugged Kelly. They meandered out to the end of the pier, chatting and laughing, then slowly returned. As they reached their cars, Al raised his right arm, clenched a fist, shook it, and called out "BE YOURSELF!"

"I wish I had a friend like Kelly," Robert had told Al. "I've never had a friend I can talk to like you talk to him." Al had keys to Kelly's apartment and stayed there often when Kelly was away. Once Al left Kelly a poem:

> Sometimes in this place, the real questions
> form as the faint - but clear - sounds
> of silver striking crystal...
> and
> the answers amplify the silence
> in increasing crescendo.
>
> This much I learned here:
> The difference between
> solitude and loneliness,
> and the need for both.

Robert had once asked Kelly how he and Al got to be good friends. "I'm not really sure," Kelly answered. "How did we, Al?"

"We played a lot of pinball together," Al laughed. They had. In 1968, Kelly, age twenty-eight, was appointed attorney-in-charge of a neighborhood law office in East Oakland. From his arrival, Kelly was charmed by Al, a dashing six-foot four-inch adventurer, ebullient story-teller and fountain of vitality. Al was similarly drawn to Kelly, a kindred dreamer, seeker and athlete, and in some ways wilder than Al. Kelly's report of his acid trips—demons, ecstasies, truths—intrigued Al but didn't persuade him to follow. Blasting his soul apart with acid, Al sensed, could leave him devastated.

Often at lunch, or for an afternoon break, Kelly and Al went to the candy store a block away and played pinball. Al was an expert, skillfully jiggling and wiggling the machine, keeping the ball alive, an art Kelly never mastered, despite Al's tutoring.

A steady stream of clients, many with unsolvable problems, flowed into their office. Within a few months of his arrival, Kelly sometimes felt overwhelmed; worse, he felt himself growing detached from clients' miseries. But his energies were revitalized when working with Al, the chief office administrator, who seemed to have a bottomless capacity to cope and care without letting his own light be dimmed. "Yeah, I want do something to change all the shit black folks gotta take," he declared. Two years older than Kelly, Al dealt deftly with workday realities. Kelly turned to him for advice about staff problems, or handling angry clients. Kelly who'd clerked for a federal judge, knew how to prepare a case and function in a courtroom, but Al knew how the local court system actually functioned—which clerks to avoid, which judges were trouble. Also, Al could deal with life on the streets.

The office had to serve a domestic restraining order on a guy named Mike, described by his ex-wife as big and mean. He was definitely hard to locate. Two process-serving companies gave up trying before Al volunteered to find him. Within days, Al had tracked Mike down to a rowdy bar in the depths of East Oakland. Al strode up to Mike, slapped him on the shoulder while reaching out his other hand and beaming "Hey, man, it's Mike!"

"Yeah," Mike responded, extending his hand.

"Hate to do it to you Mike," Al announced, laying the legal papers in Mike's open palm.

Al worked with Kelly developing major class-action cases they hoped would improve poor people's lives. They won lawsuits against arbitrary procedures of public housing and knocked down some of Governor Reagan's illegal welfare "reform." The two met with community groups from the Black Panthers to welfare rights activists. During work time, pinball games and then occasionally in bars during evenings, the two talked about reform, revolution, Black Power, the Vietnam War. Their conversations soared where neither could reach alone, and increasingly became more personal, nudging towards intimacy. They laughed together easily. "It's almost three," Kelly had teased. "Time for Al's women to start checking in. 'If Louise calls, I'm in. If Belinda calls, I'm out. If Margot calls, tell her ...'"

"Still jealous," Al had retorted. He'd first had sex when he was twelve. He'd been amused, though not surprised, at Kelly's tale of his terminal horniness growing up in a white suburb in the 50s. "Didn't get laid until your were twenty," Al laughed. "No wonder white boys are uptight!"

After they'd worked together for a couple of years, Al moved on, becoming the chief administrator of Boston Legal Services. Though he and Kelly parted casually, months later Al sent Kelly a letter. Kelly, surprised and delighted, responded quickly, and a heartfelt, if sporadic, correspondence ensued.

———

Driving with Al to a Warriors' basketball game, Kelly described his initial effort to resolve the DA's demand for money. "DA named Maureen Anderson. Wants to prove she can be as big an asshole as a guy. I told her I was an old Legal Services attorney, been contacted by some welfare rights women I used to work with. She said she won't make any deal. I kept telling her I was sure we could work something out ... I'll wear her down."

"Thanks. Man, I'd love to get it wrapped up. Once it's done, I'm ready to roll. Back to the Philippines ... Now let's go watch those black millionaires play ghetto polo."

———

During his fifth year in Boston, Al had a heart attack. Open-heart surgery. Weeks in the hospital. Thinking about his father, who died of a heart attack in his forties. As had Al's older brother. And, Al thought, I almost literally worked myself to death; yeah, yeah, all the women and partying didn't help, but it was work that did it. When he'd arrived in Boston, the Legal Services program was weak. At last, he'd known, churning with enthusiasm, I can do it. He'd helped recruit good black lawyers and staff; improved relations with neighborhood militants and city hall; got the budget under control; regularized office procedures; lead staff to working together without serious acrimony. Air-conditioners were installed in all the offices. Al never revealed whether the rumor that he'd bought them cheap because they were hot was true.

Pulling himself up in the hospital bed, Al touched the plastic tubes attached to his body. The Big Bureaucrat, he sneered. Sure wasn't worth this. As if anything's really different out there now. Ping-pong fast, belief surged back: Hey, I did do something. Now I'm weak. Give myself a break. A break, his demon volleyed back, what break? Your big fucking ego got you into this.

Well, I've always had a fine ego, Al chuckled. Born poor in Louisiana, his mother died when he was eight. After that, he'd been belted around by his father even more than he had been before. When Al was fourteen and already six feet, he swung back, catching his father off guard and knocking him down. Al ran off and hid until the next morning. After his father left for work, Al grabbed some clothes, took what little money he could find and set off for his grandmother's in Oakland. Passing for eighteen, he arrived already streetwise. Joyce did her best, but he didn't want much raising. He hustled up money, took care of himself.

He'd loved the Marines, young wild buddies. When he shouted out in the barracks "Hey—who wants to shoot pool?" some guys always did. He'd really loved being stationed in Japan. Many women there were fascinated by this immense black man who'd learned passable Japanese. After eight years in the service, Al wound up in Washington, D.C., and soon became the first black office manager of the local chapter of B'Nai Brith. Then into Legal Services, moving to Boston, and the surprise heart attack.

Every day Mil had come to visit him in the hospital. Stolid Mil. Just days before his attack, he'd again promised himself that he'd never allow her to move in with him. But when he left the hospital for dreary weeks of recovery, she took a leave of absence from her accounting work, moved in and cared for him daily. She doesn't have to say a word, Al had fretted, lying in bed, waiting for her to bring him dinner. *I owe her.*

"I set up a great disability plan in Boston," Al quipped some months after returning to Oakland. "Never thought I'd be the first to use it. So now what?" He'd been hanging out, aimless and discontent, living with Mil.

"I don't know," Kelly laughed ruefully. With two Legal Services friends, he was experimenting with private law practice. "Don't follow me—conflict, courts, paper. A stone drag ... Well, lawyering for The People sure wasn't it."

"Always the Celtic moderate," Al chuckled. "Hey, we did some good. And we had fun. You always did worry too much about results. It's all process."

"Maybe—but that process died."

"I NEED A NEW DREAM!" Al erupted.

"You've always been in some kind of public service."

"Well, it's fucked out there now," Al growled, simmering with fury. "This fucking society. White folks know what President Reagan is doing to blacks. But as long as they got a few bucks in their pocket, they just don't care."

"Correct."

"I am gonna write that novel," Al declared, raising again his unformed tale of black rage and revenge, bombs and destruction. He believed the U.S government conspired against blacks, deliberately imported drugs into the ghettos. "They do it, man! They Do! You watch. There'll be concentration camps in America." He waved his hand flashing a massive gold and diamond ring. "That's what this ring is for. I can get out fast if they try to exterminate us."

Kelly, secretly troubled as always when Al spoke like this, said nothing.

"You think you have any racism in you?" Al abruptly sprung.

"Yeah ... yeah, I'm sure I do. I just don't know what it is." He didn't reveal that he almost never found a black woman sexually appealing.

"Glad you know that you do," Al smiled, his rage suddenly contained like a window shade that had been snapped up.

Ms. Anderson's cold telephone voice threatened to take Evelyn's deposition, subpoena Robert, scrutinize wage records, tax returns.

"Ms. Anderson," Kelly tried to sound as if he were restraining rage, "Evelyn Watson has been married to the same man for over thirty years. She's held the same job as a bus driver for fourteen years. She's raising three children. Her family has barely enough to get by. I'm sure you consider yourself sympathetic to women's rights. How can you justify harassing this mother, oppressing her now, for what's years and years past?"

"It was her fault ..."

"What fault? She never lied to the Welfare Department."

"The Welfare Department never knew where to find her."

Over four months and still a stalemate. Ms. Anderson refused to settle for less than $40,000. I must do this right, Kelly belatedly realized. He went to the DA's office, searching through the case file, then the welfare department, rummaging through the bulky remains of Robert's ancient AFDC file.

All afternoon, Al sat on the Oakland pier, conjuring his dream woman while chatting with guys fishing in the Bay. Blurred images of Her, long held down by lust and variety, now lured and haunted. I gotta find her, he ached, and a pain that felt like a physical wound throbbed in his chest. He shook his head. Man, he thought, you are a cliché. The memory arose of the young, later to be famous, jazz singer who'd been his lover in Washington. He'd cried when she said it was over, but didn't yield to her desire to get married "You are a rambling man," she'd told him tearfully their last night together.

By the time he got home, Mil was asleep. She was gone for work when he woke the next morning. He lit a cigarette, but smoke didn't soothe the gnawing feelings assailing him. Yanking himself up, he wandered through the apartment. When he'd returned to Oakland, he'd settled for this bland place in a motel-style building because he'd been sure he wouldn't stay there long. Now, four years later, he glared at the big TV set and the glass lamp on a heavy gold-painted chain that dominated the dining room. I loathe this, he muttered.

Mil. I've gotta leave. Eating dinners in silence, and I don't look at her face. I don't owe her anymore. Why the fuck can't I get out?

Two paintings of jazz musicians Al had done years before in Washington hung in a hallway. Kelly, who loved painting, had called them "powerful, focused" works and suggested Al to try again. A couple of times recently he'd brought out his old box of oils, but never opened it. He stared at the paintings, feeling drained as if steel bands were being tightened inside his chest. Aw, fuck it. It was over.

The phone rang. He hesitated, then picked it up. Could be from Darlene, his troubled daughter. "Al, Rick Sermic." The real estate agent, a small man with a goatee and beguiling manner. "That house on West Street. It really is a great one!"

Al sighed. Another damn renovation project in West Oakland? He owned two already. More work, months more hassles. "I'll think about it," he told Rick. "Think!" Rick protested. "Hey, this one will go fast. You need to move!" Al hung up the phone, and some serpentine voice assuaged him—hey, you can rent it out as section 8, help out some poor black folks. You'll be doing something. Yeah, what he'd labeled his "sun voice" answered, something that traps you more. Get out.

Not to the Philippines. He'd just gotten a letter from Meena, his favorite from his Mindanao trip several years before, saying it was bad there now: Marcos, soldiers, guerrillas, bombs. Hell, he'd known that from the news, but still Meena's letter had jolted him. He hadn't been old in Mindanao—the last dream he'd lived.

Robert came over in the afternoon. Months before, he'd taught Al computer basics and Al was now up to him. Together, they'd worked at creating software programs, from a new method of listing "house for sale" to a system for winning at the racetrack. Al grabbed a floppy disk, feeling excitement course through him, "OK, let's take a look at this stuff I worked up. I may only have an hour. I'm hoping Darlene calls." He saw a disappointment flick through Robert's eyes. "OK, I promised. You got the afternoon,"

The phone rang. Don't answer, a voice told Al. Ignore it. He picked up the phone. "Rick here. Looks like there's going to be another offer soon on that West Street property. They'll take twenty-two, I'm sure." A steal, Al knew. "There's money to be made here. Don't let it slip away."

"I don't think so."

"Hey, you're a good man with a hammer."

That was true, Al knew. "I'll think about it. Gotta go."

"Another house?" Robert asked. Al nodded yes. "Going to do it?" Robert queried, impressed. He respected his dad for being a man-of-the-world, even if Al had often acted the Marine sergeant with him.

"I don't know. Maybe."

"Sounds sensible."

Al smiled. Robert the practical. Well, he could have done worse than a son finishing up his degree in computers. Had done worse, with Darlene, out with those street bums.

"Playing any ball?" Al couldn't resist asking. Their old issue: surely Robert could still play basketball while studying at Hayward State. He was a star in high school.

"No time," Robert shrugged, refusing to say again what he'd told Al many times—I just don't have the lateral movement.

Al sensed Robert pulling back. Al felt the familiar stab—I can never make up for all those years Robert had lived alone with Joyce. He'd tried, sending money to Joyce since becoming a Marine, taking Robert in when he could, helping to pay for Robert's school, and, most of all, trying to show him how to find his fire.

After three hours of computer work, Robert left. Within minutes, Al moved from energized to deflated. Darlene had not called. Worse, the West St. house clawed at him. That's crazy, his sun voice accused. You're an artist. You've got to do something from your soul.

———

"Let me show you something," Kelly handed Ms. Anderson a paper. "I found the original in Robert's welfare file. It's a note from Evelyn Watson, giving the Department her address. You can see the Department date-stamp on it. Twenty-three years ago. Mrs. Watson, is being exceedingly generous to offer to settle this case for three thousand."

Ms. Anderson silently examined the note, tapping her pencil, murmuring, "O.K., O.K. ... O.K., she did tell us..." Suddenly, she raised her head, her eyes alert and cunning. "Wait a minute! What about the father of this boy! This ... Al somebody ... Where is he?"

"Huh," Kelly shrugged, "Try finding some black guy named Al Jones who had a kid in West Oakland over twenty years ago? Forget about it."

"Yeah." Ms. Anderson nodded her head in agreement. "That's right. No chance."

———

"I'll buy the victory lunch tomorrow." Al boomed over the phone. The next day, as they finished up their second glasses of wine, Al 's celebratory mood dimmed. "I gotta move on—real soon," he announced, taking another drag on his cigarette. "Yesterday I ran into Willie, a guy I know from way back. He gives me the soul shake, high fives. I ask him how it's going. 'Oh baby,' he's all hip, 'Saturday night I had me some choice action you would not believe.' Hey, I grew up in Oakland. I know these dudes. I know he's been sitting home, TV on, up to nothing." Kelly heard pain and, more surprising, uncertainty in Al's voice. "Man, I feel like I don't belong anywhere. I'm ... killing myself staying here."

"What're you thinking about?"

"I think it's Mexico," Al tried to force excitement in his voice.

"Maybe. But I think we should take little steps. You're the one who says it's all process."

"I may buy that West Street house."

"No!" Kelly cried. "You need to get healthy and free, not sucked in." Al remained silent, and Kelly sensed he'd pushed too hard, recalling once preaching to Al about cutting out smoking and working out and Al pulling back as if Kelly were a missionary badgering a native. "Sorry man ... ah ... just trying to help."

"Yeah, I know."

More waves of frustration poured from Al, but Kelly felt there was some glass between them now. Only later did he ponder if he'd always maintained at least a bit of that glass. "I'm here if you want to talk more," Kelly urged as they parted. "Anytime. Really. Please."

Ah, what was the point of talking, Al thought, driving home. He was alone. The ache in his chest wasn't going to go away. He could never going back to the Philippines. Mexico? Sure, a huge decrepit black guy with all those honkies in Puerto Villarta. Or bumbling around Oaxaca, stumbling over Spanish and seeking authenticity. Or authentic whores. Fuck it.

His dreams were over, gone. When? "Years ago," he heard a nasty voice snarl from deep within him. He thought of that line of Fitzgerald's, "No second act in American lives." Oh yeah, Al the poet, the voice sneered. Never read a book of Fitzgerald, but you got the lines. How about one of your Omar Khyyam quotes?

"Fuck off!" he screamed. "Just mother-fucking off!" He smashed his cigarette out in the overflowing car ashtray. I'll start with stopping this this, he vowed. I'll do it.

Then I'll go find her.

Big chance, the voice sneered. All you can get is damaged goods. As if you're a fresh peach, the voice bore down. A heart that don't work right. A Johnson that can't even get it up all the time. Hey, the voice ranted—you always knew it was fucked. Yeah, yeah, you tried to outrun it, the big hero, but now you're old and fat and I'm here like I always was. What are you gonna do—sit and smoke and talk about going to Tahiti?

By the time he got home he was weary. Man, I'm bad, he agonized. Maybe I gotta try a shrink? Yeah, right, some dude asking me how I feel. I'd have a better chance if I took up skiing ... I gotta DO something. He crushed his cigarette pack.

Two days later, when Rick called, Al said he'd buy the place. He lit a cigarette and his whole body felt hot, like he'd stepped into a fire.

[1994]

MACHO

"Did I ever tell you about the time I was the ringleader in a gang fight?" Brendan asked.

"No," Kelly answered, "you certainly didn't." At least, he didn't recall it. The two men, both grandchildren of Irish immigrants, had told each other innumerable stories during their fourteen years of friendship.

"I was at a party in Pacific Palisades with some high school buddies--and there was Murphy, who'd stolen my girl, Cynthia." Nostalgia spread over Brendan's Celtic, rugged face. "Cynthia...the most beautiful woman I was ever involved with. Cover girl on a Sports Illustrated bathing suit issue. She...I won't give you the whole shot. You got it, right?" Kelly nodded. Brendan chuckled. "Actually, Murphy hadn't stolen her. We'd broken up, pretty much, a couple of months before."

"How come?"

"Oh, I was being an asshole. Instead of pleading with me to come back, she took up with Murphy, from Fremont—public school, our big rivals. At the party, we eyed each other like angry wolves. He was cocky, cool. I overheard him boast of an amazing time in a swimming race--he was a great swimmer--and I ... Let's say I indicated disbelief. 'You gonna say I didn't?' he snapped. I had to answer back. Part of the code. He clenched his fists. I turned sideways, in fighting stance, afraid he'd come after me, when I saw this buddy of his, Cogliamo--big guy, ballplayer--charging towards me. I swung. Get in the first punch, I knew that much. Later I found out he wasn't looking for a fight. He'd seen what was happening and said 'Uh oh. Better break that up.' I just nicked his shoulder with my punch. He erupted, screaming insults, and punched. I ducked and grabbed him in a head-lock and hung on...."

"Same defense I used to try," Kelly injected.

They reached Kelly's locker in the Berkeley Y, a Spartan place of dull white walls, battered orange metal lockers, wood benches, bare light bulbs and red cement floor, often awash with puddles of shower water, rumored to cause dreadful foot diseases. When their group returned from running at the Cal track, Kelly regularly changed his sweat-soaked T-shirt before moving on to the weight room. Often Brendan, unwilling to interrupt their talk, accompanied him.

Kelly grabbed a clean T-shirt. "Hold on," he called, trotting to the bathroom.

Alone, Brendan sank back into the despair that was haunting him. A man of intense, volatile emotions, no woman thought it would be easy to be married to him, though many had imagined it would be wonderful. For weeks, Brendan had been unable to shake feelings of failure, stumbling through the pressures of his lawyer's work with a tense ache gnawing deep in his chest. He was incapable of love or passion. His wife Patricia had attempted to console him; then, knowing how impenetrable he became in his darkness, she'd withdrawn.

All that day, Brendan had sat in a somber office in a San Francisco high-rise while John Smeckly, an insurance company's lawyer, ponderously grilled Brendan's client, Al Jones, on every subject conceivably related to his routine traffic accident and back injury.

"Now, Mr. Jones, you've testified that you used to play football. Did you ever injure your back at any time during your football career?"

"Career? Man, I told you. That was in high school--twenty-eight years ago."

The lawyer's methodical gaze turned to Brendan. "Mr. Reilly, will you instruct your client to answer the question."

Brendan did. Mr. Jones said no.

The lawyer looked down to his yellow pad. "Did you suffer injuries of any kind during your football career?"

Brendan sighed, knowing they'd waste hours more on what should have been covered in minutes. Smeckly charged by the hour, but Brendan doubted that he was consciously milking the case for billable time. Rather Smeckly prided himself on being a tough litigator. The odd economics of corporate litigation rendered his plodding combativeness lucrative.

During a break, Brendan meandered in the halls of Upham, Wallshaw, Farquis, Smith & Bellarmine, watching three-piece suited, muted attorneys go quiescently about their tasks, adhering to their code. The place exuded repressed, work-dominated male energy, without a drop of outlaw.

When the deposition resumed after lunch, Brendan saw, as if he were on acid, exactly what he was, a middle-aged man wasting himself on trivia, surrounded by men too blind or ambitious to see that they were trapped.

This wasn't going to happen to me, he silently berated himself. During law school, in what was now called "the 60's," he'd been a seeker. He'd worked as a civil rights lawyer in the South--Albany, Georgia and Jackson, Mississippi. Later he was a poverty lawyer in East Oakland, California. His fears that he'd be crushed by what he called "the system" had dwindled. No more bullshit. Somehow, he and his generation would create a grand egalitarian life where people weren't obsessed by success. He'd never clarified what legal work he'd do, except that it would be socially meaningful, interesting, and adequately paid. "Doing well by doing good," he now called that naive jangle of dreams and self-interest. But the wave of change he rode on flattened out. He became disillusioned with lawyering for social justice, which produced at best, mostly paper triumphs. And he realized that he no longer had--if he ever had--the soul of an activist. His passions had become private--his family, music, nature, athletics. Nevertheless, with two kids, he had to work. The Movement, smoking dope and cosmic insights surely hadn't created an economic utopia. No, money had triumphed. Kelly had joked that President Reagan thought, "Since the poor lost the war on poverty, they'll have to make reparations to the rich." Yeah, I know," Brendan answered. "And we blew it. Instead of fighting for social justice, we should have been buying real estate."

Brendan had become a partner in a three-man Berkeley law firm, which provided some satisfactions. As he said, "They can carve on my tombstone, 'At Least He Beat The Commute.'" He liked his office colleagues, and occasionally enjoyed the human drama or shark cunning of lawyering. Also, he did earn a modest living--at the cost of pressure, conflict, tension. Burdened with anxieties about his clients' cases, he was forever behind. The stack of unanswered phone messages on his desk seemed to rise inches daily. Yet, for all his hard work, and Patricia's part-time salary, they had just enough to provide adequately for their family, plus occasional splurges on a meal out or a movie. "The truth is," he'd told Patricia, "I'm almost a failure." Worse, he had no vision for change. Family life was costly, even with their frugal style. And his son would start college in less than six years. Not that he blamed his kids. He'd always wanted kids; providing was a matter of sacred duty. No, there wasn't any blame, but somehow he'd lost it. His story was over.

The night before, he'd refused dinner, then gorged on peanut butter, spooning it straight from the jar while tormenting himself with accusations of failure, as if he could only be happy if he were a grand success--a movie director perhaps, or, at a minimum, a wealthy lawyer. He lectured himself that he should be appreciative. Didn't he love his wife and kids? And he loathed self-pity. There were people in South Africa, Chile, everywhere, really suffering. And lawyering surely beat driving a bus. And ... yeah, there are so many ands, he thought, but the truth is I don't feel alive unless some part of me is living on an edge. I can't go on being just a good worker, a good father, a good husband.

Getting into bed, he told Patricia he thought the worst was over; he'd feel better in the morning.

"I think I can bear your despairs," she told him, "but I can't stand your fake optimism."

"Yeah. ...." She did know he might really lose it. "I've been thinking about my father"—an alcoholic, ineffectual man. She sighed. She'd heard of his father often recently. Brendan heard her sigh, and was reminded that their love could die, not merely pass through another drought. He felt only coldness, but knowing he should appear to try, he drew his head to hers and whispered, "I will get it back."

"Be nice if it's this year."

Tonight running, usually the most reliable of restoratives, hadn't freed him. He'd been sunk in work too long; running was all labor. Even being with Kelly, his closest friend, hadn't exorcised his demons. He needed Kelly's animal presence, but knew talk, advice, or sympathy wouldn't help. He needed faith.

Kelly finished chatting with some basketball player colleagues and returned. He reached out and touched Brendan on his shoulder. "You going to be alright?"

"It shows?"

Kelly shrugged and smiled, reminding Brendan how deeply they knew each other's souls. Since they'd first met in a poverty law office, the two had shared backpacking, parties, work-outs, hundreds of showers, and, above all, talk, often intimate discussions trying to clarify their lives, to understand how the dreams they'd released in the 60's were evolving.

"How's work?" Kelly probed.

"Oh man...." Brendan recounted the absurdity of his day. "... and they make big money from that." He shook his head.

"As you say," Kelly noted, "society rewards the wrong things."

"I did say that, didn't I?" Brendan chuckled. "At the end of it today, I ran into some lawyers I know, who invited me out for drinks. Tempting —stay and keep killing myself." Kelly, who shared Brendan's impulses to self-destruction, knew how tempting that must have been. "Somehow, I decided to come over here and try to stay alive." Brendan's face suddenly flashed defiance. For a moment, he looked like a pirate, with his roughish mustache and aura of boldness. "Ah, fuck that stuff."

"So anyway," Brendan resumed his story, "Cogliamo broke free. He was furious, screaming that I had to apologize or he'd kick my ass. Of course I couldn't apologize. He raged at me, raised his fists, and we squared off. I knew I'd have to fight—very reluctantly, 'cause I was never much of a fighter."

"I doubt that," Kelly objected. He imagined Brendan would have been a formidable opponent, with his stocky swimmer's body and his killer instinct, which surfaced now only when he did a trial, or, more frighteningly, if he thought someone threatened Patricia or his kids.

"Well, I wasn't up to Cogliamo," Brendan continued as he pushed open the door to the weight room. Its decor was similar to the locker room: white walls, bare light bulbs below metal shades and a red floor, this one with a worn carpet. The one window looked out to a small hallway. Scattered around the room were weights, benches, barbells and a few rudimentary machines.

"Oh no!" Juan, 200 pounds of muscle and grace, shouted from across the room, "I'm gonna stop smoking that funny stuff. Now I'm seeing things. Some guy just came in who looks exactly like that guy Wendon or... Brendan ... who used to come in here a long time ago—except this guy's a lot fatter."

"I repent," Brendan hollered back. "This is it. My final comeback." He ambled over to Juan and watched him finish a set of curls. "Your back's curving a lot," Brendan's voice hinted at restrained scorn, "but I guess at your age you have to start taking it easy."

They bantered on as other weight lifters smiled and laughed. Then Brendan ranged around the room, greeting many of the two dozen men there: Ben, a former pro football player, immensely strong, the papa bear of the weight room; Walt, blond, handsome, who'd once told a lover who insisted she tell him her feelings, "Look baby, you can tell me any feeling about me you want to, as long as it's approval;" Ken, whose massive body looked sculpted after a Greek archetype; Jesus, his legal name; other heavy weight-lifters. "Hey man...How's it going? ... Good to see you....Hi buddy....Trying to get it right...." Shoulder slaps, handshakes, soul-shakes, high-fives: stylized acknowledgments of respect and friendship between men who rarely encountered each other elsewhere. Before Brendan became a weight room regular, the room was often quiet. Mostly people kept to small groups, usually of their own race.

"So what happened?" Kelly asked when Brendan joined him again.

"Just as Cogliamo went for me, about ten guys grabbed us and held us back. I tried to look like I was struggling to break free, while terrified that he would. He kept hollering, 'Let me go! I'll kill the fucker!' They held on. Finally he stopped struggling and shouted, 'O.K. Brendan, we'll settle this some other time.' 'Anytime,' I snarled back. Next thing he'd set our fight for the next Saturday, at Seaside Park. 'At noon,' he taunted, 'unless you're yellow.' 'I'll be there,' I vowed."

Ray finished his stomach crunches and walked near them. "Hey Ray," Kelly waved him to stop. "I think you'll like this."

Brendan smiled at Ray. "Thank you man. I needed that run tonight." Ray, a short, stocky man who'd resigned from corporate life to become a personnel administrator for the City of Berkeley was their unofficial running leader. Brendan first led Kelly to the Y eleven years before. They'd both learned that health was basic, and lawyering sure wasn't healthy. Brendan knew he'd only maintain athletic discipline by surrendering to a group. Shortly after they began lifting weights, Ray prodded and cajoled them into trying running. Rapidly, they became the devoted nucleus of Ray's group.

"O.K.," Brendan summarized the start of his tale, feeling a surge of affection for Ray. He could pontificate, but if Brendan were starting a wartime platoon, he'd surely want Ray in it. Several years before, Ray had arrived at the Y with a large bandage covering a cheek. While running, Brendan realized that Ray was struggling painfully, though he gutted it out and finished the three miles. Walking back to the Y, Brendan insisted on learning what was wrong. Eventually, Ray revealed that he had been operated on for skin cancer that morning.

"So..." Brendan continued, "Cogliamo and I kept shouting at each other. A couple of my friends joined in, then a couple of his. Pretty soon they were almost into it. Next they were all screaming that they'd meet at Seaside Park too." He waved his wrists in circles, indicating adolescent insults and rages careening out of control. "By the time we left, we had a major battle going. Then it got real crazy. All sorts of people joined up. Guys from my high school—tough hoods I hardly knew—came up and assured me, 'Nobody's gonna kick St. Catherine's around. We'll be there.' By Monday night it was a gang fight, us against Fremont."

He paused, grinning at other regulars who'd gathered around. "By Wednesday the thing had escalated into a city-wide war—West LA against East LA. There was so much tension in school I felt I could grab it. At home I was so fearful even my little brother noticed. Of course, at school I had to look cool, while it got worse every day. Guys were talking about bringing chains, knives."

"Machine guns?"

"Really, I'm telling you. It was one of those crazy times when everything bad clicks."

Brendan felt the exuberance story telling released in him. Grab it now, he knew, nodding towards Juan at the bench press. "Can I work in with you guys in a minute?" Standard etiquette: permission was always granted.

"You mean you're going to do something more than talk?" Juan pretended to be dumbfounded.

Brendan laughed. "You know, this place is just like my grandfather's Irish bar—except that for every time he drank a shot, I lift a weight."

He returned to his tale. "So I was trapped. A couple of mean Chicanos, from some ominous street gang, came up to me and said, "'We'll be there man, backing you all the way. You better not chicken out. We're gonna whip ass.' Thursday night I felt condemned. One more day before I'd be maimed for life, if I lived. Friday morning—out of the blue—I'm called in by Father Corbett, the Principal. He looked very grave, sterner than I'd ever seen him—and he wasn't a jolly man. 'I understand you are going to participate in a fight at Seaside Park on Saturday,' he announced. I mumbled some evasion, and he cut me off. 'Do not deny it, young man. I know all about it." I just nodded my head. 'In that case,' he went on, 'clean out your locker when you leave here this afternoon. Anyone who participates in that fight will be permanently expelled from St. Catherine's.'"

Brendan grinned with animated fascination at the twists of life. "I left that office higher than I've ever been. Nothing--absolutely nothing--I've ever done in my life--not making love, not backpacking in the Sierras, not my first kid being born--nothing ever made me as happy as Corbett's edict. I had a way out. It was O.K. to call it off. I couldn't be expected to get expelled, ruin my whole life, for a fight. We were too close to immigrants for that. So I put on a grand show: 'Too bad guys, but my hands are tied.'" Brendan waved his hands freely. "Quickly, it all vanished. Nobody—not even the hoods—really wanted to fight. Certainly nobody was angry at me."

"You're up," Juan notified him.

"Ah...um..." Brendan waivered. Etiquette frowned on delay. "A couple of weeks later," he snuck in as he lay down on the bench, "I found out that Cogliamo's principal had called him in that Friday too, and told him the same thing. If he fought he'd be expelled. He--as I learned much later--was as delighted to escape as I was. And then..." he laughed, pleased with his timing, and grabbed the bar, weight 175 pounds. By the seventh rep he was panting and struggling. The tenth rep forced his limit of concentration and energy. For agonizing seconds his arms trembled as he strained to lift the bar while his audience shouted encouragement.

"PUSH! PUSH!"

"Lock it out! Lock it out!"

"PUSH!!!"

"Come on you got it."

"ALL RIGHT!!!"

The bar securely in the rack, Brendan slumped on the bench, his arms dangling by his sides.

"Good set," Walt complimented as Brendan sat up.

"It's a start. You know...this place is like life. You work hard, you can stay even." He stood up, stretching his arms high, inhaling deeply. "Ah...I think I'll live."

"And then...." He leaned forward against a wall, gathering his audience. "About four years later, my mother told me what happened. She had figured out what was going on. Added up what I'd let slip at home with what she'd learned somewhere else. Anyway, she knew. She called Cogliamo's mom and told her. They agreed: we must stop this fight, or somebody may get seriously hurt, but of course we can't let these silly boys learn we had anything to do with it. They discussed it and my mom came up with the idea of both of them calling the Principals and having them warn us we'd be expelled. Thank god for mothers."

His listeners laughed, then drifted off, resuming their exercises. For the next hour Brendan and Kelly reflected on implications of Brendan's story, and joined in the flow of energies through the weight room. Sometimes effort: strain, the clang of iron, lungs exhaling. Sometimes swirls of talk: gossip, vitamin tips, movie critiques, opinions of women, political commentary. "Let me know if the Russians get to San Jose," Juan said. "'Cause if they try to come here, I'm ready to fight."

Brendan lay down on a bench, grabbed two thirty-five pound dumbbells and muscled through a set of flies, forcing his wrists and arms up as if his demons were embodied in the force of gravity. Dropping the dumbbells, he sighed with satisfaction and stood up, reveling in the warm sensations in his muscles. Suddenly he realized that the ache buried in his chest was gone. His body was centered, whole. Feeling graceful, he ambled slowly, with a slight thrusting saunter, to the chinning bar.

"That's the way," Juan called. "You don't get this stuff from cans."

Brendan smiled. "Our Pequod," he'd once called the mix of men who shared the weight room, compatriots all, no one whose lust was money. They helped him back to his dreams. "God, I love this place," he whispered to Kelly. "If only sex were this dependable."

Brendan felt his spirit heal. He refused to be ground under by work, to devote his life to money. Undefeated, he knew the vitality surging through him would enable him to regain his vision. Kelly abruptly glanced at him as if he'd spoken his realization aloud. Their eyes met, and both grinned with affirmation.

Minutes later, they sat luxuriating in the steam room, heat soothing and revitalizing them as sweat dripped off their faces. Brendan breathed deeply, slowly, as if he'd recovered his health after an illness. Life--plain old ordinary living--was precious again. Time seemed to slow. Sensing his wildness flow untamed, and feeling at peace, with an animal optimism pervading him, he reached an arm around Kelly's shoulder. "Thank you, man. Thanks for all the years and for being a dreamer and ... All of it." He wondered what the edge he'd find soon would be.

[1983]

ESSAYS

THIRTEEN TRUE TALES OF THE SAN

FRANCISCO BAY AREA

(1) November, 1967. I'd been in the Bay area three months, working in the downtown office of Oakland Legal Services (poverty lawyers). Excited by the job, I felt I was at the forefront of a struggle for social change. Four of us left for lunch. The others were all raised in California. I was an East Coast escapee. Raised in suburban New Jersey, I'd gone to college in Massachusetts, then lived six years in Manhattan, first working there and later attending law school. One thing all that had taught me was that winters could be biting cold.

The temperature was in the mid-50s. I didn't bother to zip up my jacket, but the other three did. "Man," Mark said, "Feels like winter already. It's cold." The others agreed. You call this cold, I thought—then realized that to them it was. Man, I felt happily, I'm home. I am never moving away from here.

(2) Perhaps the only good thing I got from the Catholic church of my youth was a love of stained–glass. Within a year of moving to the Bay area, I found a San Francisco artist who taught making stained-glass windows, a craft I'd thought was a guild secret. He was a fine teacher. I studied, slowly improved my skills, and eventually made some windows.

My Legal Services friend Hayden asked me to teach him how to work with glass. I did. He made a couple of pieces, then had the idea to visit the Berkeley City Dump to look for materials he could use to hold more works—perhaps an old metal lamp, or window frame, whatever.

We drove to the Dump, on land jutting out into the San Francisco Bay, a decade before that land was transformed into a wonderful park. At the entrance to the Dump was a gate, with a gatekeeper and a sign announcing that it cost a dollar to enter the premises. I rolled down my driver's window, and handed the man a dollar. "What are you going to dump?" he asked. Nothing, I replied, we just wanted to go in. "You can't go in unless you're going to dump something," the man declared. Annoyed, I told him that that didn't make sense. The man was immediately insistent. "That's the rule. You don't have something to dump, you can't go in." I started returning his insistency—that couldn't be the rule. As my voice rose, Hayden pulled open my car ashtray, and told the man we were going to dump it. "OK," the man said.

I handed him the dollar. He took it, and handed me back fifty cents. As I stared at the change, he said, "Why should you pay a dollar just to dump an ashtray?"

(3) At the play's intermission, I walked outside the original, small Berkeley Repertory Theater, founded by a friend four years earlier. It was 1972, and smoking marijuana was still a serious criminal offense in California, though surely common practice in the quasi-hippie "counter-culture" I lived in. Walking to the corner of the Rep building, I stood slightly in shadow, my back facing out, and lit up a joint. I turned to find two burly Berkeley policemen standing in front of me. The larger one stared at me and said, "You're not doing that in front of me just to piss me off, are you?" "No sir," I replied with sincerity. "Then go do it around the corner," the cop commanded.

(4) Mark was the first of us to burn out and leave Oakland Legal Services. The work was draining and social justice elusive. He was now working part-time for a solo-practice, corporate lawyer in San Francisco. Mark hated the work. "It's like washing the floor all day—with your mind," he declared. Nor did he care for venturing to the Wells Fargo building in downtown San Francisco, and riding the elevator up to and down from the 37th floor. One afternoon, he left later than usual, after five. Conventional business types crowded the elevator, then it stopped

to allow a couple of more people to pack in. As the elevator resumed its descent, Mark announced loudly, "I am also a duck," and squatted down. Total silence until the elevator reached the ground floor, and people fled as if escaping from a fire.

(5) In the spring of '72, my love Linda and I rode my motorcycle through rural Marin County and stopped to watch a Little League baseball game in rustic Nicassio. The parents of the Point Reyes Station team were hip—stylishly counter-cultural, men in ponytails, women in granny dresses or cut-off shorts or some other latest hippie fashion (or nonfashion). Before the game, they smiled and laughed, mellow, occasionally nipping on a joint. The Nicassio parents, many drinking beer, were farmers and ranchers—big men in blue work-shirts, with gun-racks in their pickup trucks; the women were hardy, pioneer-looking.

The Nicassio kids were up first. Whatever the kids did—often strike out—their parents called encouragement and cheered, then resumed talking and laughing with each other. They did the same when their kids were in the field, no matter how poorly, or occasionally how well, their kids fielded. When the Point Reyes kids batted, their fathers turned intense and fierce, hovering on each pitch, shouting instructions: "Keep your eye on the ball!" "Level swing!" "Follow through!" By the second inning, the Point Reyes dads were yelling orders at their kids in the field: "Get in front of the ball!" "Two hands! Catch it with two hands!" "Down on grounders! Charge it!" The same lunacy that some fathers (not mine) had poisoned my Cub Scout baseball games with decades earlier.

Plus ça change. I'd mostly lost faith in lawyering for social change, but even worse, the hippie counter-culture vision had atrophied, or perhaps had never included how to live as a grown-up.

(6) I left Legal Services in 1973, burned out and knowing I was irrevocably changed. For me, life was about processes, not results. I meant to live passionately, doing processes I loved—freedom wasn't about dropping out, but dropping in.

Big deal, inner condemning voices attacked. All your "passion" and love of "processes" is just a cover for selfishness. So what if your politics remain left-wing? You won't actually do anything to help. You're just going to take and not give back.

I'm with Thoreau, my intransigence growled back: "I did not come into the world to change it, but to live in it, be it well or ill." Still, I nurtured vague hopes that following my passions would lead to contributions I couldn't anticipate. A few days after I'd quit poverty-lawyering, I walked out of my ground-floor Berkeley apartment in the evening. As usual, I'd left the living room lights on so that my stained glass windows glowed radiant-colored light out towards the street, often busy with people walking to the nearby shopping district.

A conventionally-dressed middle-aged couple, probably headed for the burgeoning Berkeley Rep paused, and the woman asked me, "Did you make those windows?" I said I had. "I just want to tell you how much pleasure you've brought us over the years," she said." We always park on this street so we can look at your art."

(7) In 1977 our Oakland law firm—Hayden, me and Merv, all of us ex-Oakland Legal Services lawyers in our early thirties—broke up. We'd managed to cope financially for three years, but then fell on hard times. None of us were from the Bay Area or had connections here to people with money. The only way we could imagine hustling up clients was to "network." As Merv put it, "That means try to hang out with rich people we don't like." Most of all, we'd all had enough of the grind and stress of private practice. At Legal Services, we'd worked for a cause—social justice. After burning out on that—specifically on using law as a means to further that—our experiment with private law was now over. My two partners had money. I had none. So they could readily move on, and did. I had to continue being a now solo-practice lawyer until my just-initiated search for other ways to make money produced results. Until then, lawyering, drag that it was, at least, as I said, "beats driving a cab," my other economic option.

I struggled by, barely. A friend asked what kinds of clients I wanted. "Anyone who can pay a hundred dollars," I replied. After almost a year, I was surviving and even had some assets—clients billed, accounts receivable, a few personal-injury cases sure to settle. What I didn't have was cash. Near broke, I cast about for alternatives to borrowing from my parents. Beyond the humiliation of a grown man having to borrow from his retired parents, I'd have the added burden of knowing that I'd rejected their hopes that I follow a traditional-lawyer career path. No, I didn't want to work for a big law firm. No, I didn't want to be a law professor. No, no, no. I wanted OUT.

I'd maintained a law-business account with the nearby bank that had handled our firm account. The banker we'd dealt with was a handsome man, also in his mid-thirties, who'd seemed to enjoy our high spirits and irreverence. Hey, I thought, I'll apply for a business loan. I'm not broke; I just have a "cash-flow" problem. The problem being that all my cash had flowed out, and none was flowing in. I got loan papers from the banker and dutifully filled them out, listing my assets, and requesting five thousand dollars, at the time enough to carry me for four to six months. On a Friday morning, I brought the papers to the banker. He looked them over, nodded his head and said that it all looked fine. Then he looked at me and smiled. "How would it be if I had the money in your account by this afternoon?" I smiled back. "That would be fine," I answered, realizing that he understood my financial reality, if not the precise details. An untypical banker, he was.

We shook hands. As I was leaving, I asked him how he became a banker. He smiled again, "Oh, I came to California a few years ago, got layed, and decided to stay."

(8) Kendell and I were out for a celebration dinner at Julius' Castle, a San Francisco restaurant on Telegraph Hill, offering gorgeous views of the Bay. Tonight, in the spring of 1977, we were in a haze of romance, magical feelings that had brought us to living together a few months before. Seated by a bay window, we were separated from other diners.

Our waiter—charming, funny, Chicano—brought us our first glasses of wine. Toasting ourselves, we spoke of our unorthodox love. She was 23, I was 37. I'd met her in Berkeley when she was the teenage actress girl friend of an actor, my then-roommate. We became friends, then better friends. Occasionally, we'd meet for lunch, or later dinner, sharing our lives: her erratic acting career, my retirement from lawyering for Legal Services. Subtly, our conversations grew more revealing and intimate. We shared much, including laughter and a love of marijuana. Then, astonishingly, we became lovers, and soon after, she moved in with me.

Our wonderful leisurely meal flowed on—more wine, more laughter and joy. Our energy radiated; our waiter joined in. After dessert, accompanied by two glasses real Sauterne, we held hands and looked out to the shimmering lights below. Our waiter returned, asking if there was anything more he could bring us.

"Only a Thai stick," I joked (my then-favorite type of marijuana). He chuckled and left.

Many of the diners had left, while we continued to linger, enchanted, when the waiter returned, holding a small silver-colored plate. On it was a joint.

"Your Thai stick," he announced. Kendell and I stared, then laughed, and I picked it up. We thanked him, and he left.

He'd also brought some matches. At least slightly protected by our semi-private seating, I lit the joint. It was indeed a Thai stick. (He later explained that he'd gone into the kitchen and said he needed a Thai-stick—not just any joint would do. Somebody gave him one.) Kendell and I smoked it, trying to appear neither furtive nor attention-seeking. Both stoned, we floated together into pure magic.

(10) In his early thirties, my Legal-Services friend Jack was stricken with severe melanoma. A superb athlete, happily married with three young children, and a still-dedicated lawyer for the poor, he'd been a vision of health his entire life. Then his wife finally compelled him to see a doctor about that spot on his back, and within hours he'd been rushed to a hospital for emergency surgery. After that, his prognosis ranged from bleak to uncertain. He had massive chemo, lost many pounds off his already lean body, and pursued every healing path he could find, from acupuncture to diet, with intense concentration on meditation and visualizations. His fierce struggle lasted months until, finally, the cancer was gone. He'd survived, and returned to his former vibrant health. I asked him what lesson he'd learned from his ordeal. He said, "Now I totally want to live life fully and intensely ... and I still have no better vision how to do that than I ever did."

(11) I'd written my first Nolo Press self-help law book, on estate planning. I'd become a writer, if not the great novelist I'd dreamt of being

when young. TV folks from the news department of a San Francisco TV network station wanted to interview me about my Nolo book "in my office." But I didn't have an office, just my home desk, so they came to my apartment, set up their lights and cameras and whatever, as I talked to the director about what they wanted. "We want to do an in-depth interview," he said. Good, I responded straight-faced, then asked how long he thought that would run. "Oh," he said, "Probably four minutes," as if that were equivalent to the length of *Gone With the Wind*. "And if it was going to be a really quick, light piece, how long would that run?" I asked. "Oh," he shrugged dismissively, "only thirty seconds."

(12) A Nolo colleague spoke of a program his wife had started, WriterCoach Connection, tutoring in Berkeley High English classes. The program seemed terrific. A coach (tutor) worked one-on-one in school with a student on his or her assignment. Crucially, every student in the class worked with a coach. No kid was singled out as needing remedial help or being dumb. Coaching seemed to be a process I could do well and would like, so I signed up.

Today's coaching group, six women and me, entered a 10th grade classroom. The teacher, a large, middle-aged man, called out seven names for the first session of coaching. A slender black teenager with a hoodie pulled over his face muttered, "I don't want no coach." I quietly told my fellow coaches, "I'll take him." As the other six students left with their coaches, the teacher walked to the hoodie student's desk and said, "Get up, you're going with your coach." The student pulled the hoodie tighter. "I said I ain't going with no coach." "Yes you are," the teacher ordered. The standoff continued for several more volleys, as I stood silently by. Eventually, the teacher announced he would call Security and have the student taken to the Principal's Office. The student slowly stood up and the two of us silently exited the classroom. We walked down the hall in continued silence, until the student abruptly threw back his hoodie, turned to me and said, "Sorry to be such a jerk, but I really hate that teacher."

(13) WriterCoach Connection had expanded to our first school in Oakland, Media Academy, one of the schools of what was formerly

Fremont High. The Media student body was about equally black and Chicano. I'd coached there for two years, and loved it—a new world for me, and often wonderfully surprising.

It was our final coaching session of the school year, 10ᵗʰ grade English. The assignment was to write a sonnet about love—a classic sonnet, fourteen lines, rhyming AB, AB, etc.

I'd only had the student once before, in the previous month. He'd had been cooperative and intelligent. I knew that he was sixteen, a three-sport athlete, handsome, big and strong and a recent transfer from Berkeley High. I asked why he'd transferred from Berkeley, certainly the better known and more prestigious school. "I wanted to live with my father," he said. Then I asked if he'd written a sonnet. [My previous student had not.]

"Yes," he said, "but it doesn't all rhyme."

I asked if I could read it, and he handed me a paper with a carefully handwritten poem of fourteen lines. Silently, I read the title, "The Greatest Gift," then the poem. It was definitely a love poem. I recall one line: "You halt my tears before they reach the floor." More, the poem seemed to be addressed to someone. "Did you write this poem to someone?" I asked.

"Yes, to my girl friend. We've been together since we were thirteen."

"It's a beautiful poem. Don't change this version for her. You have to give it to her exactly as you wrote it."

"Do you think she'll like it?" he asked sincerely.

[2012]

SEVEN TRUE TALES OF MANHATTAN

(1) In 1962, a year out of College and already parted from two ad-copy-writer jobs for obscure Manhattan publishers, I'd just completed my first week doing the same work for a larger, better-known book company. I'd instantly liked Ralph, the gracious handsome boss of the advertising department, and hoped to last in the job for a while, at least until I resolved whether to go to law school. Some weeks before I'd been hired, I'd decided to spend the upcoming weekend with my lady in my family's summer home (sounds fancier than the place was) in the Adirondacks. From Manhattan, a five hour drive, with no traffic. I left the summer-sweltering City on Friday evening so the trip took over seven hours.

Upstate, the weather was glorious, the water delightfully warm and sitting on our boathouse porch idyllic. But suddenly it was Sunday afternoon and I loathed the prospect of returning so soon to Manhattan and work. My lady said she could stay longer. So Monday morning I called Ralph and told him I was ill with a cold, but I'd be in by Wednesday.

And I was, before nine. A few minutes later, Ralph came to my cubicle. "How are you feeling?" he asked solicitously. I told him I felt much better. "You look better," he replied. "You've got a tan."

(2) On an oppressively hot, humid August afternoon I returned to my apartment building in the Upper West Side, a building mostly occupied by elderly orthodox Jews in a neighborhood becoming mostly Puerto Rican. An old man leaned slumped over by the elevator. He looked weary; his shirt was sweaty. I knew why. It was Saturday—Shabbos—and

his beliefs prohibiting him from doing any work, including pushing the elevator button. He had to wait until a goy appeared. He could have been there for hours. I pushed the button, the elevator door opened, and we entered. I asked the man what floor he wanted, knowing he couldn't push that button either. He told me, sighed, shook his head then looked at me and muttered, "Damn Stupid Religion!"

(3 A tale that has become an urban legend. I first told the tale in 1966, a few days after experiencing it in a restaurant near my apartment building. Over twenty years later, I read, to my amazement, the same basic tale, presented as if new, in the New York Times Metropolitan Diary column. Fascinating, I thought—my tale is now a Manhattan myth. Then in 2008 I read the same basic tale yet again, and again presented as freshly new, in the San Francisco Chronicle.

Here's the true tale. My lady and I were eating in a booth in a modest Chinese restaurant on Broadway. From their sighs and mutterings of annoyance, the couple in the booth directly behind me were clearly not getting along, although I couldn't make out any words. Then I heard the woman, sitting closest to me, declare loudly and emphatically, "It's not just the egg roll Frank, it's the whole last six months."

(4) After law school, I worked as a law clerk for a federal district court judge in Manhattan. He was wonderful to work for. A hard worker, he conducted many trials and loved teaching his clerks about court proceedings and how law functioned in reality. I learned much I'd never heard about in law school—from the art of cross-examination to drafting jury instructions. The legal instructions the judge gave a jury were vital, especially in criminal trials. Any miniscule mistake could be grounds for reversal by an appellate court. We were laboring to make our current criminal-trial instructions perfect, which always meant they were lengthy, when the judge exclaimed, "Just once, I'd like to say, 'Ladies and Gentlemen of the Jury: Did he do it or didn't he?'"

(5) Hard December night in downtown Manhattan rush hour, snow swirling, fierce wind stabbing, already dark. Walking from my law-clerk job to the subway, I halted with a mass of nine-to-fivers at an intersection, waiting for the red light to change. A taxi halted, the driver rolled down his window and called out in heavily-accented English, "Hey, how

do I get to the police station?" It was two blocks away. Nobody spoke, until a gruff voice barked out, "Run over a cop."

(6) Beautiful summer day in the late 1960s, some time before Manhattanites took to being nice to strangers. I was ambling in Central Park musing and looking, when I suddenly realized I might be running late for an early dinner engagement. I never wear a watch, so I approached a well-dressed man and asked as politely as I could if he would tell me the time. "What do I look like," he snarled, "a clock?"

(7) In August in the mid-1990s, I left the Port Authority bus terminal at 40th St on Manhattan's west side, after visiting my parents in New Jersey. The summer night was balmy and I wanted a walk, after spending several hours with my mother and my eighty-year old father, suffering from advanced Alzheimer's. My brother's apartment, where I was staying, was some forty blocks uptown. I'd walked five blocks up 8th Ave., when a black man roughly my size (I'm 6'1", 185 lbs.) came up and stopped directly in front of me. "Hey man, give me some money," he demanded in a tone I didn't care for. "No thanks," I replied. "Hey," he raised his voice, "Give me some money." We stood a couple of feet apart. I sensed that he was not dangerous, though I couldn't say why I sensed that. "I told you no," I said "'Look, I'm telling you, give me some money!" he insisted. I stared at him and raised my voice "I said NO!" "Listen," he replied, "you may think you're safe here—but look around you. There's nobody nearby. There's no cop here. You better give me some money!" A fury rose in me, the fury I used to feel when an opposing basketball player jabbed me with an elbow. "Don't you threaten me," I snarled at him. "I'll never give you a god-damned nickel."

He leaned back a bit, sorta smiled and said, "OK … Well, will you give me a hug?"

I looked in his eyes for a few instants, and knew he meant it. "Sure," I said.

We hugged, a real hug.

Then each of us walked on, in opposite directions.

[2012]

HAYDEN CURRY. IN MEMORIAL

[For the Yale Alumni Journal]

Hayden charmed me from our initial meetings during August 1967. We were both members of the first class of fifty trainees in the "Reginald Heber Smith Program"—aspiring lawyers for the poor. A month later, Hayden set off to work in Florida Legal Services and I went to do the same Oakland, California. After almost two years in Florida, Hayden's adventurous spirit urged change, and he contacted me, as well as several other legal services friends, looking for a job. I readily convinced the head of our program that Hayden would be a great addition, and Hayden soon joined my office—nine attorneys and seven staff in the heart of East Oakland. My deep friendship with Hayden began to bloom.

Working together on major welfare class-action cases and individual clients' problems, we discovered that we had many affinities. We were both rebels, of Celtic ancestry, and seeking a life both meaningful and exciting. We'd each grown up in East Coast suburbs, went to Ivy League schools and had "done well," a Fulbright for Hayden, Law Review for me. We'd developed a similar persona, valuing wit and quickness of mind. Our doubts about being a corporate career slave had been sharpened by the same authors and books, Sinclair Lewis, Marquand, O'Hara, *The Organization Man*, *The Man in the Gray Flannel Suit*. Why had he gone to law school, I asked Hayden. "I didn't want to write a Ph.D. thesis," he shrugged. Pure Hayden—pithy, funny and original.

174

We began to hang out together. Our conversations, the best kind, soared higher than anywhere either of us could reach alone. I was also awed by his bachelor self-sufficiency. My wife had suddenly left me a month after Hayden had arrived, and I was miserable. In contrast, when Hayden gave a dinner for seven it was a feast of exquisitely prepared crab quiche, ham with glazed-orange sauce, tiny artichokes in lemon butter, spinach and bacon salad, fine wine all garnished with literate, witty conversation. Dessert was fresh fruit in melted chocolate, accompanied by suitably strong dope. Most impressively, Hayden neither had a date nor seemed to miss one.

Women flowed through Hayden's life. He was handsome, lithe, smart, witty, and dashing—he drove a yellow Porsche convertible. As our conversations grew more intimate. I probed Hayden about love. "People have needs," he replied. I pushed—did he really not believe in love? "Love lasting forever," He chuckled. "No, I think it's like the lines in that rug." He pointed at the Oriental rug on his floor. "They come together for a while, blend, then separate." I hadn't read *Of Human Bondage,* so I thought he'd created that a simile himself.

At our work, we felt at the center of our age, on a frontline of the fight for social justice. We won some major test cases, and continued struggling with the miseries clients brought us: welfare hassles, evictions, unemployment denials, discrimination, debts, car breakdowns, beatings, scams. We began teaching welfare rights classes to welfare mothers, and attended Black Panther breakfasts.

"The soul selects her own society," Emily Dickinson stated. Hayden and I evolved into soul mates. He led me on my first backpacking trip, three nights in the Sierras. When I got to his apartment, he unveiled our camping food—a ham, chicken, candy bars, fruit, eggs, chocolate, beef jerky and two bottles of wine. "Wine?" I queried, having thought that backpacking required cutting the labels off tea bags.

"You know I like to live well."

It was 1970, then 1971, then 1972. The U. S. was in tumult. The Vietnam War ground on, impervious to protests. The "counter-culture" offered dreams of new ways of life, from "Back to the Land,' to "Turn on, Tune in and Drop Out." The Stonewall riots had erupted Manhattan, beginning the gay liberation movement. We too were experimenting—our hair grew longer, we bought motorcycles, took LSD. Deepest, we experimented with trust.

On a backpacking trip, Hayden revealed to me that he was gay. I was, he knew, incorrigibly straight. He spoke of years living in isolation. "Strange" feelings buried during puberty, secret realities hidden since his first gay sex while on his Fulbright. By the time he was in law school, he was adept at duplicity, President of the local chapter of the Law Students Civil Rights Research Council while, under an alias, pursuing his passions in Washington, D. C. "But I always knew how I'd end up," he concluded. "Alone. A sad but wise observer."

By 1975 Hayden was fully out of the closet. He revealed in the freedom of the San Francisco '70s, while he yearning for love, a partner. He'd been highly attracted to Joe, but Joe had told him he wanted to be friends, not lovers. They remained friends over a couple of years until Joe said that he now trusted Hayden enough to become his lover. Joe became the love of Hayden's life. They lived together in Oakland for decades, had many friends and shared many adventures.

In 1975, with a third ex-Oakland Legal Services lawyer, we formed the law firm of Clifford, Curry and Cherrin. We lasted three years, until we were all weary of the grind of private-practice law, most of all weary of conflicts, courts and judges. As Hayden observed, "They're SO picky." Hayden moved into buying real estate, and was very successful at it, from renovating a decayed house to digging up ground for plumbing lines to making shrew investments.

In 1980, Hayden and I collaborated on a pioneering self-help law book, "*A Legal Guide for Lesbian and Gay Couples*," published by Nolo Press. Hayden was delighted to be an author and proud of a book which could aid the gay community.

Meanwhile what was eventually called AIDs was just beginning to emerge in that community. As the danger initially became apparent, Hayden and Joe agreed—no more escapades. As Hayden put it, "We're like straight people now: monogamy and fantasy."

Through most of the 1980s, Hayden continued to live a rich, inventive, healthy, joyous life, and continued to explore. He could be a trickster; he loved theater, magic, performance. Exploring hypnotism, he eventually took over a retiring hypnotist's wares, and became, "The Duvall School of Hypnosis." Occasionally he taught hypnotism in his home. I attended one of his classes. A woman complained of a bad toothache. She would have the tooth removed in a couple of days, but could Hayden give her any help in the meantime? Hayden soothed and lulled her into a trance, then told her that her right-hand fingers were getting cold, colder, and now to touch her finger to her cheek and press them against the tooth and it would get cold and numb. And whenever her tooth started to hurt until it was removed, to touch her chin and the tooth would get numb again. He then brought her gently out of her trance and asked her how she felt. "I feel fine," she answered. "There's no pain in my tooth."

After all the class attendees had left, I said to Hayden, "I didn't know you could do that."

"I didn't either," he smiled.

In the late 80s, Joe developed a cold he couldn't shake. But——it wasn't a cold. It was pneumonia. Joe, shockingly, had AIDS. Hayden became Joe's devoted caretaker, both emotionally and then, more and more, physically. When Joe went suddenly blind, Hayden prepared every meal for him, cut up his food, and fed it to him. By the time Joe died, Hayden knew that he too had AIDs and continued his active and engaged life. As his health failed, he responded with a courage and grace that became luminous. He never complained. Two weeks before he died, he said softly to me, "It really wasn't fair. We didn't know."

There's much, much more I could add about Hayden. He loved children, including a single mother's two kids to whom who he became a close surrogate father. He loved reading, festivities, nature, skiing, travel, friends, laughter, and perceptions. He once said that what he and I were doing with our lives was "trying to bring dream and reality closer together." He did that.

He was the greatest of friends.

[1990]

REREADING LUCKY JIM

We—me and my English-major friends—all loved reading Kingsley Amis' *Lucky Jim* when we discovered it at Amherst in 1960. Beyond being hilarious, it spoke to our futures. Like Jim Dixon, we'd become professors, ending up trapped at some mediocre college. Jim is stuck teaching history at a provincial university in England during the early 1950s. Most of his students are bored; a few are ambitious pests. Far worse, Jim is powerlessness over his future. To keep his job, he must fake interest in the prattling of his department head, Welch, a domineering bore.

Reading *Lucky Jim* again four+ decades later, I'm struck by how funny it remains, and by how restricted my imagination was as a student about what my future could be. My vision then: I'd schlep through a dreaded Ph.D. program and, if I were lucky, get a college teaching job. Next, like Jim, I too would grovel, scheme for tenure, and write inane academic articles. "Let's see now; what was the exact title you've given it?'" Welch bullies Jim about an article he's written. Jim's title: "*The economic influence of the development in shipbuilding techniques, 1450 to 1485.*" Jim's thoughts on that name: "It was a perfect title, in that it crystallised the article's niggling mindlessness, its funeral parade of yawn-enforcing facts, the pseudo-light it threw upon non-problems."

Yes, Jim is funny. As we prided ourselves we were, valuing sharp, caustic humor. Not yet economic captives, we could be funny with each other, or dates, or almost anyone—except directly to authority. Our targets were usually absurdities of adults. Laughter was our art and virtue. Wit was our integrity.

Jim's humor is usually restrained to internal monologues. "He pretended to himself that he'd pick up his professor [Welch] round the waist, squeeze the furry grey-blue waistcoat against him to expel the breath, run heavily with him up the steps, along the corridor to the staff cloakroom and plunge the two small feet in their capless shoes into the lavatory basin, pulling the plug once twice and again, stuffing the mouth with toilet paper."

Rage fuels Jim's anger. Wendy Lesser aptly notes, in *Nothing Remains the Same*, that, "A kind of withheld fury, a generally silent but nearly overpowering rage lies at the heart of Lucky Jim ... The best parts of the book are about the objects of Dixon's ire." When Welch evades answering Jim's questions about job security, Jim internally responds, "For the first time since coming to the college, he thought he felt real, overmastering, orgiastic boredom and its companion, real hatred." And he yearns to be angrier. "What he wouldn't give for a purging draught of contempt, a really efficient worming from the sense of responsibility." Here's Jim on Atkinson, a fellow rooming-house boarder: "Dixon liked and revered him for his air of detesting everything that presented itself to his senses, and of not meaning to let that detestation become staled by custom."

I shared Jim's anger, raging at Amherst Puritanism (I was suspended for two weeks because of "excess chapel cuts") and at corporate-conformist life. Deep under my anger was fear. Jack, my roommate, had proclaimed since we were freshmen, "Growing up is giving up." I feared that, like Jim, I'd be unable to cope with, let alone master, money. Jim reviews "his financial position, to see if he could somehow restore it from complete impossibility to its usual level of merely imminent disaster." Worse was Jim's fear, again like mine, of unemployment. Jim worries that Welch might fire him, "What would he do afterwards? Teach in a school? Oh dear no. Go to London and get a job in an office? What job? Whose office? Shut up."

Jim and I shared other distressing characteristics. We drank too much. Here's Amis' classic description of Jim waking up with a hangover. "A dusty thudding in his head made the scene before him beat like a pulse. His mouth had been used as a latrine by some small creature of the night and then as its mausoleum. During the night, too, he'd somehow been on a cross-country run and then been expertly beaten up by secret police. He felt bad."

Equally distressing, Jim and I seemed to have no ambition, beyond our shared desire to have a good time and avoid responsibility. College teaching seemed my only viable way to earn a living—high school teaching would be far too much of a grind. A few Beatniks lived freely, but for that you had to be an artist, didn't you? That took a lot of guts—rejecting a career and living without a regular paycheck. I'd never felt a passion to teach, and had learned that I was no scholar, but what else could I do? Corporate life was absurd, as I'd learned through reading—Sinclair Lewis, J.P. Marquand, *The Man in the Grey Flannel Suit*, *The Organization Man*. What else was there? Lawyer? Corporate mouthpiece or ambulance chaser? Advertising? Paid professional liar?

College teaching had some appeal. I loved literature, or more accurately, reading fiction. Favorite English professors had awoken me to intellectual life and the satisfaction, as well as the struggle, of trying to write well. Those inspiring teachers seemed to live large, satisfying lives. Perhaps I could inspire new generations to love reading great books and to write well. But even beyond my lack of calling, I had other hesitations about college teaching. First, jobs were scarce. More importantly, my father, a math professor at a college he considered inferior, regarded many of his colleagues as small-minded and thought academic politics dismal. He found the men he met in his other career, international quality-control consultant, far more interesting and enjoyable.

Still, in my junior year, I signed up for an advanced Latin seminar, because good grades in college Latin should help in getting into a top graduate school. (I'd had three years of Latin in high school, sort of liked it.) When I told my favorite English teacher of my decision, he smiled and said "Oh, going to be a great man, huh?" I attended two Latin classes before acknowledging I was overwhelmed and uninterested. My fantasies of being a great man perished, never to return.

Later that year, a professor in an English honors class asked me whether a poem was properly classifiable as "gothic or romantic." What difference does that make," I snarled. "I want to know if it's good." He peered disdainfully at me, then warned, "You're going to have to know how to make this kind of distinction when you get to graduate school." Then I'm not going, I silently vowed.

But I wavered—being a professor meant summers off and a salary. Otherwise, back to the what-else dilemma. From a third generation Irish-American family, on scholarship, without influential connections, I could do——what? Start a small business? Literally inconceivable. As far as I knew, the only businesses Irish-Americans ran were bars. None of my college friends' dads were entrepreneurs. No one I knew at college, from friend to professor, ever mentioned, let alone dreamed of, opening a small business. It just wasn't done. Somehow I'd absorbed an erzatz version of the English upper-class scorn of being in "trade." Graduate from Amherst, which spoke of its students as "future leaders," and run a little store? I think not.

Neither Jim nor I understood women or love. Though I proclaimed myself a romantic and dreamt of falling in love, women were as mysterious to me as they were to Jim. The woman in Jim's life is Margaret, another teacher, "small, thin, and bespectacled, with bright make-up," neurotic and apparently his fate. Although Jim doesn't understand how it's happened, somehow they're a couple, sort of. Not that she understands him. "She had been known to interpret some of his laziest or most hurtful actions or inactions in this light [positively], though not, of course, as often as she'd interpreted some gesture of support as lazy or hurtful." Jim's love life is as mired as his career. "He'd never be able to tell Welch what he wanted to tell him, anymore than he'd be able to do the same with Margaret." He muddles on, unsure if she cares for him, let alone if he cares for her.

Then Christine appears, the gorgeous young girlfriend of Welch's son, Bertrand, a self-proclaimed-artist. "The notion that women like this [Christine] were never on view except as the property of men like Bertrand was so familiar to him that it had long ceased to appear an injustice." Bertrand has returned to the university in hopes of meeting the wealthy Gore-Urquhart, Christine's uncle, and landing some vaguely defined job. Christine initially appears to be as pretentious as Bertrand. When Jim verbally jabs at Bertrand for his gushing admiration of the rich, Christine takes offense. "I'd rather you didn't talk in that strain … I always get a bit irritated by that sort of thing. I'm sorry. I can't do anything about it; it's just a thing about me, I'm afraid."

"Seen anybody about it yet?" Jim snaps back.

Soon however, Jim discovers that she has a rebellious streak, and mutual attraction follows. Plot complications ensue, but neither can summon the courage to take decisive action. "It's just the sort of stodgy, stingy caution that's the matter with us," he tells her. "You can't even call it looking after number one."

As Wendy Lesser observed, Christine is a "physically-attractive cipher." Readers never see her inner life. Jim, however, occasionally, sees his isolation from women. "Dixon fell silent again, reflecting, not for the first time, that he knew absolutely nothing whatsoever about other people or their lives." Me too, usually after some brutal shock from a woman I'd been going with: she would transfer to the University of Kansas or had tried to commit suicide or had decided to marry her old prep-school sweetheart. As with Jim, these occasional shocks did not provoke curiosity, let alone awareness, of my isolation from intimacy, let alone any intention to try to do something about it.

Jim lives in a pre-sexual liberation world. He and Christine don't kiss, let alone make love. Indeed, we discover that Christine hasn't made love with Bertrand. Christine exists, as far as Jim and Amis see, to make a man happy. For Amis, a woman's role is to be desirable; he is surprisingly comfortable with male dominance. "It was queer how much color women seemed to absorb from their men friends, or even the man they were with for the time being. That was only bad when the man in question was bad; it was good when the man was good."

My college love life was sadly like Jim's. Those were Puritan, pre-pill, pre-feminist times. No girls were ever allowed in Amherst bedrooms. During those twilight years of "the feminine mystique," the major task of most women at Smith or Holyoke (the nearby women's colleges) was, I realized much later, to become engaged.

Jim's career careens downward. Welch pushes him into giving a speech on "Merrie England" to a town-gown function. Everyone who matters is there, including Gore-Urquhart. Jim drinks (surprise) and delivers his talk in an increasingly-rambling parody of Welch's bombastic style. Welch promptly fires him.

E.M. Forster declared: "Happy endings are a novelist's prerogative." Amis employs that prerogative. Love conquers all. Jim ends up with Christine. And Jim's rebellious wit, his inability to put up with fools, appeals to Gore-Urquhart, who hires Jim as his private secretary. Jim's job duties: "It'll be mainly meeting people or telling people I can't meet them." Hey, I thought at age twenty, finally a job I'd be good at. With the job, Jim gets to move to London and be free. "Doing what you wanted to do was the only training, and the only preliminary, needed for doing more of what you wanted to do." He certainly isn't going to teach. "There were compensations for ceasing to be a lecturer, especially that of ceasing to lecture."

No one would remember or praise *Lucky Jim* today if it were viewed as a romance. Christine is only a device. Lesser correctly notes that, "the weakest parts of the book are the love scenes." The book continues to appeal because of its savage humor, and the appeal of the inept rebel who somehow prevails.

Occasionally, a contemporary critic revisits *Lucky Jim*, and finds it remains hilarious. A New Yorker review praised: "Today, you're impressed by how much *Lucky Jim* has retained its fizz. How does a bright mind cope with creeping boredom? Trying to pass as a capable young man, Dixon indulges in a full repertory of facial expressions … and anti-cant exercises." Christopher Hitchens agreed, stating in an Atlantic Monthly essay that the book is "wildly and anarchically funny." Jonathan Yardly also concurred in the Washington Post. "Remarkably, *Lucky Jim* is as fresh and surprising today as it was in 1954." Roger Kimball, as managing editor of The New Criterion, stated, "*Lucky Jim* is one of the funniest novels ever published."

Lucky Jim is a funny comic fable, young-man department. Jim even gets to belt Bertrand, flattening him after Bertrand provokes a fight. After rereading the book and seeing its limits, I wondered—why do I want to there to be more in it? So what if it's only a witty fairy-tale? Hilarity should be enough. So what if Amis/Jim doesn't comprehend women at all? So what if the characters are always consistent? Yes, Bertrand is always pompous, Margaret always neurotic. Consistent is what comic characters are. So what if no demons lurk in Jim's soul and he's just a rascally troublemaker we're meant to love? Hey, wasn't I too a loveable rascal at Jim's age?

I wanted a book that had spoken to me so deeply almost fifty years ago to have more depth. I'd remembered *Lucky Jim* as being both hilarious and right-on about life, offering a vision of what living authentically required. But the book doesn't have that vision. Instead, much as I still loved the book's wit, I was also reminded that I'd been mistaken back then to see wit as THE essential quality, rather than one of many.

While Jim has doubts, questions and insecurities, his enemy is clear—authority. Sure, he drinks too much and rages, but that's just "part of his charm" (in Ring Lardner's great phrase). The potential dooms he faces are humiliation or poverty, not self-destruction. No demons lurk in Jim's soul; there's no hint that he needs to seek inward, learn how to take care of himself both spiritually and physically, try to understand love and women.

We English majors were similar. While we loved to talk and laugh, candor wasn't part of our agenda. Nor did even the best English classes pierce to the intimate. I didn't know what was deep inside even my closest friends. No candor with a girl friend either, and certainly not with myself. Oh sure, I felt tension at times and got angry. But who didn't? As I went through college, I became adept at projecting and believing in my seemingly confident, witty self, and increasingly able to unconsciously smother inner conflicts or fears, aside from about earning a living.

Some of my college friends became English teachers and liked it, becoming neither Jims nor Welchs. I went another way. After two years in Manhattan publishing—if Jim thought teaching was horrible, try writing ad copy for textbooks or mediocre books on nursing—I went to law school, interested in some kind of public service (and hoping that law would offer tolerable ways of earning a living.) Next I moved to Oakland, California, working in Legal Services in a mostly poor black neighborhood and plunging into "the Sixties:" Anti-Vietnam War protests, growing my hair long, sex-drugs-and-rock-and-roll, and most of all, seeking.

That seeking included uncovering inner demons. I'd continued to drink too much through the years I lived in Manhattan. We were, as a friend from those days later put it, "All in a pre-alcoholic state." On the other hand, I did have the ironic good fortune that there was only one drug I could abuse then. (Unlike Jim, I wasn't a smoker.) In California, with a panoply of drugs available for experimenting, my addict-demon had much to work with. But I'd begun to work out regularly and had resumed playing basketball, a passion of my youth. These required developing sufficient control over my persistent addict demon. For years, during afternoon drives to work out or play basketball, I'd struggle against a beguiling voice urging, "Take the day off. Have a couple of drinks. Smoke a joint. You've had a rough day. You deserve to enjoy." I evolved several methods of caging that demon, including regularly meeting a good friend at the Y. "Hey, I can't stand him up," I'd tell the demon. Eventually I'd simply think, and sometimes shout aloud, "Oh, you again. Just shut up."

My most ferocious demon proved to be fear itself. The depth and virulence of fear was revealed in my first (very painful and very truthful) LSD trip. I saw, felt, and knew that buried, unconscious fear had warped my life. Fear far deeper than over earning money. Fear of women, fear of love, fear of rejection, fear of failure, fear, Fear, FEAR.

Why such fear? I can't give a definitive answer, nor comprehend which factors contributed what to my pervasive fear: My parents were from the Depression generation and passed their economic fears onto me? I wasn't by nature a fighter, but, unless a Gore-Urquhart showed up, still had to struggle to create my place in the "real" world? I felt I would never be passionately loved by a woman? Perhaps fear was innate, born in me? Whatever—the fear was there. What mattered was to recognize it and learn to manage it. An onion-peeling process if there ever was one.

While engaged with that, I lived an economic life that proved to be far more prosperous and open than Jim's, or of my fearful college imagination. (How about that: I'd worried about the wrong things.) Legal services was a great boon, both "doing well by doing good" and on-the-job-therapy. Once, as I ranted against the evil U. S. government and its Vietnam War to my father, he wryly observed, "True, but it's not every country that would pay you to fight it." Burning out on legal do-gooding after six years, I started a law firm with two Legal Services colleagues. Although without connections, we managed to support ourselves for three years and remain friends. Then we burned out on practicing law, period. I stumbled economically on, supporting myself as a lawyer-for-hourly-hire, a Kelly-girl of law. Earning enough to get by, I loved having ample free time. Freedom—that's what I wanted. Whether I was an artist or not, I was certainly a bohemian.

An old friend, who I'd met through Legal Services, led me to Nolo Press, in Berkeley, the pioneer publisher of self-help law books. I became an author, if not the novelist I'd fantasized becoming when young. Over the last three decades, Nolo and I have done well financially. "Royalties" is a magnificent word and an even better reality. So surprise, I earn my living from participation in American free enterprise, a system so diverse and vibrant that even I could find a satisfying place in it.

In college, I'd assumed that my economic possibilities were as bleak as Jim's were in impoverished, post-World-War-II England. I believed in *Lucky Jim*, because it presented wit and not-suffering-fools as the only and sufficient qualities to lead me to freedom. If I held to those qualities I too could (somehow) be free. Believing in *Lucky Jim* was one aspect of my general belief in that I'd discover freedom by reading fiction—in some mystical way, reading novels would lead to illumination, wisdom, Truth with a capital T. Well, sometimes I'd learn from a novel, especially when I identified with a character. Novels taught me I wanted no part of corporate life. But mostly my learnings provided only hints of how to live, little clues of who I was. Robert Frost famously defined poetry as, "a momentary stay against confusion." That applies equally to my novel reading. What I couldn't see when young was the momentary part. Which of course is no fault of *Lucky Jim*. Just that rereading that novel brings back my youthful naiveté about what literature could offer me.

On rereading now, *Lucky Jim* it strikes me as an innocent book from an innocent time. Perhaps that's why, for all its superb humor, it seems to have faded for the reading public, despite an occasional critical rave. I couldn't find it in any of Berkeley's bookstores, though it remains in print. The book would seem speak to today's college students, especially English majors. College teaching prospects, except perhaps for untenured gypsy scholars, are far worse for English Ph.D.s than when I graduated. Plus the larger economic world has certainly grown harsher. But the book seems little known on college campuses. The college English professors I know report that their students aren't familiar with *Lucky Jim,* though some enjoy Amis' son Martin's novels.

Finally, rereading *Lucky Jim* brings back how little I knew myself back then. But at least I mostly enjoyed myself, naïve as I was. My friend Patsy said of our college days, "That was before we knew we were intense." My friend Ellen observed about us when young, "That was before we knew that we hated ourselves." I could say that I wish I'd been able to plunge into inner learning when I was in college, but that ignores how repressed Amherst and most of the U.S. was, as well as myself. Understanding who I am, how to live authentically, how to love, proved to be long and winding process. And I can certainly be a slow learner. Fortunately, I was still young during "the Sixties." I wanted to rebel and explore, and I lived in a culture that stimulated and sustained my instincts—although as a quasi hippie-seeker I couldn't see that the process was endless. Looking back to my youth through the prism of *Lucky Jim,* I wonder at the me before change, the innocent, volatile, bottled-up bundle of energy I was in college, and marvel that I managed to have as much fun as I did. And I still enjoy *Lucky Jim* for its ferocious humor, even if it's not the beacon for existence I once took it to be.

[2008]

FOR MY AMHERST 50TH REUNION
(2011)

Resume Life: After graduation, two years in Manhattan publishing (Maxwell Perkins I wasn't); next Columbia Law School, Law Review (There's a story to that); then clerked for a federal judge in Manhattan (good year, learned a lot). Moved to Berkeley in 1967 to work for Legal Services in Oakland until 1973. Partner with two legal services friends in Oakland law firm, 1975-1978. Author of a number of self-help law books published by Nolo Press, Berkeley, 1978 to present.

Life: Divorced in 1971, I lived a sometime tumultuous, sometimes ecstatic, sometimes lonely love life until I encountered Naomi Puro in 1981. We've been together since.

I love living in Berkeley and the Bay area, my spiritual home. At Legal Services I met many of my (still) closest friends. Eight of us are members of a poker group that has met for forty+ years.

For me, living is process, not results. If the process isn't satisfying, I prefer not to do it, no matter how lofty the goal. Satisfying does not (necessarily) equate with enjoyable. I've become (among other things) a painter. Painting is often a struggle, but a one I find, ultimately, satisfying. Over years, I've discovered much I love, including: love itself; friends; family; painting; writing (I'm a mostly-unpublished essayist); travel (especially to France); speaking and studying French; reading (even including poetry; I'm a member of a poetry reading group—excellent poets—we're not poetry writers); nature; athletics, especially basketball; cooking, good food and wine; dancing tango (most recent passion).

A friend once commented on the number of passions I live. I replied, "Yes, I've unleashed a herd of turtles."

My web site: denisclifford.com

I benefited considerably from being at Amherst. Above all, I made life-long friends, and was taught by Roger Sale, who became a friend over two decades ago. In freshman English I-II, Sale broke through my substantial resistance to awaken me to intellectual, interior mental life. When I finally wrote a passably honesty English I paper, he wrote, "At last, you're out in the open, where I can get at you." Sale demonstrated by his being as well as his insights that it was vital and compelling to try to see, to perceive what was truly going on.

I had other excellent teachers: English—DeMott, Baird, Art history—Trapp, History—Sedlow, Philosophy—Epstein, and probably others I've forgotten.

Much of my development at Amherst was social, including exploration of the mysteries of girls and sex. With the guys I recall a blended haze of good times—the Deke house bar and lawn, all-night poker games, playing basketball or Frisbee, learning to rock dance, much wit and laughter, and above all, wonderful conversations.

Our learnings, both from each other and from Amherst, were sadly restricted by the repressed 50s East Coast WASP culture we lived in. While at Amherst, I had no sense that I could be intimate, truly open my heart and soul, with anyone, including myself. I can't recall a single serious conversation about love or sex, though they were certainly central to me.

Much was wrong with the institution of Amherst, from the absurdity of required chapel to its Puritan hysteria prohibition about girls in dorm rooms. The Administration's "Underachiever Program," abruptly proclaimed during spring 1959, manifested the narrowness of spirit and smug certainty of the college rulers. "Underachievers," if you recall, were students deemed by the Administration to be failing to live up to their "potential" (however that was determined). Underachievers would be placed on probation or suspended from the college for at least a semester.

The administration lied about consulting with parents and students, or giving "underachievers" any warning at all prior to suspension or probation. I was placed on probation for having a C+ average for the second semester of my sophomore year. At the end of the first semester of my junior year, my grades were (as I recall): A+ A B+ and D+. The Faculty Dean (Porter) wrote my parents that because my semester grade average was a B, I would be taken off probation, but the college remained dissatisfied with my performance, stating: "We would prefer that he get all Bs." My mother said, "They really are crazy, aren't they."

Soon after the "Best and the Brightest" of Them created and perpetuated the Vietnam War. A few years ago Sale asked me why I'd been angry at Amherst. I answered that I knew now that I would have been angry at any college I went to, then added, "But there was something else. Amherst was trying to make a little McGeorge Bundy out of me." Sale laughed and said, "Well, that's true."

At Amherst, we were told and assured that we were "future leaders," which meant we were being trained to become members of the Establishment. I feared and loathed this Amherst culture, not accepting then (or now) Amherst's definition of ambition, which to me meant being a man of emotional repression.

While at Amherst, I lacked the vision to do more than rebel, have fun, try to fathom love and sex, and learn to love reading and writing (though that's a pretty good list). But I didn't explore what else I might be passionate about. I didn't even develop my love of basketball, which I've played for the rest of my life (well, until my hip-joint replacement). Nor did I investigate painting, or take art classes, although I'd loved painting as a young kid.

But all that is subsumed by the reality that I was young, so young. And that the world I lived in then did not encourage looking deeply inside or exploring passions unrelated to ambition (or fun).

As a senior, I took the Shakespeare class taught by Professor Baird, that compelling, formidable man, well into his sixties. I always sat by the window on the third-floor classroom, looking out to the Johnson

Chapel, the administration building. One spring morning Baird suddenly halted his talk, nearly leapt off the podium and moved rapidly to the window. "There they go, the bastards," he snarled. I looked down. Dean Porter, Dean Esty and other administration minions were walking on the sidewalk from the chapel. "Every morning at ten twenty … out for coffee … the bastards …," Baird snarled on. He rose and looked directly at us. "Outlive the bastards," he proclaimed, " a small victory but a real one." [2011]

ON TIPPING

We Americans tip. Although we rarely reflect on that custom, beyond a vague acceptance, we may soon need to ponder its worth. Some major restaurants have recently eliminated tipping, replacing it with a fixed service charge, usually 20%. A few op-ed writers urge abolishing tipping altogether. To them, tipping compels coerced servility; accepting tips means being a toady. Nonsense, I say. Tipping is a good thing. It allows brief personal connection between us and someone who serves us. Yes, it's an atypical form of personal connection—it's transitory and done through money—but when we tip we're personally acknowledging a human being, the one who waited on is. Surely most of our financial life is sufficiently impersonal. Ending tipping would remove moments of humanity and spontaneity from our economic life, and entail a variety of other losses—including the loss of signs encouraging tipping.

- If You Fear Change, Leave It Here
- Tip Big, and Cheat on Your Taxes
- Tips Create Great Karma

Tipping is neither a conventional market transaction nor mandatory. We tip when we chose to. When we tip, it's only after service was performed; we don't bargain over the amount of the tip to secure the service. Many might say that they tip simply because they know the worker depends on tips. However, I suggest that tipping survives not only because of a sense of duty, but because most of us are generally satisfied by the service-tipping process. We enjoy the human interplay involved.

We're pleased at being briefly removed from conventional capitalism. I am paying the waiter, not The Boss (or alternatively, I briefly become a Boss). There are no filters or hierarchies between myself and my tip to the person who served me.

Astute tip seekers understand that success comes by performing as well as by serving. We tend to be more generous with servers who've engaged and related with us than those who haven't. Not that engagement requires intrusion. The finest performance I've witnessed was by a middle-aged waiter in a Parisian restaurant, decades ago. My friend Hayden and I had finagled onto a two-week charter tour of European capitals. For the first time in my life, I was going to have dinner in a Michellin-stared restaurant. But we couldn't find the place, searching with anxious frustration until someone finally directed us to it, hidden in an alley. Apologetic and sweaty, we arrived over half an hour late. The young owners graciously welcomed us to their intimate, stylish restaurant. Promptly, Hayden and I became exuberant Californians, delighting in food more delicious than any we'd ever tasted, passing forks of treats back and forth, laughing with pleasure. Our waiter laughed with us, heartily offered recommendations (I still recall that chestnut soufflé), and seemed pleased with our sometimes-fumbling French.

Half-way through our leisurely meal, a dignified couple in their 60s sat at the table closest to us. I over heard the waiter's quiet, "Bonsoir, Baron et Baroness." Addressing them as if he were in the court of Louis the 14th, he held his body formal and stately. Then he slowly turned towards us; by the time he faced us, he was again the relaxed, friendly man he'd been before. Throughout our meal, he repeated his act several times, starting from either direction. All of us, including the Baron and Baroness, understood precisely what he was doing: performing the waiter appropriate to each of us.

- Atipaclypse Now
- Feeling Tipsy
- Show Your Gratitude, Leave Big Tips

There are, of course, many ways to perform. An essential is doing the job right. A waiter recommends what he knows is the best on the menu. A cab driver glides through city traffic, not careening recklessly as if in a NASCAR race. Then there's charm or flirtation, admirable arts when practiced skillfully. (Overdo them, though, and you have entered the world of servility.) Here's the legendary San Francisco columnist Herb Caen's report: "Smart waiters' tricks. A man received in his restaurant change a $5 bill on which someone had drawn a butterfly and the message 'If you love your money, set it free.' And yes, he left it as a tip."

Tipping allows you to feel generous, at relatively little cost. My mom, still exuberant in her late 60s, mentioned that supermarket clerk clerks in our suburban hometown disappeared when she wanted help carrying grocery bags to her car. I asked if she tipped them. She did—a dime. Mom was frugal by nature and necessity, having raised seven children. But now, in the 1980s, she and my father were quietly astonished at their prosperity in retirement.

Mom knew that I believed (devoutly) in being a good tipper. The ample tips I had received working in a parking lot during four college-year summers had enabled me to escape the cramped finances normal for an Ivy-league scholarship student. I suggested to Mom that we do some dollar calculations about her tipping. How often was she in a situation where she "should" tip? Grocery boys, Christmas tips to mailman, occasional cabs in Manhattan—all of it. How much did she estimate that she tipped now in a year? Now, how about a really good tip each time— not a dime at the supermarket, but a dollar, maybe two dollars. Then we added up the difference. Somewhat over $200 a year. "Mom, for only a couple of hundred bucks, you to get to be a Sport. You'd love it. Try it."

A few months later, she reported that she'd become a big tipper, and was delighted at the results. Grocery clerks now rushed to her, volunteering to carry bags to her car. Taxi drivers smiled and thanked her when she left. Best of all, she loved feeling she was a Sport—generous, expansive.

- To feel good is to give—so please tip
- Your gratuities help defray our servers' education expenses, and they all thank you.
- A tip a day keeps the doctor away

The parking lot was at the Enchanted Forest, in the upstate New York Adirondacks. Age eighteen, I became a parking lot attendant, and my colleague Bob introduced me to tips, or more precisely, the art of extracting tips. We wired Forest signs to car bumpers, unless the driver refused one. "Is there a charge?" many drivers asked. "No, but you may tip if you like," we'd reply. Bob and I joked with drivers, deciphered license plates ("We've been waiting for you. You're the folks from Utica"), and sang along with songs blaring from park loud speakers. Many people did tip—usually a quarter, occasional more, rarely as little as a dime. For the first time in my life, I experienced prosperity. More valuable for a dreamy English major, I learned I could hustle money. American capitalism wasn't exclusively the realm robber barons and soulless corporations. Even I might turn out to be an entrepreneur, or at least a hustler.

Bob occasionally expounded on the art of tipping. People who tipped us were Sports; those who didn't tip but wanted a sign were Stiffs. Sports included most all fast drivers, Italians and anyone smoking a cigar. Stiffs include many red heads (Scotch?) and almost all rich people in their Cadillacs and Imperials. Sports seemed to enjoy life, while Stiffs seemed fearful.

- Excuse me while I Tip This Guy
- God Knows When You Don't Tip
- Our Heartfelt Thanks for Your Notable Tipping Abilities

Opponents of tipping usually base their case on supposed moral grounds. Steven Shaw, in the New York Times, argued that tipping forces waiters to be "a team of pseudo-contractors rather than employees," freeing employers from paying them a living wage. What did Mr. Shaw hold up as a model? McDonald's! "...service at (tip-free) McDonald's is far more reliable than the service at the average upper-middle-market restaurant." [Oh come on] And why Mr. Shaw, is this?

"... because they [McDonald's employees] are well-trained and subject to rigorous supervision." Great—just what we need to encourage relaxed restaurant dining: poorly-paid, over-controlled employees.

Revealingly, "moral" concerns seem mostly to benefit owners. A few years ago, the owner of Per Se, an elite Manhattan restaurant, instituted a 20% service fee on all bills (although tips averaged 22%) because, he asserted, the kitchen help weren't getting a fair percentage of waiters' tips. There was, he stated, an "Imbalance of earnings." This "imbalance" would be corrected by reducing waiters' income, not by the owner paying decent wages to the kitchen help. The owner didn't consider diminishing his profits at a restaurant where (the N.Y. Times reported) "… customers have been begging for a chance to pay $175 or more for a single dinner there."

More recently, several elite Bay Area restaurants, following the lead of Berkeley's world-renown Chez Panisse, eliminated tipping and added a 20% service charge. The restaurant owners cited a need to equalize pay to all employees, especially now that local minimum-wages laws had risen to the apparently-ruinous levels of around $11 dollars an hour. Once again, the owners didn't mention the possibility of lowering their profits.

Tipping evoked moral outrage in *The Itching Palm, a Study of American Tipping*, by William Scott (1916). Excoriating "the moral malady of flunkyism," he railed against the "willingness to be servile for a consideration. It is democracy's deadly foe. The two ideas cannot live together except in a false peace." Scott somehow overlooked the reality that the "willingness to be servile for a consideration" is essential for many jobs (perhaps he wasn't aware of Corporate Life.). Scott further argued that the Bible opposes tipping. Perhaps, yet somehow tipping has survived since at least Roman days.

Some American crusaders have attempted to make tipping illegal, because of its allegedly anti-egalitarian and therefor immoral nature. Around 1900, a few states passed laws prohibiting tipping, but they were generally ignored, and later repealed. In France, the Popular Front government in the 30s "abolished gratuities as humiliating," allegedly imposing a servile status on the tippee. Tips were replaced "by a percentage added to the bill. Tips, of course, continued to be given and expected, but the spirit changed." (*The Hollow Years*). This experiment was soon abandoned and the French settled on their current practice: "service compris" in the bill, and paying a bit more, maybe 5% if service was good. Finally, a few cultures do regard tipping as improper. In Japan tipping remains insulting, being regarded as noting inferiority. But the worldwide trend seems to be going the other way. Even in China— where the communists prohibited tipping for decades—the custom now is to tip 3% in major cities. Similarly in Denmark, which had a tradition of no-tipping because all workers received a decent wage, Danes now often tip a little bit extra.

A perhaps-moral argument for tipping is that the person served can reward good service and punish bad. The tip is a service rating. Maybe. But how harsh to be if service was below par? Refusing to tip when service was mediocre seems harsh, when you can always tip small. What about lousy service? Then the question become why. Perhaps the server is inexperienced, or overwhelmed. My generous friend Toni is still more accepting; she declares, "Always tip an incompetent waitress. It encourages improvement." She makes exceptions for bad attitude. If a server is unpleasant, dismissive or hostile, it's O.K. to stiff him or her. Still, that's rare. We value tipping not for the occasional times we try to teach the server a lesson by leaving nothing, but for the many times we want to demonstrate our appreciation for service well done.

+ Tips: For To-Go Coffee and Just Cuz
+ Tips: Thanks a Latte
+ Tips: Support "Counter" Intelligence

Some people abhor tipping because deciding when or how much to give is confusing and painful. Esther, the heroine of Syvia Plath's *The Bell Jar* hadn't known that she should have tipped a Manhattan bellhop. Her roommate tells her: "'You ninny, he wanted his tip.'" Esther thinks: "Now I could have carried that suitcase to my room perfectly well by myself, only the bellhop seemed so eager to do it that I let him. I thought that sort of service came along with what you paid for your hotel room. I hate handing over money to people for doing what I could do just as easily myself, it makes me nervous. "

Later, she gives a cab driver a dime tip for a dollar ride, thinking that the tip was "exactly right and (I) gave the driver my dime with a little flourish and a smile ... But he started telling, 'Lady, I gotta live like you and everybody else' in a loud voice which scared me so much I broke into a run."

Well, it's true, tipping requires that you learn unwritten rules. A tip lover will face inconsistencies. If I tip because I value personal contact as well as service, why do I leave a tip for hotel maids, even if I never see them? I guess because I want reward the maids their specific work for me. But if I'll I tip all those who do me a personal service, why don't I tip my dental hygienist? It doesn't occur to me, because her job is professional, and one rarely tips professionals. Similarly, I never tip an owner. Tips to my haircutter ceased when she became the proprietor and was presumably earning profits.

- (near Christmas) Please, No Tips: Ruin My Holidays
- Tipping makes you sexier-try it Darling
- (near Halloween) Tip or Treat

Tipping "really belongs to what sociologists call a gift economy rather than a market one," states James Surowieki, in *The New Yorker*. By "gift economy" I take it he means things "we do not get by our own efforts," as Lewis Hyde defined that term in his brilliant book *The Gift*. Actually tipping doesn't fit into readily either a market or gift economy. Gifts are made freely, from love or generosity. We do not acquire gifts in recompense for our own efforts. We do not make gifts to others because they've served us. Tipping is a market/economic transaction, but a unique one, dependent upon feelings, communication, cultural-tradition, and performance, as well as service. That reality annoys some people. Another moralist, Kelly Seagraves, asserted in *Tipping: an American Social History,* her diatribe against tipping, that "The (Boston) Irish tipped lavishly because they can't help it. It's one of the penalties of Hibernicism." No evidence was offered for her generalization. None could be.

My approval of tipping is not a product of my Celtic genes. I simply enjoy and value the talking and connection tipping encourages, and appreciate that I'm sufficiently affluent to be able to tip. Sometimes I'll tip when it's not expected. I've tipped cheerful cash register clerks at Long's and Safeway, friendly toll-takers, and considerate employees of fast food joints—as a surprise reward for their upbeat attitudes in tough jobs. The tips have always been received with delight, sometimes mingled with astonishment. And I feel good—I don't get to feel generous often enough.

Lets Keep On Tipping.

[2009] [2014]

THE FAN WHO LEFT

I've been a Giants fan since 1947, when I was seven. My devotion was total, passionate as only someone can be who falls in love with a team as a child. "Yea Giants!" was the caption under my picture in my junior high school yearbook.

Nine years after the Giants moved to San Francisco, I followed them from Manhattan. Through bad years and oh-so-close years, decade after decade, I kept my fan's faith. Someday, the Giants would win it all, and I'd be watching. The only time they did win during my 50+ years of rooting, in 1954, my father had a year's job in France, and I learned of the Giants' triumph through brief reports in the Paris Herald Tribune.

Last spring, I agreed with the team's president, Peter Magowen: This was the best Giants team in years. And now they were in the World Series! And leading three games to two, and up 5-0 in the 6th game. By the start of the 7th inning, my hope surged to confidence. We couldn't lose, not with our big lead, and Ortiz pitching well, and our excellent bullpen. I told Naomi, who'd become a fan as an adult, that I could smell Victory (whatever Victory smells like). Then disaster—the Giants lost, 6-5. Devastatingly pained, I felt as if every woman who'd ever rejected me had combined for one crushing blow. "I can't believe it!" I cried. "I just can not believe it! … How could we …" I ranted on, until, to my surprise, I erupted with fury. "I'm sick of being hurt," I screamed. "I'm fed up with the Giants and disappointment. I've had it!" Naomi said my response was turning weird. I raged on for another hour until suddenly I calmed—astonishingly, I now didn't seem to care very much.

Within a day, I realized why. My seven-year fan/fanatic felt he'd been burned once too often. Impulsively and decisively, he'd grabbed his glove and bat and went away. I sensed that he'd never return. No longer was my soul welded to the Giants' fortunes. There was no "we" of the team and me. Abruptly, I'd become a sixty+ years old adult who'd once been die-hard Giants fan. I was now mildly interested in the 7th game, which I didn't expect the Giants to win. During the game, which Naomi watched, I sorta listened while paying bills; I asked Naomi to call me if something good was happening. When the Giants lost, I was briefly, mildly disappointed.

I certainly didn't choose or decide that my fan should leave—he just left. As Wordsworth wrote, "Whither is fled the visionary gleam? Where is it now, the glory and the dream?" Gone, gone. I may miss that boy, especially if the Giants ever make it back to the World Series. Still, his departure allowed me to see, by the time the Giants lost the Series, that they'd had a magical year, even if the magic finally deserted them. And perhaps I'm saner with this odd detachment I'm left with. At the least, given the Giants' history, I'm sure to feel much less pain during future baseball seasons.

[2002]

Postscript, 2014. The Giants win three World Series in five years! Astounding. WHAT FUN! Of course I resumed being a fan, though not with the devotion I'd had before 2002. My fandom remained diminished. Baseball was truly only a game. As I said after one painful Giants' loss a decade ago, "This hurts so much, it's a lucky thing it doesn't matter."

ROCK AND ROLL

Rock & Roll was liberating. In 1954 I was fourteen and going to the American Community School of Paris (my father had a year's job with the Marshall Plan) when rock and roll erupted. "Rock Around the Clock," Chuck Berry's "Maybellene," Fats Domino's "Blueberry Hill." Rock captivated me instantly. I could try to reconstruct now why I loved rock but I didn't ponder it then. Rock & Roll MOVED, exuding energy, sensuality, and was inherently rebellious, not music for Puritans. Even I, no dancer before, wanted to boogie to rock & roll.

Before Rock, there'd been a nadir of pop music. Eddie Fischer, Patti Page, Teresa Brewer, Perry Como. Bland music, sappy lyrics, or worse: "How Much is that Doggie in the Window?" "Oh Mein Papa." I'd never imagined that pop music could speak to me, until suddenly it did.

From 1955 to '57, back in my New Jersey suburb, the early flood of great rock singers and songs captured me. My buddies and I listened to rock on the radio, bought 45 records, played them at home or at parties. Little Richard, Jerry Lee Lewis, Buddy Holly, Carl Perkins, The Everly Brothers, more Fats Domino, more Chuck Berry. "Blue Suede Shoes," "Whole Lotta Shaking Going on," "Johnny B. Goode." I loved them all, and Berry the most. As John Lennon aptly said, "If Rock and Roll had a name, it would be Chuck Berry." None of us dreamt of attending a rock show, or even knew that they existed. Then the King, Elvis: "Hound Dog," "Don't be Cruel," "That's Alright Mama." You had to move to Elvis. The youth of America literally moved to Elvis. His music (if not his lyrics) and his Elvis-the-Pelvis performance were erotic. My parents, not instinctively partial to rock & roll, thought it absurd that the Ed Sullivan TV show showed Elvis only singing from the waist up. In the snarky, apt words of Bob Dylan, "Something is happening here and you don't know what it is, do you, Mister Jones?"

Next, college days at Amherst. Freshman year a lifelong friend introduced me to Jimmy Reed, Bo Diddly, Muddy Waters. Then Tex introduced us to Johnny Cash. Later we discovered Ray Charles, and his epic "What'd I Say?" the most overtly erotic song yet. We played our discoveries at our fraternity weekend parties, in our rooms, and dancing with weekday Smith dates at the City Café, a semi-dive bar in Northampton with a superb rock juke box.

Into the 60s, when rock reached a peak, or, in my view, its highest peak. Our heroes from before rolled on, except for the tragic death of Buddy Holly. Plus—The Beatles, The Rolling Stones, Simon and Garfunkle, Aretha Franklin, The Who, The Kinks, Janis and Big Brother, Jefferson Airplane with Grace Slick, the Grateful Dead, Creedence, Motown, Roy Orbison, The Beach Boys, The Doors, Crosby Stills Nash & Young, and many, many more. And of course Dylan, going electric with "Subterranean Homesick Blues." Dylan our prophet; "Twenty years of schooling and they put you on the day shift." Got that right, Bob. "I Ain't Gonna Work on Maggie's Farm No More." Me neither, Bob.

A Golden Age of Rock, music for "The Movement," the Counterculture, a wave of young Americans determined to live authentically (whatever that would turn out to mean.) Sometimes rock lyrics spoke directly to us. Lots of Dylan. And Creedence's "I ain't no millionaire son;" the Stones' "I can't get no satisfaction;" CSN&Ys' "We can live in peace;" The Grateful Deads's, "What a Long Strange Trip It's Been." But deepest, rock remained ecstatic, tribal. Moving to San Francisco in 1967 ("the summer of love") I soon went to shows at the Fillmore and the Avalon Ballroom. Stoned and more than a bit intimidated by the wildly dancing crowd, I also felt that the world (well, at least the U.S.) must be moving my way. My boss at Legal Services, married with four young children, said, "We sure got better music than the bad guys."

But that didn't turn out to be determinative. Ronald Reagan was elected President in 1980. Even earlier, in 1976 The Bee Gees turned to disco, which became a brief rage. Rock slowly diminished into sometimes-terrific music, but without a Movement to interact with. More often, to me, rock seemed to have become corporate, homogenized, and dull. But perhaps it's only that I became forty. Surely in recent decades there have been great rock performers: Bruce Springsteen, Bonnie Raitt, Bob Seeger, The Talking Heads, Mark Knopfler, many more. My soul-mate Merv mentioned to his daughter recently that he'd heard a new rock band called "The Killers," that he really liked. She said, "Dad, they've been my favorite band for six years." As Neil Young sang, "Rock and Roll will never die."

[2011]

Made in the USA
San Bernardino, CA
13 February 2015